Alan J. Weisbard

BECOMING A LAWYER:
A HUMANISTIC PERSPECTIVE
ON LEGAL EDUCATION
AND PROFESSIONALISM *(1981)*

By

ELIZABETH DVORKIN
Member of the New York Bar; formerly Assistant
Professor of Law, University of
Hawaii School of Law

JACK HIMMELSTEIN
Director, Center for Law and Human Values; Coordinator of
Professional Responsibility Programs, City University
of New York Law School at Queens College

HOWARD LESNICK
Distinguished Professor of Law, City University of New York
Law School at Queens College

In collaboration with a group of law school teachers, students
and administrators working with the Project for the Study
and Application of Humanistic Education in Law

ST. PAUL, MINN.
WEST PUBLISHING CO.
1981

D1373064

COPYRIGHT © 1981 by WEST PUBLISHING CO.
All rights reserved
Printed in the United States of America

Library of Congress Catalog Card Number: 80-6225

ISBN 0-8299-2126-5

Dvorkin et al. Legal Education

2nd Reprint—1987

CONTRIBUTORS TO THESE READINGS

Barbara Bezdek
> An attorney with a public-interest law firm; a student at Columbia Law School at the time her comments were written.

Elizabeth Dvorkin
> A staff member of the Project for the Study and Application of Humanistic Education in Law and a teacher at Columbia; a student at Columbia when she began writing for this book.

Marcia Eisenberg
> An attorney with a New York City law firm; a student at Columbia at the time her comments were written.

Michael Sidley Evans
> A teacher at the University of San Diego School of Law and participant in the first summer educational program offered by the Project.

Gary Friedman
> An attorney in solo practice in California, teacher at Golden Gate and New College Law Schools, and consultant to the Project.

Jack Himmelstein
> A staff member of the Project and a teacher at Columbia.

Michael Kushner
> A student on leave from Columbia working with a public-interest law firm.

Howard Lesnick
> A teacher at the University of Pennsylvania Law School and participant in the Project's first summer educational program.

William McAninch
> A teacher at the University of South Carolina Law School and participant in the Project's first summer educational program.

Leonard Riskin
> A teacher at the University of Houston College of Law and participant in the Project's second summer educational program.

Peter Swords
> An administrator and teacher at Columbia and participant in the Project's first summer educational program.

Joseph Tomain
> A teacher at Drake University Law School and participant in the Project's second summer educational program.

*

SUMMARY OF CONTENTS

*

TABLE OF CONTENTS

TABLE OF CONTENTS

TABLE OF CONTENTS

TABLE OF CONTENTS

ACKNOWLEDGEMENTS

This book was first developed in a collaborative effort by Elizabeth Dvorkin, Jack Himmelstein, Barbara Bezdek, Marcia Eisenberg and Peter Swords, with the assistance of Gary Friedman. We have benefited from Ruth Dvorkin's editorial assistance and from the ideas, suggestions and support offered by a number of participants in the educational programs of the Project for the Study and Application of Humanistic Education in Law. The Project was supported by a grant from the National Institute of Mental Health (Grant No. 5 T24 MH–14938, Center for Mental Health Services Manpower Research and Demonstration). Howard Lesnick spent a portion of his time as a Rockefeller Foundation Humanities Fellow in work on this book.

We are grateful to the following authors and publishers, who have granted us permission to use excerpts from their works. (All selections have been edited. Footnotes have generally been deleted; where retained, footnotes bear their original numbers.)

John Ayer, "The Make Believe World of the Lawyer," from *Learning and the Law*, Vol. 4, No. 1, Copyright © 1977, American Bar Association.

Arnold Beisser, "The Paradoxical Theory of Change," in GESTALT THERAPY NOW, Fagan & Shepherd eds., Copyright © 1970. Reprinted by permission of Science and Behavior Books.

Robert Bellah, "The New Religious Consciousness and the Secular University," Reprinted by permission of DAEDALUS, Journal of the American Academy of Arts and Sciences, Boston, Massachusetts. Fall 1974, *American Higher Education Toward an Uncertain Future I.*

Curtis Berger, "The Legal Profession's Need for a Human Commitment," *Columbia University General Education Seminar Reports*, Vol. 3, No. 2 (1975).

Robert Bolt, A MAN FOR ALL SEASONS. Copyright © 1960, 1962 by Robert Bolt. Reprinted by permission of Random House, Inc.

George Brown, HUMAN TEACHING FOR HUMAN LEARNING. Copyright © 1971 by George Brown. Reprinted by permission of Viking Penguin Inc.

Fritjof Capra, THE TAO OF PHYSICS. Copyright © 1975 by Fritjof Capra. Reprinted by special arrangement with Shambhala Publications, Inc., 1123 Spruce St., Boulder, Colorado 80302.

A. James Casner and W. Barton Leach, CASES & TEXT ON PROPERTY. Copyright © 1951. Reprinted by permission of Little, Brown & Co.

Roger Cramton, "The Ordinary Religion of the Classroom," 29 *J. Legal Educ.* 247 (1978).

James Elkins, "The Paradox of a Life in Law," 40 *U. of Pitt.L.Rev.* 129 (1979).

John Enright, "One Step Forward: Situational Techniques for Altering Motivation for Therapy," *Psychotherapy: Theory, Research and Practice*, Vol. 12, No. 4, Winter 1975.

ACKNOWLEDGEMENTS

Viktor Frankl, MAN'S SEARCH FOR MEANING. Copyright © 1962 by Viktor Frankl. Reprinted by permission of Beacon Press.

Edwin Greenebaum, "Attorneys' Problems in Making Ethical Decisions," 52 *Ind.L.J.* 627 (1977). Copyright © 1977; Proprietorship, Trustees of Indiana University.

Charles Hampden-Turner, "Essay," Unpublished, 1978.

Frank Haronian, "The Repression of the Sublime," in THE PROPER STUDY OF MAN, James Fadiman, ed. Copyright © 1971 by James Fadiman, Ph.D., California Institute of Transpersonal Psychology, Menlo Park, California.

John Holt, FREEDOM & BEYOND. Copyright © 1972 by John Holt. Reprinted by permission of the publisher, E. P. Dutton.

K. N. Llewellyn, THE BRAMBLE BUSH. Copyright © 1960 by K. N. Llewellyn. Reprinted by permission of Dean S. L. Mentschikoff.

Christopher Logue, NEW NUMBERS. Copyright © 1970 by Christopher Logue. Reprinted by permission of Alfred A. Knopf, Inc.

Archibald MacLeish, RIDERS ON THE EARTH. Copyright © 1978 by Archibald MacLeish. Reprinted by permission of Houghton Mifflin Company.

Peter Marin, "The New Narcissism," *Harper's Magazine,* October 1975. Reprinted by permission of International Creative Management. Copyright © 1975 by Peter Marin.

Abraham H. Maslow, "The Jonah Complex," in HUMANITAS, Journal from the Institute of Man, Vol, III, No. 2, Fall 1967. Copyright © 1967 by the Institute of Man, Duquesne University. Reprinted from the edition of 1967–1968, Pittsburgh First AMS EDITION published 1972.

Rollo May, LOVE AND WILL. Reprinted by permission of W. W. Norton & Company, Inc. Copyright © 1969 by W. W. Norton & Company, Inc.

Paul Nash, "Dialogue," in THEORY AND PRACTICE OF HUMANISTIC EDUCATION (unpublished).

Douglas Phelps, "Law Placement and Social Justice," 53 *N.Y.U.L.Rev.* 663 (1978).

Robert Pirsig, ZEN AND THE ART OF MOTORCYCLE MAINTENANCE. Copyright © 1974 by Robert M. Pirsig. About 2,180 words (as scattered quotations). Reprinted by permission of William Morrow & Company.

Erving & Miriam Polster, GESTALT THERAPY INTEGRATED. Copyright © 1973. Reprinted by permission of Bruner/Mazel, Inc.

Charles Reich, THE SORCERER OF BOLINAS REEF. Copyright © 1976 by Charles Reich. Reprinted by permission of Random House, Inc.

Carl Rogers, ON BECOMING A PERSON: A THERAPIST'S VIEW OF PSYCHOTHERAPY. Copyright © 1961 by Carl Rogers. Reprinted by permission of Houghton Mifflin Co.

Carl Rogers, "Toward a Modern Approach to Values," *Journal of Abnormal & Social Psychology,* Vol. 68, No. 2, 1964. Copyright © 1964 by the American Psychological Association. Reprinted by permission.

E. F. Schumacher, A GUIDE FOR THE PERPLEXED. Copyright © 1977 by E. F. Schumacher. Reprinted by permission of Harper & Row Publishers, Inc.

Thomas Shaffer, "Christian Theories of Professional Responsibility," 48 *So.Cal.L.Rev.* 721 (1975).

William Simon, "The Ideology of Advocacy," 1978 *Wis.L.Rev.* 30.

John Steinbeck, THE GRAPES OF WRATH. Copyright © 1939, 1967 by John Steinbeck. Reproduced by permission of Viking Penguin Inc.

William Stringfellow, MY PEOPLE IS THE ENEMY. Copyright © 1964 by William Stringfellow. Reprinted by permission of Holt Rinehart and Winston, Publishers.

ACKNOWLEDGEMENTS

Leo Tolstoy, A CONFESSION, translated by Aylmer Maude (1921). Reprinted by permission of Oxford University Press.

Scott Turow, ONE L. Reprinted by permission of G. P. Putnam's Sons. Copyright © 1977 by Scott Turow.

Mark Twain, "The War Prayer," from EUROPE AND ELSEWHERE by Mark Twain. Copyright © 1923, 1951 by the Mark Twain Company. Reprinted by permission of Harper & Row, Publishers, Inc.

Richard Wasserstrom, "Postscript, Lawyers and Revolution," 30 *Univ. of Pitt.L.Rev.* 125 (1968).

Richard Wasserstrom, "Lawyers as Professionals: Some Moral Issues," 5 *Human Rights* 1 (1975).

"With the Editors," 84 *Harv.L.Rev.* vii (Dec. 1970).

ELIZABETH DVORKIN
JACK HIMMELSTEIN
HOWARD LESNICK

*

BECOMING A LAWYER
A HUMANISTIC PERSPECTIVE ON LEGAL EDUCATION AND PROFESSIONALISM

THE PURPOSE AND DESIGN OF THIS BOOK

The purpose of this book is to explore a humanistic perspective on teaching and learning law. The editors developed the book as part of the work of the Project for the Study and Application of Humanistic Education in Law. The Project, based at Columbia Law School and supported by a grant from the National Institute of Mental Health, is a nationwide effort by legal educators to respond to those aspects of legal education that leave the professionalization process narrowly role-defined, limiting the ability to perceive and appreciate the human concerns and values that underlie law and lawyering. We are seeking new approaches that would better reflect these dimensions and be more responsive to the individuals in the learning process, especially to their deeper aspirations in choosing a career in law. In this book we explore our concerns about the professionalization process and the issues raised in considering the relevance of humanistic education to law.

We have found it fruitful to begin by examining the process that transforms a lay person into a lawyer. We believe that a subtle process of professionalization occurs during law school without being addressed or even acknowledged. This learning by inadvertence means that the participants often fail to consider fundamental questions about the identity they are assuming, and its relation to their values. These questions about professional identity are difficult and elusive, hard to capture as they arise moment-to-moment in the classroom or practice, and hard to respond to. They are also vital, it seems to us, to anyone who is choosing to spend three years in law school, and anywhere from a few years to a lifetime in the practice of law. Their importance also extends to the greater community; the construction of a professional identity for lawyers helps determine what the practice of law, and law itself, will mean for society.

The lawyer's professional identity is shaped in part by the boundaries we adhere to in deciding what is appropriate and inappropriate to legal education. In general we emphasize the ability to analyze and advocate, placing a high value on the capacity to be precise, logical and objective. Law students learn that because the legal system is proof-oriented, they should make statements that can be defended through objective criteria. In order to identify and then respond to the specific legal issues posed by the problems presented, they develop and refine their ability to set aside their personally-held beliefs. When it is time to argue "policy" the frame of reference moves from what objectively "is" to what "ought to be," but this "ought" is still largely determined by outside forces; there is no necessary connection between the lawyer's (or the client's) beliefs and the legal argument.

The task of learning these skills is a difficult, perhaps never-ending one, and it is not surprising that it absorbs most of the energy of teachers and students. Legal argument has a narrowing and focussing nature and when issues are put beyond the scope of what is legally relevant, by such concepts as precedent, justiciability or procedure, it does not seem fruitful to put class time into them. From accepting their irrelevance to the argument, we often move imperceptibly to thinking them irrelevant altogether. Questions of the sort we deal with here—the nature of the lawyer's role, the relationship between an individual's values and who he or she is as a lawyer, what legal issues mean to a client in the context of his or her life—do not, in general, fit into this accepted analytic scheme.

We become acculturated to an unnecessarily limiting way of seeing and experiencing law and lawyering, a way which can separate lawyers (as well as the other actors in the legal system) from their sense of humanity and their own values. When that separation occurs, the profession easily becomes experienced as only a job or role, and human problems as only legal issues. Care and responsibility yield to exigencies and stratagems; and legal education, instead of reflecting the aspiration and searching that embody law and lawyering, can all too easily become an exercise in attempted mastery and growing cynicism. In short, the search for competence can lead lawyers and law students to become constricted by the roles and patterns of thinking they have adopted and unable to move beyond these confines when they work.

This limiting way of professional life is not, of course, solely the result of the professionalization process that occurs in law schools. There are strong economic, cultural and psychological forces at work within the profession and the larger society that influence both the experience of the practicing attorney and the direction of legal education, making it all the more difficult to bring meaningful change to law schools. These forces are supported by, and reinforce, an atomistic and manipulative view of our relation to the world. The focus on the parts to the exclusion of the whole results in peoples' becoming cut off from their own sense of humanity, aspirations and values, and from their responsibility towards self and others.

An example is the prevalent assumption that clients' only needs are to maximize their wealth or freedom of action. Similar assumptions are made for lawyers, that their significant needs in professional life are for financial earnings, prestige and autonomy. The professional model justifies satisfaction of these ends, while other needs, such as the expression of concern or regard for others, are assumed to be non-existent or of minimal importance. As law students become professionalized they tend not to consider the possibility that other models of legal professionalism can exist. A resistance to creative change and development is thus built into the profession. We do not mean to suggest that the legal profession is devoid of recognition of the underlying aspirations and values of all persons, both members of the profession and the general public, whose lives are affected by law. The history of the profession and its underlying ideals evidence the humanistic base of the law and the lawyer's role. We do believe that we can move much closer than we are to having that humanistic base as the principal force guiding conduct and content in education and in practice.

A humanistic perspective on learning and teaching law, as we develop it here, broadens the scope of traditional education to include a focus upon the persons of teachers and students, the human dimensions underlying the subject matter, and the experience of learning. The goal of this perspective is not to replace the traditional strengths of the profession but to include them in a larger context. For example, the point is not that concern with human aspirations and values should replace technical mastery and analytic rigor. What is needed is a way of bringing together mastery with aspiration, intellect with experience, rigor with value, pragmatism with idealism, competence and skill with caring and a sense of meaning. We are searching for ways of experiencing and thinking in law school and lawyering inclusive of these different poles of human life. When we look at legal education in this light we see several issues of importance: the need to complement the traditional focus of legal education on intellectual analytic skill with attention paid to moral sensitivity, personal values and social awareness; the proper role of authority in education; the importance of encouraging the assumption of personal responsibility by teacher and student and by lawyer, client and others in the practice of law; and the difficulties we face in developing the ability and will to adhere to a sense of personal integrity and value within the rewards, demands and pressures of the educational environment, the profession and society.

In this book, we do not seek to describe a humanistic legal education or to articulate the concrete changes that would be necessary to bring this perspective into the classroom. We are just beginning to consider the bearing which the work in humanistic education can have on legal education and the law. Our attempt here is to point to the direction in which meaningful development can occur. The changes necessary for education to move in this direction may be small or radical. For law teachers, change may include differences in their understanding of the nature and purposes of professional education, in the relation of their own values and ideals to their role as teachers, in their relation to students and the profession, and in their focus and approach in the classroom. For law students and lawyers, the necessary changes to move in this direction may mean an understanding of the place of professional work as an expression of one's total life and the place of professionalism in the larger context of the development of humankind, with potentially important personal, social and political implications for those within and outside the profession. The challenge here is great. These issues are very hard to grapple with, especially since they are so intertwined with the way we experience the world. This book reflects the challenging and evolving nature of these issues; it is more tentative, more open-ended than definitive.

The organization of the materials reflects the questions that arise when, as people involved in legal education, we begin to consider these changes. The particular form of this book attempts to respond to the difficulty of understanding and expressing a humanistic perspective on legal education in a way that does it justice and connects with the readers' own experience. Each chapter is composed of selections from relevant published writings followed by short essays describing how the issues raised in the passage affected us from our own viewpoints as persons involved in the law school community—touched us as a student, teacher, lawyer or administrator. (The authors of the essays are identified on the page following the title page above.) We use this form of personal writing in order to understand and communicate both the idea expressed in a passage and the experience that underlies the idea.

In working on the book we have found that some topics have greater importance for our lives than others. We imagine that this will be true for the readers, too. We suggest that in reading this book, you actively relate what you read to your own experience—focus on the parts that seem important to you, and on the ways the ideas and experiences expressed relate to your life. We encourage you to write on the themes you find relevant, in whatever form seems appropriate to you. Because the concepts presented here have a tendency to develop and take on new meaning, we also suggest returning to the book, or to selected portions of it, over time.

A humanistic perspective on teaching and learning law builds upon our experience—on the way we actually live our lives, on our inner reality —as we study, teach or practice law. This focus on experience can enhance the personal involvement of the learner in the educational environment. It also has the potential for encouraging us—students, teachers and lawyers —to confront and express the vision of law, of justice and of liberty that we hold inside ourselves and to begin to experiment with ways of making that a part of our daily lives as professionals.

1. ADDRESSING A LIMITING VIEW OF PROFESSIONALISM

A. IDENTITY AND ROLE

Thomas Shaffer, *Christian Theories of Professional Responsibility*
48 So. Cal. L. Rev. 721, 731-734 (1975).

If I close my eyes and imagine a lawyer, I expose myself to a *role*. If I close my eyes and see me, I expose myself to an *identity*. And if I close my eyes and see myself as a lawyer, I expose myself to the conflict between my role and my identity. The role concept is sociological—seen from the outside in; the identity concept is psychological—seen from the inside out. The conflict is existential, of course, and perhaps best approached in the context of the lawyer acting in the lawyer-client relationship. The lawyer receiving a client sees his client and he sees himself; he sees his client looking at him and he sees himself looking at the client. He has expectations of himself and he knows that the client has expectations of him. In trying to discover what those two sets of expectations are, he asks himself, "What does a *lawyer* do now?" That is the role question. . . .

These immediate and conflicting perceptions of role create anxiety in students and thoughtful practitioners over one's ability to be honest, thoughtful, knowledgeable, dependable, dominant, attentive, and careful. The anxiety turns on the fact that the lawyer constructed through these images is not real. What is real is the whole person, a reality more grand than the subject of a role because it involves aspiration. This illustrates the distinction between role and identity. The concept of role arises from viewing the lawyer from the outside; identity, on the other hand, is a matter of the lawyer looking out from the inside. He sees himself as a *Student* and as a complex *Person*, and in these capacities he looks afresh at his *Lawyer* dimension. All three dimensions—Student, Person, Lawyer, and probably more—are encompassed in the notion of identity. This multidimensional characteristic of identity becomes even more complex when the lawyer perceives the client also observing all three of these dimensions.

Thus, the lawyer-client interaction becomes considerably more complex for the lawyer when perceived in terms of identity rather than role. This multi-dimensional identity, like role, is not free from internal conflicts. . . .

Comment

Shaffer's terminology and his presentation of the tensions and conflicts that exist for lawyers and students fit my own experience. Students appear to move easily into roles. They assume roles as students and seek a way to become comfortable with roles they are about to assume as attorneys, often separating themselves in the process from some of their own aspirations about law and humanity. In the face of difficult questions about what it means to be a lawyer in society, they are understandably moved to settle for learning the mores and the attitudes that will identify them as legal professionals. With the added external emphasis that law school, the legal system and our society place upon performance, it is understandable that concern over role is so paramount and the deeper questions of who we are as people move into the background, and there are forgotten.

What is true here for students and lawyers is also true for me as a teacher. There is a way I have of experiencing myself from within, my identity, and a way I have of experiencing myself from the outside, my role. It is unfortunate, and true, that the two are often in tension. I can get so wrapped up in figuring out what to do as a teacher that I can lose touch with the essence of *who* I am as a teacher. The students, too, conspire with me and the institution to see me only in my role as a teacher. It can be so comfortable to be seen as the professor, as the authority, that I can forget sometimes that in accepting the role I can adopt a way of being that separates me from myself and what I truly want as a teacher. In effect, by making my role my identity, I distance myself from my own aspirations and my connection with other human beings.

Such patterns, developing from an over-identification with role, are hard to break. Being on a first-name basis with the students is not the answer. Indeed, any shift in the trappings of role, although potentially valuable, can simply shift the forms of the issue and leave the role-identity tension basically untouched. Nor is the answer to deny the differences between student and teacher, for that, too, can do injustice to the truth of our relationship as human beings learning together. The problem lies deeper; in any overly limiting concept of ourselves. For just as we can limit ourselves through role, any partial concept—including unnecessarily restrictive concepts of identity itself—can keep us from the fullness of the human condition. The challenge of finding a way, individually and collectively, that fully honors our frailties, abilities and aspirations is a large one. The security of role is only one tempting escape.

Yes, these patterns are hard to break, but rewarding to do so—and necessary: The costs are too high not to.

J.H.

Charles Reich, *The Sorcerer of Bolinas Reef*
pp.24-43 (Bantam 1976).

After my clerkship ended, I wanted to stay in Washington. I went to work for a law office noted for its identification with Yale Law School, New Deal liberalism, and civil liberties.

The firm was an elegant place. I got a spirited greeting from the receptionist when I arrived; then I sat back in my swivel chair, feeling that I was able to cope with the world. It was in many ways a highly privileged existence. Lawyers arrived at work well after the early-morning rush. I would get myself some coffee from the large percolator down the hall and then enjoy the luxury of settling back with *The New York Times* and the *Post*—even reading the comics. . . .

There was a great sense of importance. Consider a conference with a high government official, along with two senior partners. I strode purposefully from the office, turning around at the door to say impressively, "We'll be at the Department of Justice." We hailed a taxi and got in. Then there was the monumental facade of the building on Constitution Avenue. The marble hallways, the elaborate reception room, the office of the official, an American flag behind his desk, a view of the Capitol Building from the long windows, portraits of predecessors in office and the official himself asking us to be seated. While the other men did most of the talking, and I returned their glances solemnly, I was inwardly telling myself, "This is what everyone wants! This is really living!" Where these men ate lunch, where they went for recreation, what they talked about, and what they wore was what everyone else wanted and tried to copy.

But even in these moments I could not keep up the pretense that everything from arriving in the morning . . . to such a conference was really a meaningful experience. What was happening at the conference was so detached from our real feelings as to make it an inhuman thing—no better, really, than listening to announcements by the stewardess on a coast-to-coast airplane trip. The participants spoke lines, they did not communicate. I wish I had dared look someone in the eye or smile at the high official or just yawn.

I liked to work; it was not self-punishment. I simply enjoyed functioning in a way that felt powerful and competent. And I liked the people I worked with in the firm. They were politically liberal, intelligent, sophisticated, lively, entertaining, and excellent lawyers. They were dedicated craftsmen, devoted to their profession. Yet I felt that they, and I, were all victims of our work.

Our work was detrimental to us; it left us depleted. The moments of enjoying work did not last very long. Something about the firm crept in to interfere. The most obvious forms of interference were interruptions, phone calls, distractions. But these had to be expected in a lawyer's life: a lawyer took whatever came along, without priority, form, turn, or order; he had to glory in his ability to play many parts instead of one. No, the trouble went beyond interruptions and multiple tasks.

The atmosphere in the firm was so often full of tension, over-concern, and uncomfortable pressure that it was hard to maintain a high style. More serious still, what I wrote usually met with some objections from the senior men and eventually ended up as a product different from what I had originally written. They always wanted everything put more strongly. . . .

The opposition were always "those sons of bitches" or "those bastards" or worse. I never felt the need to make the other side seem so evil. But such an objective memorandum would not do. "It isn't positive enough," they would object. "You can put our position more strongly." My own exact voice, then, was not what they wanted to hear. My expression, my thought, must fit larger objectives. I must present an argument with a conviction I did not necessarily feel, an eagerness that was not necessarily in me, a certainty that I might not possess.

Much of my work consisted of talking to people—colleagues, people from outside, public officials. It was much easier than writing, but was not completely satisfying either. All of these people had a professional, or public, self. They all represented a particular interest or point of view, and they took this position with what seemed to be their heart and soul. If positions had been taken in a purely detached manner, there might have been some zone for genuine human contact between the participants. But detachment did not win ball games; everyone must ring with seemingly true belief. After such a performance, there was little room left for a "real" person to show himself. One put one's entire self—writing, voice, manner, personality, personal appeal, even physical stance—at the service of the matter at hand. One coated over one's real self with a public self—every pore covered, if one were really professional, until the public self became first the only visible self, then the only real self.

Whatever they really felt, the other lawyers liked to adopt the appearance of being cynical about the law and its processes, the causes and clients for which they worked, and the firm itself. Deprecation of everything was almost a way of life with them. Winning and losing cases was a game. Questions of justice, wisdom or good policy were irrelevant for lawyers. They were, in one partner's memorable phrase, hired knife-throwers.

But they did not play it as if it were a game. At the heart of their conversations were tension, anxiety, and a total absorption in their work. I could not accept that lack of distance from work, that lack of a sense of irony or humor. They embraced it, they ate and drank it, they knew no moment away from it, it was life and love to them. It was a case of too much.

When I went to lunch with a couple of young lawyers from the firm, there was lots of animated talk, but I was deeply withdrawn. We talked about politics, but it seemed as if they were simply making an effort to sound clever and amusing. The young men waited eagerly for a chance to seize the center of the conversational stage. They did not really listen to each other, they prepared their own remarks for the moment when the person who was speaking finished. They listened only for the purpose of replying. What they said seemed always to be addressed not to the others at the table, but to some invisible judge or authority figure. So even at a casual moment, when there was no authority present, the conversation continued to be an oratory contest, the brilliant speakers impatiently waiting their chance to earn an A in Lunch. . . .

The lawyer's life had a fundamental lack of limits. This was even made into a virtue. You could be unexpectedly asked to work nights, Saturdays, Sundays. You might arrive in the office and be told to get on a plane and fly to New York. You might be fully occupied with one job and then abruptly put on another with both to be done in the time allotted for one. Work at the firm simply did not include a factor that showed respect for the needs of the individuals. That would have been considered an inexcusable form of softness.

I think that even worse than the violation of spirit was the destruction of consciousness. Few people respected my right to have my own thoughts and feelings for very long. Usually the whole day was one series of things that jangled the mind until it could no longer function. When I spent a long day at the office without access to my thoughts and feelings, I felt that every moment was one of outside pressure. And my real self was driven far inside. This destruction of thought and feeling plus the repressed anger that went with it made it impossible for me to regain any sense of self when the working day was over. You cannot strike your head all day with a hammer and then expect that the person within will want to come out when you get home. . . .

There was one part of me who walked through each day at the office with a tense, set determination, numb to the cries of pain or anger within myself. I could bear anything, endure anything, and do my job. I told myself, accept whatever the job brings with it, so long as you work here. Then there was another part of me which actually felt pain, fear and anger, who could only take so much and then would go into a fury. There was so much pressure. Any of the partners could assign me work, and none checked with the others to see how much my work load totaled. It was up to me to tell a partner no if I was already too busy, but I never knew how much was expected of me, how much anyone else did, or whether my no would be believed or considered a form of malingering. There was so much boredom and waste of time, such as at long conferences where nothing of real substance happened. There was so much to cause anger, delays, explosive frustration, tension, anxiety, rebellion at what seemed to be stupid instructions, a work rhythm of undue hurry and undue delay, an ethic that required one to endure fools, bullies and petty tyrants with silence or even a pleasant smile. Under my tense and straining facade I boiled and seethed. But it was their firm, not mine.

When the invasion of my inner being became too great, I would disappear to one of my sanctuaries. . . .

In the library of the Supreme Court—ornate, rich, magnificent, and hushed—I could have an immensely long and splendid wooden table to myself and the grave courtesy of attendants; even the washroom was of marble and scrupulously clean. Very few people used the library, and it was open only to former law clerks and members of the Supreme Court bar. It was like the interior of a place of worship, imposing a silence on everybody. Here I could feel like the privileged law clerk again, the private assistant to the Senior Justice, and not like some sweaty and harassed lawyer. Here I could work the way I liked to work, with moments of contemplation, short interruptions to glance idly at the shelved books or recent periodicals; here all was dignity, repose and silence, with ornamented chairs and table lamps, carpeted floor and carved woodwork.

. . . .Wasn't this work what I should be doing? I asked myself. I did want public service, I did want to learn a craft, I did want to work on something important.

I was actually working on arguments to be presented to a government regulatory agency in a long-drawn-out proceeding involving a license to construct a dam on a navigable river. The problem was profoundly important: issues of conservation, recreation, natural beauty, preservation of salmon runs, electric rates to consumers, and private versus public power were in dispute. To work on this problem was, surely, to be involved in society in a meaningful way. It was the word "meaningful" that was the joke. The more one knew about how decisions were actually made, the more one felt one was laboring only with appearances. . . .

Many of my friends fell back on craftsmanship as a justification for their work, virtuosity for its own sake, a job that other professionals could appreciate. Medicine, painting, and physics were also crafts. But the craft must be morally and socially responsible—at least that is what I believed.

And a craft should be fulfilling as a form of self-expression. How could our craft be this when it was carried out, not only without concern for its social consequences, but also under tremendous pressure, urgency, drive—all of which produced not a work of art to be contemplated, but a product fed into the whirring wheels.

I couldn't help but feel the immense wastefulness of pouring so much energy, so many people's time, so much telephoning, typing, printing, traveling, into an activity that was fundamentally without direction. At the firm we spent by far the better part of our lives doing this work; how could that be justified? Was the society as a whole equally engaged in activities with little social value?

The truth was that I was spending my life in ways that were never what I really wanted to do. I did not want to be in Washington, I did not want to work for a law firm or even be a lawyer, I did not feel drawn toward the people I spent time with. I wanted to be somewhere else, doing something totally different, with people who were exciting and adventurous. No matter how hard I tried to believe that my work was a sign of my "maturity," I found myself full of yearning for something else.

Could one make a life out of this? Could one be a hired knife-thrower and enjoy it? For what pay or for what prestige could it make sense for a person to spend his days this way? . . .

When the day at the office ended, I drove home to my apartment house. I stepped out of the elevator at the eighth floor, and walked swiftly down the modernistic, carpeted corridor past a long line of identical doors to my own apartment. I opened the door and felt the cool, dry, air-conditioned air and the silent neatness. The hard, hot Washington day pulsing with government business, throbbing with urgent, important matters, was over. The door closed with a metallic click.

The first thing that greeted me was a feeling of personal emptiness. . . .

At the office, with the phone ringing, the typewriters clicking, everyone in a hurry, there was no time to feel depressed. But in the apartment everything was absolutely motionless: some very austere furniture, the lifeless view out the windows, and silence.

Comment

In disagreement with Reich, I do feel, on the whole, that the opposition is evil. The interests they represent are selfish and anti-egalitarian. Yet I, too, sometimes have problems taking it all very seriously. My work is purportedly in the public interest, and involves millions of dollars of municipal funds, yet it is abstract; the causal link between my actions and any particular effect on individuals is so diminutive that I begin to feel aimless. I represent consumer interests, yet I have as little in common with our clients as I do with the utilities and oil companies we fight. And I take it further: I am beginning to feel that the entire legal structure with which I deal and of which I am a part is corrupted and corrupting.

It isn't easy for me to say, as Reich does, that "it's their firm, not mine." My firm exists to further a cause I believe in. I came here because I would be able to do "good work." I was right; those are the issues I am working on, but something is wrong. The principles I believe in are not alive for me in my work or in the way we work together. Behind the facade of bureaucratic formality, I can see all of the characteristics I most detest in myself and in others—jealousy, pettiness, vindictiveness. I am disturbed when I find myself becoming antagonistic to those at the ministerial levels of various agencies. It is disconcerting to hear myself saying, to one of the attorneys at my office, that I think they finally hate me at the Department of Energy because I accused them of not doing their job. The attorney looks at me, pats me on the shoulder. You're a member of the club, kid.

I recall being given the following assignment: a corporation against whom we had been litigating for years kept threatening to sue us for various reasons, none of which are relevant here. I was asked to find some statute that would provide a civil or criminal penalty for this continued "intimidation." They had, in fact, done nothing but make idle threats and, indeed, would probably go no further than that. My instinct was that such a statute didn't exist. These kinds of parleys went on all the time, I thought: You can't send someone to jail for threatening to sue! But it was my assignment, so I researched it.

As I suspected, I found nothing, and reported my lack of findings to the attorney in charge of the case. His reaction astounded me. He got very red in the face, sank down in his chair, and said, looking very bitter, "That's not the answer I wanted." I said I was sorry (I really wasn't . . .), but no such statute exists. He screamed at me: "I asked you to be creative. Don't they teach you how to be creative at Columbia?" I felt smaller than I ever remembered. I stayed and worked until midnight that evening. I arose at six the next morning, shaking with fear and guilt at not having performed the way I was expected to perform. After all, this man might be occasionally unreasonable, but I respected him as one of the most brilliant lawyers in his field, and I honestly cared about how he viewed my work. By noon that day, I had completed a memorandum in which I reiterated my conclusion that no such statute existed, and then went on to outline several contrived strategies we could use to "counterscrew" the opposition. I had faith in none of these strategies; they were neither legally sound nor, in my mind, exemplary of fair dealing. Yet I breathed a sigh of relief knowing that I had at least not given a negative answer.

That evening, I began to feel resentment towards this attorney and towards myself. Is this what they call creativity in the legal world? To try to slam the opposition with absurd legal contentions? To waste my time and our client's limited resources just to obviate my own guilt and to appease an attorney who had so lost any sense of perspective or detachment that he would want to see the opposition's counsel threatened with imprisonment?

This, I believe, is what Reich terms the "destruction of consciousness." It is bad enough that lawyers thrive on stirring up trouble rather than working towards conciliation. It seems as if conflict becomes imbued in a lawyer's mental processes. I find it in myself. I am essentially unstimulated by the memoranda, petitions and briefs I write or help write, so I indulge myself by inserting some acerbic wit (inevitably excised by the time it gets to final form), attempting eloquence in phraseology, or finding new ways to say "arbitrary and capricious." This grasping at the air is ultimately unsatisfying. It is hard enough to get people to listen carefully to what you have to say; asking them to care *how* you say it is beyond reason when, to paraphrase Reich, they listen to you only so that they may reply. And the pleasures of contentiousness are not the sum total of what drew me to this work.

I should be pleased to be able to make a living working for a cause in which I can believe. This, I have found, gets me only so far. Then I am relegated to the familiar existential abyss. The moment I feel that I'm on the right side of the issue, I am forced to stare into the circus mirror of my self-righteousness; no attempt at shifting positions will correct my distorted reflection. I find that I must try very hard to believe the words I speak. I am comfortable neither with moral certitude nor moral relativism. Yes, I'm supposed to be fighting the bad guys, but when everyone's wearing the same uniform and fighting with the same weapons it gets difficult to tell who's who.

M.K.

With the Editors
84 Harv.L.Rev. vii (Dec. 1970).

Each Sunday from early spring to early fall, hundreds of young people gather in the Cambridge Commons. It is a varied group in appearance and mood. Bright and outlandishly romantic costumes are set against drab proletarian outfits, smiles of companionship juxtaposed with wan, blank faces. A band plays; there is some marijuana; sailing frisbees define the perimeter of the group.

Here in Gannett House—across Massachusetts Avenue—work proceeds as usual. An editor and an author dispute the most effective way of countering a troublesome argument: drop it to a note or meet it head on in the text? A quick glance at the Sunday *Times;* a cold Pepsi at eleven in the morning; a glance out the window into the Commons. And back to work.

Cambridge Sundays are a plain metaphor of the gulf between law and life which deeply disturbs many of us. The eight to ten years in which a young person attends law school and makes his way into the partnership ranks of a firm have heretofore been years of intense and virtually exclusive involvement in acquiring the lawyer's skills of rationality and judgment. Perhaps prior generations of young lawyers felt no isolation in these olympian confines because they knew where they wished to be at the end of the long hard road of legal apprenticeship. Most wanted to be practitioners. Many could confidently postpone the integration of law with life until security had been assured and the burden of total devotion passed along to the newer, and younger, men in the firm.

But the sacrifices inherent in a diligent apprenticeship grow increasingly difficult to make. Few of us know where we are headed, and even fewer believe that the slow seepage of personal vibrancy which follows from single-minded devotion to legal studies is worth whatever additional skills may be exercisable upon "arrival" at the unknown point of aspiration. Not only is there no sharp vision of future reintegration to sustain us, but we also wonder whether it will ever be possible fully to reawaken our esthetic and emotional dimensions after they have fallen into disuse during the long period of legal development.

Legal institutions are responding to the need of young lawyers to find moral worth in their professional activities, but there is little indication of sensitivity to the more subtle discontent we describe. Nor are we so lucky that the remedies for one malady will alleviate the other. The gulf between law and life cannot be cured by sprinkling an appealingly modern seasoning into the law school curriculum, so long as total devotion to things legal and analytical are the stuff around which even the newer courses are built. More flexible selection processes for legal journals will not explain to newly chosen editors why they must become library fixtures at the age of twenty-two. And the law firms will not satisfy the yearnings of our generation through collateral mechanisms, however praiseworthy, for promoting the public good. For conscience, after all, is very different from spirit. . . .

Robert Bolt, *A Man For All Seasons*
pp.xi-xiv (Vintage 1962).

. . . Thomas More, as I wrote about him, became for me a man
with an adamantine sense of his own self. He knew where he began and left off, what area of himself he could yield to the encroachments of his enemies, and what to the encroachments of
those he loved. It was a substantial area in both cases, for he had
a proper sense of fear and was a busy lover. Since he was a clever
man and a great lawyer he was able to retire from those areas in
wonderfully good order, but at length he was asked to retreat
from that final area where he located his self. And there this sup-
ple, humorous, unassuming and sophisticated person set like
metal, was overtaken by an absolutely primitive rigor, and could
no more be budged than a cliff.

This account of him developed as I wrote: what first attracted me was a person who could not be accused of any in-
capacity for life, who indeed seized life in great variety and
almost greedy quantities, who nevertheless found something in
himself without which life was valueless and when that was
denied him was able to grasp his death. For there can be no
doubt, given the circumstances, that he did it himself. If, on any
day up to that of his execution, he had been willing to give public
approval to Henry's marriage with Anne Boleyn, he could have
gone on living. Of course the marriage was associated with other
things—the attack on the abbeys, the whole Reformation
policy—to which More was violently opposed, but I think he
could have found his way round those; he showed every sign of
doing so. Unfortunately his approval of the marriage was asked
for in a form that required him to state that he believed what he
didn't believe, and required him to state it on oath.

This brings me to something which I feel the need to explain,
perhaps apologize for. More was a very orthodox Catholic and
for him an oath was something perfectly specific; it was an invitation to God, an invitation God would not refuse, to act as a witness, and to judge; the consequence of perjury was damnation,
for More another perfectly specific concept. So for More the issue
was simple (though remembering the outcome it can hardly
have been easy). But I am not Catholic nor even in the meaningful sense of the word a Christian. So . . . why do I take as my hero
a man who brings about his own death because he can't put his
hand on an old black book and tell an ordinary lie?

For this reason: A man takes an oath only when he wants to
commit himself quite exceptionally to the statement, when he
wants to make an identity between the truth of it and his own

virtue; he offers himself as a guarantee. And it works. . . . Of course it's much less effective now that for most of us the actual words of the oath are not much more than impressive mumbo-jumbo than it was when they made obvious sense; we would prefer most men to guarantee their statements with, say, cash rather than with themselves. We feel—we know—the self to be an equivocal commodity. There are fewer and fewer things which, as they say, we "cannot bring ourselves" to do. . . . But though few of us have anything in ourselves like an immortal soul which we regard as absolutely inviolable, yet most of us still feel something which we should prefer, on the whole, not to violate. Most men feel when they swear an oath (the marriage vow for example) that they have invested something. And from this it's possible to guess what an oath must be to a man for whom it is not merely a time-honored and understood ritual but also a definite contract. It may be that a clear sense of the self can *only* crystallize round something transcendental, in which case our prospects look poor, for we are rightly committed to the rational. I think the paramount gift our thinkers, artists, and for all I know, our men of science should labor to get for us is a sense of selfhood without resort to magic. . . .

Another thing that attracted me to this amazing man was his splendid social adjustment. So far from being one of society's sore teeth he was, like the hero of Camus' *La Chute*, almost indecently successful. He was respectably, not nobly, born, in the merchant class, the progressive class of the epoch, distinguished himself first as a scholar, then as a lawyer, was made an Ambassador, finally Lord Chancellor. A visitors' book at his house in Chelsea would have looked like a sixteenth-century *Who's Who*: Holbein, Erasmus, Colet, everybody. He corresponded with the greatest minds in Europe as the representative and acknowledged champion of the New Learning in England. He was a friend of the King, who would send for More when his social appetites took a turn in that direction and once walked round the Chelsea garden with his arm round More's neck. ("If my head would win him a castle in France, it should not fail to fall," said More.) He adored and was adored by his own large family. He parted with more than most men when he parted with his life, for he accepted and enjoyed his social context.

One sees that there is no necessary contradiction here; it is society after all which proffers an oath and with it the opportunity for perjury. But why did a man so utterly absorbed in his society, at one particular point disastrously part company from it? How indeed was it possible—unless there was some sudden aberration? But that explanation won't do, because he continued to the end to make familiar and confident use of society's weapons, tact, favor, and, above all, the letter of the law.

For More again the answer to this question would be perfectly simple (though again not easy); the English Kingdom, his immediate society, was subservient to the larger society of the Church of Christ, founded by Christ, extending over Past and Future, ruled from Heaven. There are still some for whom that is perfectly simple, but for most it can only be a metaphor. I took it as a metaphor for that larger context which we all inhabit, the terrifying cosmos. Terrifying because no laws, no sanctions, no *mores* obtain there; it is either empty or occupied by God and Devil nakedly at war. The sensible man will seek to live his life without dealings with this larger environment, treating it as a fine spectacle on a clear night, or a subject for innocent curiosity. At the most he will allow himself an agreeable *frisson* when he contemplates his own relation to the cosmos, but he will not try to live in it; he will gratefully accept the shelter of his society. This was certainly More's intention.

If "society" is the name we give to human behavior when it is patterned and orderly, then the Law (extending from empirical traffic regulations, through the mutating laws of property, and on to the great taboos like incest and patricide) is the very pattern of society. More's trust in the law was his trust in his society; his desperate sheltering beneath the forms of the law was his determination to remain within the shelter of society. Cromwell's contemptuous shattering of the forms of law by an unconcealed act of perjury showed how fragile for any individual is that shelter. Legal or illegal had no further meaning, the social references had been removed. More was offered, to be sure, the chance of slipping back into the society which had thrust him out into the warring cosmos, but even in that solitude he found himself able to repeat, or continue, the decision he had made while he still enjoyed the common shelter.

Note

Robert Bolt's play gives poetic expression to the thoughts of a man who will not surrender his own self. In the early months of his emerging conflict with his friend King Henry, More encounters his wife's dismay at his unwillingness to tell the King what he wants to hear:

MORE   (Taking in her anxiety) Well, Alice. What would you want me to do?

ALICE   Be ruled! If you won't rule him, be ruled!

MORE   (Quietly) I neither could nor would rule my King. But there's a little . . . little, area . . . where I must rule myself.   (p.34)

To his close friend, the Duke of Norfolk, a practical man—aristocratic, far from bright, loyal and decent; and the man perhaps least able to understand and share More's agony—he is most explicit:

NORFOLK   All right—we're at war with the Pope! The Pope's a
Prince, isn't he?

MORE   He is.

NORFOLK   And a bad one?

MORE   Bad enough. But the theory is that he's also the Vicar of
God, the descendant of St. Peter, our only link with Christ.

NORFOLK   (Sneering) A tenuous link.

MORE   Oh, tenuous indeed.

NORFOLK   Does this make sense? You'll forfeit all you've got—
which includes the respect of your country—for a theory?

MORE   (Hotly) The Apostolic Succession of the Pope is—(Stops;
interested) . . . Why, it's a theory, yes; you can't see it; can't
touch it; it's a theory. But what matters to me is not whether it's
true or not but that I believe it to be true, or rather, not that I
believe it, but that *I* believe it.   (pp.52-53)

Later, when the pressure from the King has become more threatening,
More, in order to protect Norfolk, is attempting to provoke him into
breaking off their friendship:

MORE   The nobility of England, my lord, would have snored
through the Sermon on the Mount. But you'll labor like Thomas
Aquinas over a rat-dog's pedigree. Now what's the name of those
distorted creatures you're all breeding at the moment? . . .

NORFOLK   Water spaniels!

MORE   And what would you do with a water spaniel that was afraid
of water? You'd hang it! Well, as a spaniel is to water, so is a man
to his own self. I will not give in because I oppose it—I do—not
my pride, not my spleen, nor any other of my appetites but *I*
do—*I*. (MORE goes up to him and feels him up and down like an
animal. . . .) Is there no single sinew in the midst of this that
serves no appetite of Norfolk's but is just Norfolk? There is!
Give *that* some exercise, my lord!   (pp.71-72)

Even when Norfolk is questioning More in prison, as a member of an official Commission, the genuineness of the personal link between these two
friends breaks through:

NORFOLK   Oh, confound all this . . . I'm not a scholar, as Master
Cromwell never tires of pointing out, and frankly I don't know
whether the marriage was lawful or not. But damn it, Thomas,
look at those names . . . You know those men! Can't you do what I
did, and come with us, for fellowship?

MORE   (Moved) And when we stand before God, and you are sent to
Paradise for doing according to your conscience, and I am

damned for not doing according to mine, will you come with me,
for fellowship?   (pp.76-77)

More's daughter Margaret is the only person in the play whom he
regards as his intellectual equal—and the only one to whom he can say, as
he does moments before his death: "You have long known the secrets of
my heart." They each take pleasure in intellectual banter—and they each
can rely on the other's capacity to distinguish it from something more:

ROPER   Sir, come out! Swear to the Act! Take the oath and come
    out!

MORE   Is this why they let you come?

ROPER   Yes . . . Meg's under oath to persuade you.

MORE   (Coldly) That was silly, Meg. How did you come to do that?

MARGARET   I wanted to!

MORE   You want me to swear to the Act of Succession?

MARGARET   "God more regards the thoughts of the heart than
    the words of the mouth." Or so you've always told me.

MORE   Yes.

MARGARET   Then say the words of the oath and in your heart
    think otherwise.

MORE   What is an oath then but words we say to God?

MARGARET   That's very neat.

MORE   Do you mean it isn't true?

MARGARET   No, it's true.

MORE   Then it's a poor argument to call it "neat," Meg. When a
    man takes an oath, Meg, he's holding his own self in his own
    hands. Like water. (He cups his hands) And if he opens his
    fingers *then*—he needn't hope to find himself again.   (pp.80-81)
                                                              H.L.

Richard Wasserstrom, *Lawyers as Professionals: Some Moral Issues*
5 Human Rights 1, 2-22 (1975).

The primary question that is presented is whether there is
adequate justification for the kind of moral universe that comes
to be inhabited by the lawyer as he or she goes through professional life. For at best the lawyer's world is a simplified moral
world; often it is an amoral one; and more than occasionally,
perhaps, an overtly immoral one. . . .

It is, I think, at least a plausible hypothesis that the pre-
dominance of lawyers [in Watergate] was not accidental—that

the fact that they were lawyers made it easier rather than harder for them both to look at things the way they did and to do the things that were done. The theory that I want to examine in support of this hypothesis connects this activity with a feature of the lawyer's professionalism.

As I have already noted, one central feature of the professions in general and of law in particular is that there is a special, complicated relationship between the professional, and the client or patient. For each of the parties in this relationship, but especially for the professional, the behavior that is involved is to a very significant degree, what I call, role-differentiated behavior. And this is significant because it is the nature of role-differentiated behavior that it often makes it both appropriate and desirable for the person in a particular role to put to one side considerations of various sorts—and especially various moral considerations—that would otherwise be relevant if not decisive. Some illustrations will help to make clear what I mean both by role-differentiated behavior and by the way role-differentiated behavior often alters, if not eliminates, the significance of those moral considerations that would obtain, were it not for the presence of the role.

Being a parent is, in probably every human culture, to be involved in role-differentiated behavior. In our own culture, and once again in most, if not all, human cultures, as a parent one is entitled, if not obligated, to prefer the interests of one's own children over those of children generally. That is to say, it is regarded as appropriate for a parent to allocate excessive goods to his or her own children, even though other children may have substantially more pressing and genuine needs for these same items. If one were trying to decide what the right way was to distribute assets among a group of children all of whom were strangers to oneself, the relevant moral considerations would be very different from those that would be thought to obtain once one's own children were in the picture. In the role of a parent, the claims of other children vis-a-vis one's own are, if not rendered morally irrelevant, certainly rendered less morally significant. In short, the role-differentiated character of the situation alters the relevant moral point of view enormously.

A similar situation is presented by the case of the scientist. . . .

In both of these cases it is, of course, conceivable that plausible and even thoroughly convincing arguments exist for the desirability of the role-differentiated behavior and its attendant neglect of what would otherwise be morally relevant considerations. Nonetheless, it is, I believe, also the case that the burden of proof, so to speak, is always upon the proponent of the desirability of this kind of role-differentiated behavior. For in the absence of special reasons why parents ought to prefer the interests of their children over those of children in general, the moral point of view surely requires that the claims and needs of all children receive equal consideration. But we take the rightness of parental preference so for granted, that we often neglect, I think, the fact that it is anything but self-evidently morally appropriate. My own view, for example, is that careful reflection shows that the *degree* of parental preference systematically encouraged in our own culture is far too extensive to be morally justified.

All of this is significant just because to be a professional is to be enmeshed in role-differentiated behavior of precisely this sort. One's role as a doctor, psychiatrist, or lawyer, alters one's moral universe in a fashion analogous to that described above. Of special significance here is the fact that the professional *qua* professional has a client or patient whose interests must be represented, attended to, or looked after by the professional. And that means that the role of the professional (like that of the parent) is to prefer in a variety of ways the interests of the client or patient over those of individuals generally.

Consider, more specifically, the role-differentiated behavior of the lawyer. Conventional wisdom has it that where the attorney-client relationship exists, the point of view of the attorney is properly different—and appreciably so—from that which would be appropriate in the absence of the attorney-client relationship. For where the attorney-client relationship exists, it is often appropriate and many times even obligatory for the attorney to do things that, all other things being equal, an ordinary person need not, and should not do. What is characteristic of this role of a lawyer is the lawyer's required indifference to a wide variety of ends and consequences that in other contexts would be of undeniable moral significance. Once a lawyer represents a client, the lawyer has a duty to make his or her expertise fully available in the realization of the end sought by the client, irrespective, for the most part, of the moral worth to which the end will be put or the character of the client who seeks to utilize it. Provided that the end sought is not illegal, the lawyer is, in essence, an amoral technician whose peculiar skills and knowledge in respect to the law are available to those with whom the relationship of client is established. The question, as I have indicated, is whether this particular and pervasive feature of professionalism is itself justifiable. At a minimum, I do not think any of the typical, simple answers will suffice. . . .

The job of the lawyer, so the argument typically concludes, is not to approve or disapprove of the character of his or her client, the cause for which the client seeks the lawyer's assistance, or the avenues provided by the law to achieve that which the client wants to accomplish. The lawyer's task is, instead, to provide that competence which the client lacks and the lawyer, as professional, possesses. In this way, the lawyer as professional comes to inhabit a simplified universe which is strikingly amoral—which regards as morally irrelevant any number of factors which nonprofessional citizens might take to be important, if not decisive, in their everyday lives. And the difficulty I have with all of this is that the arguments for such a way of life seem to be not quite so convincing to me as they do to many lawyers. I am, that is, at best uncertain that it is a good thing for lawyers to be so professional—for them to embrace so completely this role-differentiated way of approaching matters.

More specifically, if it is correct that this is the perspective of lawyers in particular and professionals in general, is it right that this should be their perspective? Is it right that the lawyer should be able so easily to put to one side otherwise difficult problems with the answer: but these are not and cannot be my concern as a lawyer? What do we gain and what do we lose from having a social universe in which there are professionals such as lawyers, who, as such, inhabit a universe of the sort I have been trying to describe?

One difficulty in even thinking about all of this is that lawyers may not be very objective or detached in their attempts to work the problem through. For one feature of this simplified, intellectual world is that it is often a very comfortable one to inhabit.

To be sure, on occasion, a lawyer may find it uncomfortable to represent an extremely unpopular client. On occasion, too, a lawyer may feel ill at ease invoking a rule of law or practice which he or she thinks to be an unfair or undesirable one. Nonetheless, for most lawyers, most of the time, pursuing the interests of one's clients is an attractive and satisfying way to live in part just because the moral world of the lawyer is a simpler, less complicated, and less ambiguous world than the moral world of ordinary life. There is, I think, something quite seductive about being able to turn aside so many ostensibly difficult moral dilemmas and decisions with the reply: but that is not my concern; my job as a lawyer is not to judge the rights and wrongs of the client or the cause; it is to defend as best I can my client's interests. For the ethical problems that can arise within this constricted point of view are, to say the least, typically neither momentous nor terribly vexing. Role-differentiated behavior is enticing and reassuring precisely because it does constrain and delimit an otherwise often intractable and confusing moral world. . . .

[I]t is clear that there are definite character traits that the professional such as the lawyer must take on if the system is to work. What is less clear is that they are admirable ones. Even if the role-differentiated amorality of the professional lawyer is justified by the virtues of the adversary system, this also means that the lawyer *qua* lawyer will be encouraged to be competitive rather than cooperative; aggressive rather than accommodating; ruthless rather than compassionate; and pragmatic rather than principled. This is, I think, part of the logic of the role-differentiated behavior of lawyers in particular, and to a lesser degree of professionals in general. It is surely neither accidental nor unimportant that these are the same character traits that are emphasized and valued by the capitalistic ethic—and on precisely analogous grounds. Because the ideals of professionalism and capitalism are the dominant ones within our culture, it is harder than most of us suspect even to take seriously the suggestion that radically different styles of living, kinds of occupational outlooks, and types of social institutions might be possible, let alone preferable. . . .

[E]ven if on balance the role-differentiated character of the lawyer's way of thinking and acting is ultimately deemed to be justifiable within the system on systemic instrumental grounds, it still remains the case that we do pay a social price for that way of thought and action. For to become and to be a professional, such as a lawyer, is to incorporate within oneself ways of behaving and ways of thinking that shape the whole person. It is especially hard, if not impossible, because of the nature of the professions, for one's professional way of thinking not to dominate one's entire adult life. Thus, even if the lawyers who were involved in Watergate were not, strictly speaking, then and there functioning as lawyers, their behavior was, I believe, the likely if not inevitable consequence of their legal acculturation. Having been taught to embrace and practice the lawyer's institutional role, it was natural, if not unavoidable, that they would continue to play that role even when they were somewhat removed from the specific institutional milieu in which that way of thinking and acting is arguably fitting and appropriate. The nature of the professions—the lengthy educational preparation, the prestige and economic rewards, and the concomitant enhanced sense of self—makes the role of professional a difficult one to shed even in those obvious situations in which that role is neither required nor appropriate. In important respects, one's professional role becomes and is one's dominant role, so that for many persons at least they become their professional being. This is at a minimum a heavy price to pay for the professions as we know them in our culture, and especially so for lawyers. Whether it is an inevitable price is, I think, an open question, largely because the problem has not begun to be fully perceived as such by the professionals in general, the legal profession in particular, or by the educational institutions that train professionals. . . .

[Wasserstrom goes on to discuss the ways that the relation between attorney and client typically denies the latter the respect and dignity accorded an equal. He concludes his explanation of the reasons for this situation in these words:] Finally, as I have indicated, to be a professional is to have been acculturated in a certain way. It is to have satisfactorily passed through a lengthy and allegedly difficult period of study and training. It is to have done something hard. Something that not everyone can do. Almost all professions encourage this way of viewing oneself; as having joined an elect group by virtue of hard work and mastery of the mysteries of the profession. In addition, the society at large treats members of a profession as members of an elite by paying them more than most people for the work they do with their heads rather than their hands, and by according them a substantial amount of social prestige and power by virtue of their membership in a profession. It is hard, I think, if not impossible, for a person to emerge from professional training and participate in a profession without the belief that he or she is a special kind of person, both different from and somewhat better than those nonprofessional members of the social order. It is equally hard for the other members of society not to hold an analogous view of the professionals. And these beliefs surely contribute, too, to the dominant role played by a professional in any professional-client relationship. . . .

Thus it is, for example, fairly easy to see how a number of the features already delineated conspire to depersonalize the client in the eyes of the lawyer *qua* professional. To begin with, the lawyer's conception of self as a person with special competencies in a certain area naturally leads him or her to see the client in a partial way. The lawyer *qua* professional is, of necessity, only centrally interested in that part of the client that lies within his or her special competency. And this leads any professional including the lawyer to respond to the client as an object—as a thing to be altered, corrected, or otherwise assisted by the professional rather than as a person. At best the client is viewed from the perspective of the professional not as a whole person but as a segment or aspect of a person—an interesting kidney problem, a routine marijuana possession case, or another adolescent with an identity crisis.

Then, too, the fact . . . that the professions tend to have and to develop their own special languages has a lot to do with the depersonalization of the client. And this certainly holds for the lawyers. For the lawyer can and does talk to other lawyers but not to the client in the language of the profession. What is more, the lawyer goes out of his or her way to do so. It is satisfying. It is the exercise of power. Because the ability to communicate is one of the things that distinguishes persons from objects, the inability of the client to communicate with the lawyer in the lawyer's own tongue surely helps to make the client less than a person in the lawyer's eyes—and perhaps even in the eyes of the client.

The forces that operate to make the relationship a paternalistic one seem to me to be at least as powerful. If one is a member of a collection of individuals who have in common the fact that their intellects are highly trained, it is very easy to believe that one knows more than most people. If one is a member of a collection of individuals who are accorded high prestige by the society at large, it is equally easy to believe that one is better and knows better than most people. If there is, in fact, an area in which one does know things that the client doesn't know, it is extremely easy to believe that one knows generally what is best for the client. All this, too, surely holds for lawyers.

In addition there is the fact, also already noted, that the client often establishes a relationship with the lawyer because the client has a serious problem or concern which has rendered the client weak and vulnerable. This, too, surely increases the disposition to respond toward the client in a patronizing, paternalistic fashion. The client of necessity confers substantial power over his or her wellbeing upon the lawyer. Invested with all of this power both by the individual and the society, the lawyer *qua* professional responds to the client as though the client were an individual who needed to be looked after and controlled, and to have decisions made for him or her by the lawyer, with as little interference from the client as possible. . . .

Comment

Wasserstrom sees lawyers adopt role-differentiated behavior for its moral comfort in light of the ambiguous position that society asks lawyers to fill. I certainly feel that to be true for me.

In lawyering and teaching, I often see the seeming arbitrariness of my decisions and actions. What I mean is that having certain power in a society and world beset by ills, I am constantly in the position of not pursuing certain goals in favor of others, not taking certain actions in a case I am handling or in a course I am teaching. Inevitably, this is *my* decision—I am choosing how to spend my time and lead my life. But I have often tried to content myself with saying "this is what a lawyer does," or "this is what a teacher does," thus seemingly avoiding my responsibility for the choice I am making.

Although defining reality on the basis of professional norms can often seem comforting at the time, I find that on a deeper level it is ultimately unsatisfying. I become alienated from myself. It is not that "what a lawyer would do" is irrelevant; it is that doing "what a lawyer (or teacher) would do" can become a substitute for my examining what I personally believe is right, and when that happens I have somehow lost myself and my connection with my own ideals in the process. If I am to compromise or settle for less than what I deeply hold true, at least I would rather see that that is what I am doing. If I do not see, I will fool myself into believing reality is different from what it is. I will learn to see and accept "reality" in terms constructed to exclude any possibility of expressing my own most deeply held values, and my actions will be based on my self-limiting vision.

It is not only because the moral dilemmas we face as lawyers are confusing: Wasserstrom also suggests that we accept the path of role-differentiated behavior because being present as ourselves is hard. I am more "skilled" at being an attorney or a teacher than at being myself. At least it seems that way. It seems safer somehow. I feel less vulnerable while maintaining that stance and that distance. And what is most disturbing about Wasserstrom's suggestion, because it feels so true, is that it is not simply a question of our letting go of role-differentiated behavior in some formalistic sense. There are many ways that I have made the characteristics of "lawyer" the characteristics of "me." In the law school we seem to spend much of our time thinking like lawyers, acting like lawyers, and arguing like lawyers, even when we are *not* in role. I am not sure how much it has to do with the fact, as Wasserstrom writes, that one's professional role becomes one's dominant role, and how much it has to do with the correlative apparent fact that we are attracted to professions in which our personality traits can have professional expression. In me, both feel true.

What is clear is that this "internalized role" affects much that I know I do, and probably much that I am not aware of. As I accept that effect, as a teacher and a lawyer, I inevitably restrict my human and moral universe in ways that limit who I am and what I am trying to serve. Much of me that is important and vital can be left out of my role and many of my thoughts, acts and arguments seem almost designed to keep me from seeing that. Therefore, it is crucial for me to be increasingly aware of and face these roles which can all too easily define and limit the full human dimensions of my work and life.

J.H.

William Simon, *The Ideology of Advocacy: Procedural Justice and Professional Ethics*, 1978 Wis. L. Rev. 30, 36-38, 52-59.

[By "The Ideology of Advocacy," Simon means "a framework of certain common, unquestioned principles," adherence to which he asserts is prevalent within the legal profession. He describes these principles in these words:

The first principle of conduct is the principle of neutrality. This principle prescribes that the lawyer remain detached from his client's ends. The lawyer is expected to represent people who seek his help regardless of his opinion of the justice of their ends. [When] he takes a case, he is not considered responsible for his client's purposes. . . . The second principle of conduct is partisanship. This principle prescribes that the lawyer work aggressively to advance his client's ends. The lawyer will employ means on behalf of his client which he would not consider proper in a non-professional context even to advance his own ends. . . .

[T]he principle of procedural justice [is] that there is an inherent value or legitimacy to the judicial proceeding (and to a more qualified extent, the entire legal system) which makes it possible for a lawyer to justify specific actions without reference to the consequences they are likely to promote. The . . . principle of . . . professionalism [is] that [ethical] questions are to be resolved in terms of legal doctrine and that they should be resolved by lawyers collectively in their occupational capacities and not by lawyers individually in terms of personal or social norms or by broadbased political institutions.]

The [Positivist*] lawyer purports to assist his client by using his objective knowledge of the precise, regular, mechanical operation of the legal system to predict the consequences of alternative courses of action. The lawyer assumes specific courses of action as factual hypotheses and reasons from them in accordance with the rules of the legal system in order to determine the consequences in terms of state action which follow from them. Yet, by itself, this type of assistance is of little use to the client. The client is not interested in the consequences of *any* course of action. Of the infinity of possible courses of action, he is interested in only those which might advance his ends. . . .

The Positivist version of the Ideology of Advocacy focuses on the person for whom the law is a mystery. Such a person, even if conscious of and articulate about his ends, would not know which aspects of them the lawyer would need to understand in order to gauge the impact of the legal system on his life. In order to isolate these aspects, he would need the legal knowledge for which he relies on his lawyer. The lawyer, on the other hand, has

---

* [Simon's use of Positivism has been described in Bellow & Moulton, The Lawyering Process: "In the 'positivist' version . . . ends are seen in Hobbesian terms as 'natural, individual, subjective and arbitrary,' and society is pictured as an aggregation of competing individuals. The lawyer's role is justified in such circumstances as an extension of the client's will in a system in which the client could not realize his or her entitlements without such assistance." (pp.106-107 n.37)]

no reliable way of learning the client's ends on his own. Because these ends are subjective, individual, and arbitrary, the lawyer has no access to them.[56] Because the lawyer's only direct experience of ends is his experience of his own ends, he cannot speculate on what the client's ends might be without referring to his own ends and thus biasing the neutral predictive analysis he is supposed to perform. Any attempt to frame inquiries to the client concerning his ends or to interpret the client's ambiguous replies will necessarily involve the intrusion of the lawyer's own ends. Thus, consciously or not, the Positivist lawyer is faced with a dilemma: On the one hand, he cannot give intelligible advice to his client without referring to ends; on the other hand, he cannot refer to ends without endangering the client's autonomy, and thus, undermining the basic purpose of his role.

The strategy [for dealing with the dilemma] is to impute certain basic ends to the client at the outset and to work to advance these imputed ends. . . . The Positivists seem to assume that, if the ends imputed are sufficiently . . . widespread, the risk of interference in the client's autonomy can be minimized. By imputing ends to the client at the outset, the lawyer obviates dangerous inquiries into the particular ends of the particular client. On the other hand, if most people actually do share the imputed ends to some degree, then the lawyer will usually advance the client's actual ends when he works to advance the imputed ends. The ends which Positivism imputes are derived from the basic Positivist premise of egoism, but they go beyond this initial premise to emphasize characteristics of extreme selfishness. The specific ends most often imputed are the maximization of freedom of movement and the accumulation of wealth. . . .

This Positivist strategy is a complete failure. It can only precipitate, rather than mitigate, the lawyer's subversion of the client's autonomy. . . . Unlike the hypothetical person assumed by the Positivist advocate, actual people have not just a few, discrete ends, but rather many ends which are interrelated in a complex fashion. Moreover, these ends are set in a social context in which the individual's fulfillment depends on his relations with others. Even assuming the basic Positivist psychology of egoism to be accurate, it would not follow that a person's ends could be reduced to a few crude presumptions. On the contrary, a person's fulfillment is likely to depend on a complex balance among many different satisfactions. Moreover, the attainment of individual satisfaction depends on the cooperation of others. . . .

56. Cf. S. Wolin, Politics and Vision: Continuity and Innovation in Western Political Thought 341 (1960) ("The basic assumption [of liberal political thought], that each was the best judge of his own interests, rested squarely on the belief that no individual could truly understand another").

Thus, when the client comes to the Positivist seeking to protect the delicate rhythms of his private life from disruption by the mechanical operation of the state, the lawyer will implement the very result he was supposed to prevent. The lawyer explains to the client the probable impact of the state, not on the client's own life, but on the life of the hypothetical person assumed in the Positivist model whose simple, crude ends bear only the most problematical relation to those of the client. This advice is much worse than useless to the client. Though it will often be irrelevant to his ends, the client may not be in a position to reject it. The client of whom Positivism is most solicitous is the naive person, face to face with the alien force of the state, threatened with a massive disruption of his life. Confronted with the need to act in this strange situation, the client must make sense of it as best he can. The lawyer puts himself forth quite plausibly as the client's best hope of mastering his predicament. If he is to avoid being overwhelmed by chaos, he must acquiesce in his lawyer's definition of the situation. He must think in a manner which gives coherence to the advice he is given. He may begin to do this quite unconsciously. If he is at all aware of the change, he is likely to see it as a defensive posture forced on him by the hostile intentions of opposing parties, of whom his perception is mediated by the categories of his lawyer's framework of analysis. His only strategy of survival requires that he see himself as the lawyers and the officials see him, as an abstraction, a hypothetical person with only a few crude, discrete ends. He must assume that his subtler ends, his long-range plans, and his social relationships are irrelevant to the situation at hand. This is the profound and unintended meaning of Holmes's remark:

> If you want to know the law and nothing else, you must look at it as a bad man, who cares only for the material consequences which such knowledge enables him to predict, not as a good one, who finds his reasons for conduct, whether inside the law or outside of it, in the vaguer sanctions of conscience.

The role of the bad man, conceived as an analytical device for the lawyer, becomes, under pressure of circumstances, a psychological reality for the client.

The image of rational choice by the client in response to neutral analysis by the lawyer is the shabbiest fiction of the Ideology of Advocacy. . . . Even where the issue is formally submitted to the client as a matter for his decision, the client's choice is determined, or at least strongly biased, by the way in which the lawyer defines the question.

Thus, a lawyer representing a murderer does not discuss

society's feelings about the nature of the crime, the legitimacy of the state's attempt to punish him, the client's own views of his actions, or their effect on his life in society. In advising him about whether to cooperate with the authorities, he will not explain the complex functional and extrinsic policies behind the privilege against self-incrimination. As a scrupulous professional, all he can do is explain that, of two courses equally incomprehensible to the client, one will probably lead to prison and the other to release. Similarly, the good Positivist advocate does not explain that the obligation made unenforceable by the Statute of Frauds would be binding but for a formality. Neither will he inquire into the fairness of the bargain, the nature of the relationship between the two parties, or the effect of not paying on the client's future business dealings or his standing in the community. His analysis must leave the client to decide whether or not he wishes to be coerced by the state to pay a sum of money to the plaintiff.

Of course, in practice, lawyers often do not even go through the motion of presenting critical questions to the client as occasions for choice. They decide the questions unilaterally in terms of the imputed ends of selfishness[64] . . .

Despite its complete irrationality, this Positivist strategy for dealing with the problem of inaccessibility of personal ends has become so widely accepted that many lawyers have come to

---

64. E.g., L. Auchincloss, The Partners (1974):

> She asked him to review one of her estate plans whereby the rich husband of an incompetent was enabled to set up a trust in such a way as to throw the bulk of his estate taxes on his wife's children by a prior marriage, leaving the trust principal intact for his own.
> "But the widow's property will all be gobbled up!"
> "I don't know what you mean by 'gobbled up,' Mr. Simmonds."
> "I mean that Mr. Pierson will have shoved the taxes that properly belong on his estate off on his wife's. His children will end up rich while hers are bust."
> "It's an odd situation, certainly. I think I have handled it to the advantage of my client."
> Ronny stared. "But does Mr. Pierson *know* about his wife's will and the effect of this?"
> Mrs. Stagg smiled thinly. *"One thing you'd better learn right away, Mr. Simmonds, is never to ask what clients know. Mr. Pierson does not*

come to One New Orange Plaza for spiritual advice. He wants to look after his incapacitated wife with the minimum injury to *his* offspring. I think that is precisely what my plan will effect." Id. at 32-33 (second emphasis added).

Mrs. Stagg is engaging in the strategy of imputed ends. For her, the issue is whether or not the client wishes to save money for his family, and the answer is sufficiently self-evident to make formal inquiry of the client superfluous. For Mr. Simmonds, the issue is whether the client wishes to save money for his family at the expense of his wife's family. Mrs. Stagg thinks that putting the question this way makes impermissible assumptions about the client's ends. The desire to save money for one's own family is sufficiently simple and basic an end to be imputable to the client. On the other hand, the concern for more remote relatives would implicate far more particular and subjective considerations. Since this concern is clearly on the far side of the line which separates the realm of imputable ends from the realm of pure equate the manipulation of the client in terms of imputed ends with neutral advice to the client on his rights. . . . The Positivist lawyer is not an advisor, but a lobbyist for a peculiar theory of human nature.

Positivist lawyers fail to see that the kind of behavior they impose on their clients is meaningless when it originates in the lawyer's conception of his own role rather than in the will of the client. And yet, because the imputed ends cannot approximate the complexity of the client's actual ends, Positivist advocacy cannot join forces with the will of the client. This is so even in the area of criminal defense, where the Positivist case for an imputed end is strongest, but nevertheless insufficient. It may be true that the desire to escape criminal punishment is basic and widespread. But the standard adversary defense cannot be justified by routinely imputing such a general desire to every client. The actual and specific ends of even a purely selfish individual may not be served by an adversary defense. For instance, such a defense may merely prolong and intensify an ordeal regarded as more terrible than the threatened punishment.[67] Or it may make the punishment, if it should occur, more difficult to endure by forcing the client to struggle against it and to deny its legitimacy.

The Positivist psychology either makes advocacy impossible or forces the lawyer into the strategy of imputed ends.

subjectivity, there is no more reason to present this consideration to the client than there is to ask him whether he wishes the trust assets to be invested in companies which do business with South Africa. In attempting to speculate on his client's actual ends, Mr. Simmonds has really been trying to foist his own personal ends on the client.

See also Patterson & Cheatham, [The Profession of Law], at 86: "The layman might well view [pleading the Statute of Frauds] as being unfair, but the advocate does not. The duty of loyalty to his client requires the plea, regardless of the merits of the claim." Notwithstanding the fact that the client, presumably a layman, might regard the plea as "unfair," the authors do not speak of consulting him, and they assume that the Statute will be routinely pleaded when it is available. The "duty of loyalty" thus appears to be, not to the client's actual ends, but to the imputed ends.

67. See, e.g., F. Dostoevsky, The Brothers Karamazov, at 552-53 (Magarshack trans. 1958). During the investigation by the examining magistrate and the public prosecutor, Dmitry Karamazov's fear and discomfort increase as the officials emphasize his procedural rights:

"You see, gentlemen," he said suddenly, restraining himself with difficulty, "you see—I listen to you and I seem to be haunted by a dream —you see, I sometimes have such a dream—a curious kind of dream—I often dream it—it keeps on recurring—that someone is chasing me— someone I'm terribly afraid of—chasing me in the dark at night—looking for me, and I hide somewhere from him behind a door or a cupboard— hide myself so humiliatingly—and the worst of it is that he knows perfectly well where I've hidden myself from him, but he seems to be pretending deliberately not to know where I am, so as to prolong my agony, to enjoy my terror to the full. . . . That's what you're doing now. It's just like that!"

Because the imputed ends ignore the most important dimensions of the client's personality, the strategy leads to the manipulation of the client by the lawyer in terms of the lawyer's own moral and psychological prejudices. In this manner, the lawyer becomes the agent of the result he was supposed to prevent. He subverts his client's autonomy. . . .

B. PERSONAL AWARENESS IN
PROFESSIONAL DEVELOPMENT

Curtis J. Berger, *The Legal Profession's Need for a Human Commitment*
3 Columbia University General Education Seminar Reports No.2,
pp.13-15 (1975).

.... I believe that legal education is too single-mindedly absorbed in affairs of the head and too inattentive to—indeed, rejecting of—matters of the heart. Legal education is an intensely cerebral pursuit. The highest praise we can bestow upon our students is to tell them that they "think like a lawyer," which requires a wholly analytical matrix for dealing with problems. Not logic alone, as Justice Holmes taught, but even as we factor social policy, or economics, or political theory into our analysis, we are calculating in the way we proceed. Our mindset is, how can we draw upon the wellsprings of our knowledge to make the best *lawyer's* argument for the conclusion we have reached.

That we prize intelligence is not an indictable offense. But I do charge our law school—and nearly every other law school—with encouraging the belief that high intelligence is virtually all that matters during law school and in the practice of law. That we deify high intelligence becomes evident to our students even before they arrive. This week's issue of the Law School News carries a story that our entering class is the finest first-year class we have ever matriculated. How do we value our students? How do we judge their worth? Their median LSAT score is 690; their median grade-point average, 3.6. Within a week after our first-year students arrive, they have heard about Law Review. And it becomes an *idée fixe* that their careers cannot amount to much if Law Review, the quintessence of intellectual meritocracy, eludes their grasp. But, in fact, that will happen to 90 percent of our students. Within the classroom, they hear their instructors brilliantly, but often aridly, dissecting court opinions, ridiculing fuzzy-headed thinking, stifling passions as unprofessional. Students learn quickly that if we, their instructors, are to judge them highly, they must prove themselves with their heads.

I believe that the head is attached to the heart—not only biologically—and that it is the pulsating heart of the professional man or woman that legal education has avoided. I do not assert that legal education makes our graduates evil, but I do believe that legal education makes our graduates less feeling, less caring, less sensitive to the needs of others, less tolerant of the frailties of their fellow creatures, even less alarmed about the injustices of our society, than they were when they entered law school. What concerns me is the mind-set and the heart-set into which we mold our students: that it is better to be smart than passionate; that people who feel too deeply tend not to think too clearly; that a fine intellect can rationalize any position or state of affairs, no matter how outrageous or indecent or unjust. . . .

At the risk of sounding simplistic, we should train our students to deal with other human beings, so they will begin to understand that when a client comes into a lawyer's office he is usually a disturbed person, so they will begin to appreciate that very often what surfaces as a legal problem has its roots in deep-seated social problems. Above all—and this has nothing to do with the curriculum—I think that we as teachers must let our students know that we value them, and not only for their intellectual abilities. For unless lawyers value the compassionate in their own beings, I think they will be incapable of caring about the human needs of others.

Scott Turow, *One L*
pp.91-92 (Putnam 1977).

All of our teachers tried to impress upon us that you do not sway a judge with emotional declarations of faith. Nicky Morris often derided responses as "sentimental goo," and Perini on more than one occasion quickly dispatched students who tried to argue by asserting supposedly irreducible principles.

Why, Perini asked one day, is the right to bargain and form contracts granted to all adults, rather than a select group within the society?

Because that was fundamental, one student suggested, basic: All persons are created equal.

"Oh, *are* they?" Perini asked. "Did you create them, Mr. Vivian? Have you taken a survey?"

"I believe it," Vivian answered.

"Well, hooray," said Perini, "that proves a great deal. How do you *justify* that, Mr. Vivian?"

The demand that we examine and justify our opinions was not always easily fulfilled. Many of the deepest beliefs often seemed inarticulable in their foundations, or sometimes contradictory of other strongly felt principles. I found that frequently. I thought, for example, that wealth should be widely distributed, but there were many instances presented in class which involved taking from the poor, for whom I felt that property rights should be regarded as absolute.

Yet, with relative speed, we all seemed to gain skill in reconciling and justifying our positions. In the fourth week of school, Professor Mann promoted a class debate on various schemes for regulating prostitution, and I noticed the differences in style of argument from similar sessions we'd had earlier in the year. Students now spoke about crime statistics and patterns of violence in areas where prostitution occurred. They pointed to evidence, and avoided emotional appeals and arguments based on the depth and duration of their feelings.

But to Gina, the process which had brought that kind of change about was frightening and objectionable.

"I don't care if Bertram Mann doesn't want to know how I *feel* about prostitution," she said that day at lunch. "I *feel* a lot of things about prostitution and they have everything to do with the way I *think* about prostitution. I don't want to become the kind of person who tries to pretend that my feelings have nothing to do with my opinions. It's not *bad* to feel things."

Gina was not the only classmate making remarks like that. About the same time, from three or four others, people I respected, I heard similar comments, all to the effect that they were being limited, harmed, by the education, forced to substitute dry reason for emotion, to cultivate opinions which were "rational" but which had no roots in the experience, the life they'd had before. They were being cut away from themselves.

Comment

I haven't been able to resolve this clash between the whole of me, which includes my feelings, and law school. It hurts me that my own experiencing is not thought relevant to the civilized intellectual analytic gymnastics for which courses are designed. The most painful example I can give is the Constitutional Law classroom treatment of abortion. I was seething with rage, that there in that book were my rights about my body and my ability to choose my life. Furious at how those rights reached existence—through men who were judges, lawyers, doctors, psychiatrists, hospital administrators, legislators. Terrified at how fragile those rights might become. Wounded by injustices of centuries. And pricked by my conscience and religion (what's left of it) because I'm not sure that I would exercise the freedom I see as requisite to justice for women.

More immediately, in that class, with all this turmoil inside, I was furious, frustrated and pained not to be able to get it out. There were different restraints operating on me then. One was my own fear of speaking out in a class that size, as a woman, in what I knew would be a very emotional way. Also, I knew that I wanted to explode emotionally, and it was

very clear, from the professor's handling of the material, which was absolutely frigid, and from every message I'd received since I'd first walked
into that law school a year and a half before, that emotionally charged
discussion was highly inappropriate. I did not know how to bridge the gap
between all of my feelings about abortion and the normal classroom intellectual style. I said nothing.

B.B.

Comment*

I often respond to a comment or question in a way that blunts the
political challenge or the emotional content that animates it, and thereby
avoids the anxiety that would be produced by permitting the challenge to
surface or by allowing the student's unwelcome feelings or unfocused
groping to come out unimpeded. Many times I realize (as soon as class is
over) that someone asked a question or made a comment that obviously
reflected an unexpressed challenge. A common example is a question that
asks for information, but that covers skepticism or hostility toward my
perceived views or those reflected in the course materials. In one instance,
I had been considering eligibility requirements in unemployment in-
surance and had been developing the point that the contours of those requirements were affected by the fact that the experience-rating system
gives the employer a financial stake in its employees' eligibility for
unemployment benefits. A student asked in a bland, guarded way what
the objection was to letting the employer's financial interest influence the
eligibility rules. The student obviously thought that such an interpenetra-
tion between financing methods and eligibility rules was self-evidently
sensible. But he did not *say* that, and I answered the question as he chose
to put it: He asked for the objection, and I gave it to him, fully and in an
expository manner. When I finished, he had no response, and I went on.
The real issue he was raising—that he saw controlling significance in the
employer's perspective, and was surprised and vexed to realize that
others did not—was never explored, although it was exactly the issue I
most want students to recognize and grapple with. By coming close to
confronting the basic policy choice, he gave me a fine opportunity which I
turned aside before it surfaced visibly.

Why did our interaction take this self-defeating form? For his part,
the student was channeled to respond in the form of a question seeking information, rather than through a direct challenge to my priorities. To do
so seems more "legal" and analytical; it blunts the challenge to the
teacher's authority; it minimizes the student's exposure of his own value
system; it is less likely to engender hostility from classmates.

I in turn allowed the veiled quality of the challenge to keep it from surfacing, and collaborated in a dialogue that skirted the issues I wanted to
expose. I could have commented directly to him on what appeared to

* This Comment is a revision of a portion
of an essay published, with others, as
Reassessing Law Schooling: The Sterling
Forest Group, 53 N.Y.U.L. Rev. 561, 565
(1978).

underlie his question, but I did not. I could have asked the class for reactions to it, which might have flushed the issues out, but I did not. The choice made was made reflexively—but was nonetheless a choice—to take the "safe" road; it probably responded to my fear of embarrassment or politicization, my desire to prevent the surfacing of a distasteful problem at a time when I most feel the need to be able to move quickly and surely over the changing ground of class discussion.

I do not know as a teacher how to react to interpersonal hostility among students in a constructive way so that the dialogue does not simply call forth discord, but acknowledges and confronts it, and goes on to grapple in class with its relevance to the setting of public policy and to the practice of law. By turning aside nascent—or full-blown—manifestations of hostility, I contribute to a shared exaggeration of their destructiveness and inappropriateness, of their irrelevance to "law." Issues of distributive justice are unquestionably divisive and depressing. They are not resolved by good lawyering. If the issues we talk about in class, or their implications, are just plain upsetting, there may be an unspoken agreement to try to steer clear of them. By subscribing to this agreement, we make their airing seem even more fearsome than it need be.

H.L.

George Brown, *Human Teaching For Human Learning*
pp.10-12 (Viking 1971).

The position of most educators at all levels is that the primary function of schools is to teach the learner to be intellectually competent. The position is described by those who hold it as realistic, hardheaded, and a number of other fine-sounding things. Our belief is that this position is instead most unrealistic and illusionary. Oh, yes, it would greatly simplify matters if we could somehow isolate intellectual experience from emotional experience, but at the moment this is possible only in textbooks and experimental designs. The cold, hard, stubborn reality is that whenever one learns intellectually, there is an inseparable accompanying emotional dimension. The relationship between intellect and affect is indestructibly symbiotic. And instead of trying to deny this, it is time we made good use of the relationship. Indeed, the purest, highest form of abstract thinking is coupled with congruent feelings on the part of the thinker, even in the grossest sense of pleasure, boredom or pain. Or, as Michael Polanyi has observed, it is the passion of the scholar that makes for truly great scholarship.

The more of reality a person has available to him, the more effective he becomes in work, in play, and in love. What has happened to most of us is that we have learned to continually substitute fantasies for reality. This is aggravated by the fact that we share many of these fantasies; that is, they are socially reinforced. This is a large and complex area. But here is a somewhat oversimplified description of how the substitution of fantasy for reality can occur.

As children, we are unable to separate the acts we do from the feelings or impulses that accompany them. When we are punished for a naughty act, we also assign the punishment to the feelings that precipitated and sustained the act. What we feel is thus as bad as what we do. As we become socialized or learn to behave in acceptable ways, we not only restrain our "bad" acts but also repress our "bad" feelings. There are a number of psychological mechanisms that enable us to do this, but whatever the means we use, we are forced to deaden ourselves. We must deny feeling. The more we deaden our bad feelings, the more we deaden all feeling, for apparently we have no way of selecting for elimination only those unacceptable feelings. The deadening is an over-all process. As the process of deadening persists, we lose touch to the extent that we are no longer aware of what we really do feel. We eventually reach a point where we have little choice about how we behave, for, deprived of feelings to tell us what we want or don't want, we react primitively, compulsively, ritualistically. It is not surprising, then, that without access to their feelings a large number of people really do not know that they want.

We do not suggest as an ideal the hedonistic, anarchistic individual who expresses his feelings no matter what, where, when, or who. This sort of person is as "out of it" as the one who has no feelings. A healthy individual has a mind and uses it—not to deny the existence of feelings but to differentiate how, when, and with whom it is appropriate to express feelings spontaneously from occasions when one must wait. When he chooses to postpone or control the *expression* of his feelings, however, he does not at the same time deny to himself that *they exist. . . .*

Comment

"The more of reality a person has available. . . ." George Brown's words are, for me, a simple and profound justification for seeking a humanistic education in law. If I refuse to acknowledge a part of reality, then I have that much less reality available. If my vision is based on a distorted view, then I diminish what I can contribute and receive. If together we collude in the denial of aspects of reality—Brown notes the role of social reinforcement in maintaining the power of an illusion—then together we will fail to see. And, conversely, the more of reality we have available, the more we can see, and do.

Brown's criticism of all education for magnifying the role of intellectual experience while denying the emotional is pertinent to legal education. Curtis Berger has pointed to the exaltation of the head over the heart, and we can add other examples—pragmatism over idealism, information over understanding, the hard over the soft, and the objective over the subjective. Our tendency as members of the legal profession to value certain aspects of reality over others is no secret, even from ourselves. We know of the lawyer's mindset. We know of the way we can lawyer students and colleagues, friends and family. We are so skilled at putting reality in boxes that it comes as no surprise to discover we have boxed ourselves in in the process. Whether we justify our methods or decry them, we easily become their prisoners—our illusions have us trapped.

There is inevitably a price to be paid for this denial of reality. What we do not admit to be real does not disappear. Our denial only diminishes our ability to see and appreciate, and to act on what we see. If we deny the validity of the emotional aspects of reality they only move underground— their experience and expression become masked. From my perspective, the emotional dimensions, for teacher and student alike, permeate the law school and affect learning in vital ways. Feelings of frustration, cynicism, anger, arrogance as well as insecurity, poignancy and caring abound—the former expressed more easily, although hardly acknowledged, the latter more commonly suppressed, in experience as well as expression.

For me, a search for a humanistic education in law will mean finding ways to include and validate the subjective dimension of our experience. The subjective dimension includes the emotional and much more in addition; the way we experience the world, our self-images, our thinking processes, our values and beliefs and our sense of purpose and meaning. To deny that dimension does not deny the force of our subjective colorations, it is only to pretend to others and to ourselves that they are not there. It is holding on to a false illusion of objectivity, which is not only untrue, but a distortion of objectivity itself. It may be essential to include an awareness of the subjective dimension of reality if we are to understand and communicate—with one another and within ourselves. How often does the intellectual power of our arguments sting with a force we do not admit or have an impact we do not understand? Ironically, our search for an objective shared reality would seem to demand an increasing recognition of our subjective lenses.

Yet when I think of this task I find it hard to know where to begin or how to proceed. When I ask myself how to make more of reality available when I am with my students, or my colleagues, or by myself, I find no simple answer. I am tempted even to put the question out of mind, to hide even that, along with the unknown and feared pains and frustrations, rewards and joys that attempts at answering the question could bring.

When I turn to my students, I am filled with doubts about what Brown says. There are materials to master, skills of analysis to learn; there are judges who decide on narrow grounds, employers and clients who pay for tunnel vision, adversaries ready to take advantage of any departure from a narrow norm. Is that what we mean by the "real world," a world in which we collude in the denial of a reality that includes so much more? Who am I to invite students to ask these questions when they must go out into the "real world?"

Must the process of obtaining mastery necessarily mean a denial of so much of reality, a self-imposed and self-fulfilling imprisonment, of oneself and others? The questions will not go away, nor the hopes that balance the fears. Is there any way for our lives in law to open to more?

J.H.

Comment

The significant lesson I learned while in law school is that for me everything does start with my caring. That is what commits the whole of me to what I am doing; care is what taps into my most effective energy. I learned that it is possible and essential to me to care, and that caring is not sentimentality that should be separate from my professional life. It's a fact, too, that I am like this, and it is a part of my lawyering every bit as much as it is a part of me. I will not put the caring down in order to have law. Until I learned this, it seemed that this noble thing, The Law, would reject me, because these feelings continually surfaced in me and I could not keep them hidden: My clients suffered, the remedies didn't remedy, classmates were miserable, I felt inadequate. I was depressed, and I wanted to talk about these things and more.

But if I paid attention to them, wouldn't they take over and wipe out the pieces of the legal craft I was trying to learn? I feared they would. The model of a lawyer that I picked up along with most of the law students I know did not include feelings. A good lawyer was dispassionate and analytical and therefore able to work cleverly and creatively to the good of the client. The first experience I had with the inadequacy of that model was with a clinical client whose possible contract action was a good ten years old. Starting with the basics of legal procedure in the real world, the answer to his question was clear to me: "No, I'm very sorry, you cannot proceed because the statute of limitations has run." I could not let it stop there. I could not answer, "No case, I can't help you." When I tried to remain dispassionate, I found I didn't know how.

I tried drawing lines on what I could properly do for clients and I couldn't stay within the bounds I drew. Extraneous passions *roared* through me, physically. I worried that I would lose control. I feared the effect on me of listening to the feelings inside triggered by what I saw in my clients' lives. I feared, "Oh my God, I can't make it as a lawyer." Then I discovered nascent feelings that my own hurting was OK (maybe). And it has turned out to be so in all my clinical work. The feelings I was experiencing do not have an adverse effect on my lawyering; in fact, they motivate me to better lawyering all around. They need not and do not interfere with my legal craftsmanship; they do allow me to feel that it is me being a lawyer, not a stranger or a mask.

B.B.

Erving & Miriam Polster, *Gestalt Therapy Integrated* pp.211-228 (Bruner/Mazel 1973).

At its best, awareness is a continuous means for keeping up to date with one's self. It is an ongoing process, readily available at all times, rather than an exclusive or sporadic illumination that can be achieved—like insight—only at special moments or under special conditions. . . . Furthermore, focusing on one's awareness keeps one absorbed in the present situation. . . .

[W]e would like to call attention to four main aspects of human experience where awareness can be focused. They are: awareness of sensations and actions, awareness of feelings, awareness of wants and awareness of values and assessments. . . .

Identifying basic sensations is no easy task. If the gap could be closed between basic sensations and more complex behavior, there would probably be fewer instances of incongruent or out-of-touch actions. It is common for an individual to eat, for example, not only because he is hungry but also because it is mealtime, or because he may not be in the right situation to eat later on when he expects he *will* be hungry, or because he likes company rather than eating alone, or because he can get a particular kind of food now and won't be able to get it later or when he is in another place. It is only too plain that the individual's sensations and what he does about them are often only distantly or obscurely related. So it is not surprising that the resulting muddle only adds to the oft-lamented crisis of identity—how *can* one know who he is without at least minimally knowing what goes on inside? And how can he know what is going on inside when so much of his experience seduces him away from honoring the process? . . . And so, the fact is that people who are lonely sometimes eat, those who are angry make love, and those who are sexually aroused make speeches. In such perversions of the relationship between feeling and doing lies the crux of self-alienation. . . .

While it is true, of course, that the feeling level of personal experience is inextricably related to sensation, feelings do have a quality which goes beyond the range of rudimentary sensation. When a person says he is afraid, he is telling what his feeling is. Subsumed within this feeling-tone, perhaps even supporting it, he may recognize specific sensations such as heart palpitations, sweaty palms, fluttery stomach or shortness of breath. On the other hand, he may feel afraid without these sensory accompaniments; experiencing and knowing his fear clearly and intuitively but without awareness of any of the subsidiary sensations.

Feelings include a personal assessment, an attempt to fit this particular event into the larger scheme of one's experience; sensations can be accepted piecemeal and do not seem to require or elicit this sense of fit. Heart palpitations in and of themselves say very little about a person's total being because they are non-specific; one's heart may beat rapidly under conditions which differ as widely as fear may differ from eager anticipation. . . .

Awareness of wants, like awareness of any experience, is an orienting function. It directs, it mobilizes, it channels, it focuses. A want is a blip into the future. People who have no wants— depressed people, for example—have no future. Everything seems worthless or hopeless, so nothing matters enough even to want it. If something does happen, and if the depressed person is not too desensitized, perhaps he may acknowledge the happening, but his own experience leans into nowhere.

A want is a linking function, integrating present experience with the future where its gratification lies and also with the past which it culminates and summarizes. Wants grow from where one has been; making sense out of the sensations and feelings which lead to this moment of wanting. Only by touching into where one is and what one wants right now can one forge the central link in the chain of events and experiences which make up one's life.

It seems axiomatic to say that one needs to know what one wants before he can be gratified, but in fact this is not invariably true. Many satisfactions come about without our ever becoming aware of wanting them. I see you smile and I light up too, but I didn't experience *wanting* you to smile—it just happened. Since many experiences like this do just happen, unplanned and spontaneous, many people come to *depend* on these happenings as their primary means of gratification. The problem is, though, that while these experiences are enriching and inevitable in life's unpredictable benevolence, they are like bonuses—unfortunately, undependable. Much of the gratification available requires us, like a sunflower, to face in the right direction and to move, literally or figuratively, in that direction. Knowing what we want, as the sunflower *knows* it wants sunlight, arouses us to move. . . .

Comment

Awareness of values and assessments—the ability to recognize one's values and assess whether they are relevant to the present situation or only important to who one was in the past—hit me during one class in a way that is related to the questions Wasserstrom poses about the lawyer's role: Does the lawyer's role have a particular form? What is wrong with acting as a traditional professional? What would be best? What is effective? I believe that holding onto the questions is valuable, even if I have no answers. Asking the questions changes my perspective on how I have to be as a student or as a lawyer.

As a student, I generally do my reading before class, take notes, expect the teacher to tell me what is important, accept his or her judgment, and speak up to answer a question or when called on. I don't presume to know the direction the course or any particular class should take. The role of law student I had adopted is that of a passive receiver of information.

In this particular class the teacher made a comment about women that infuriated me. I had previously had the experience of being deeply disturbed by things said in class. I had reacted by turning off, shutting down, counting the minutes until the end of the class and leaving physically as quickly as possible. This time I actually asked myself questions like those I listed above. Do I want to react normally? What else could I do? What is most effective? As I asked the questions I was flooded with answers. I realized that I could do any number of things: react normally, speed up my normal reaction by walking out, challenge his statement on intellectual grounds, tell him during class that I feel personally insulted by what he said, speak to the teacher privately about my reaction, make a general appeal to the class to refuse to put up with his nonsense, or make a formal complaint to the powers-that-be.

When I focused on what I, Liz, a person who is a student in this class, wanted to do, I made a choice and I acted on it. I spoke up, without raising my hand, and made an emotional statement challenging his comment on intellectual grounds. That experience has been very important for me. I did some things that Liz, the student, doesn't do: volunteer a comment in a large class without waiting for the teacher's permission to speak, show my strong feelings about a real world and legal problem in the classroom, challenge a teacher as I would challenge a peer, and draw on my outside experience when speaking in class. What was most important to me was that in deciding to do all these things that I would usually never even dream of doing, I did what the whole of me wanted to do instead of subordinating most of myself (my experience, my feelings, my beliefs) to my role. And what has stayed with me most clearly since then is my surprise and then delight at the awareness that I have any number of choices; the boundaries of the role I have adopted are not the limit of what I can do.

E.D.

Robert Pirsig, *Zen and the Art of Motorcycle Maintenance*
pp.304, 306-307 (Bantam 1975).

Of the value traps, the most widespread and pernicious is value rigidity. This is an inability to revalue what one sees because of commitment to previous values. . . .

The most striking example of value rigidity I can think of is the old South Indian Monkey Trap, which depends on value rigidity for its effectiveness. The trap consists of a hollowed-out coconut chained to a stake. The coconut has some rice inside which can be grabbed through a small hole. The hole is big enough so that the monkey's hand can go in, but too small for his fist with rice in it to come out. The monkey reaches in and is suddenly trapped—by nothing more than his own value rigidity. He can't revalue the rice. He cannot see that freedom without rice is more valuable than capture with it. The villagers are coming to get him and take him away. They're coming closer . . . closer! . . . now! What general advice—not specific advice—but what *gen-*

eral advice would you give the poor monkey in circumstances like this?

Well, I think you might say exactly what I've been saying about value rigidity, with perhaps a little extra urgency. There is a fact this monkey should know: if he opens his hand he's free. But how is he going to discover this fact? By removing the value rigidity that rates rice above freedom. How is he going to do that? Well, he should somehow try to slow down deliberately and go over ground that he has been over before and see if things he thought were important really *were* important and, well, stop yanking and just stare at the coconut for a while. Before long he should get a nibble from a little fact wondering if he is interested in it. He should try to understand this fact not so much in terms of his big problem as for its own sake. That problem may not be as big as he thinks it is. That fact may not be as small as he thinks it is either. That's about all the general information you can give him.

Comment

There are many ways to deny myself a full awareness of what is important to me. I can prize what I value so highly that, like the monkey, I am apt to hold tightly and firmly to it. That seems such a logical thing to do that it takes parables like this (or sheer exhaustion) to make me realize that I am prizing holding on more than what I value or more than the process that leads me to discover what I value.

I can do that with my teaching, with a concept, with a feeling. Clearly the closed fist approach keeps me from discovering what is valuable *now:* not forever, of course, because if I don't change then I will be forced to, but it will be a grudging and highly unsatisfying effort. That seems true to me as well for legal education and the legal system. Both often seem to be holding so tightly to old forms that they resist being open to the new values and new forms that might serve them, or even to keeping the old values truly alive in the present reality.

Of course, this could be seen as a recipe for valuing nothing or simply following any passing mode, and that is not what I'm saying. The impulse that led the monkey to close his fist seems fine; the refusing to let go is the problem. It is not that the monkey should never again close his fist on rice. It is that *holding* is not the value. For me it is important to remember that it is the discovery and shared experience of values that I am seeking. That I would like to hold to . . . lightly enough to make it possible.

J.H.

Carl Rogers, *Person to Person*
p.88 (Pocket 1975).

Being real involves the difficult task of being acquainted with the flow of experiencing going on within oneself, a flow

marked especially by complexity and continuous change. So if I
sense that I am feeling bored by my contacts with this student,
and this feeling persists, I think I owe it to him and to our relationship to share this feeling with him. But here again I will want
to be constantly in touch with what is going on in me. If I am, I
will recognize that it is *my* feeling of being bored which I am expressing, and not some supposed fact about him as a boring person. If I voice it as *my own* reaction, it has the potentiality of
leading to a deeper relationship. But this feeling exists in the
context of a complex and changing flow, and this needs to be
communicated too. I would like to share with him my distress at
feeling bored, and the discomfort I feel in expressing this aspect
of me. As I share these attitudes I find that my feeling of
boredom arises from my sense of remoteness from him, and that
I would like to be more in touch with him. And even as I try to express these feelings, they change. I am certainly *not* bored as I
try to communicate myself to him in this way, and I am far from
bored as I wait with eagerness and perhaps a bit of apprehension
for his response. I also feel a new sensitivity to him, now that I
have shared this feeling which has been a barrier between us. So
I am very much more able to hear the surprise or perhaps the
hurt in his voice as he now finds *him*self speaking more genuinely because I have dared to be real with him. I have let myself
be a person—real, imperfect—in my relationship with him.

Comment

Recently I have begun to seek out the personal dimension in my encounters with people I meet in my capacity as a law school administrator,
at least to the extent that I remember to do so. Sometimes then I notice
that the person I am with is troubled or in pain. It comes as a shock. The
meeting will have been progressing easily, with me trying to be open and
friendly, when all of a sudden I see that the other person is in pain. I do a
sort of awareness gasp—"Hey, this is a lot more important than I
thought"—and shift down to a level where I feel much more concern. I get
frightened. The meeting becomes a great deal more serious than I had an-
ticipated. This kind of unanticipated turn disturbs me. Also, in addition to
the shock of the unexpected, I have terrible difficulties being with someone in pain. My infant daughter's crying unnerves me, as does my wife's
anxiety about her.

Of course, I don't have to go deeper. I can continue the meeting on a
very matter-of-fact basis. The ostensible point of these meetings is
usually easy to deal with, e.g., an employee asking to take a little extra
time at lunch or students asking for permission to post flyers on our
classroom doors. It is far "easier" to keep it on the matter-of-fact level and
I worry about my competence to reach out to someone in pain. How could
I possibly help? Recently however, I have tentatively tried it. It is very
new for me and I am not too clear about what happens, but what is ex-

tremely clear is that I come to know the other person as a person, not just as a request or a problem. In most instances he or she will take the opportunity, and the situation will become real in a way and dimension that had been lacking before. I come to feel very relaxed and at ease with the person. We resolve the immediate problem and we do something more: We acknowledge one another's reality and importance.

P.S.

2.   THE SEARCH FOR MEANING

> And now, perhaps, I ought to
> have done. But I know that some
> spirit of fire will feel that his main
> question has not been answered. He
> will ask, What is all this to my soul?
> You do not bid me sell my birthright
> for a mess of pottage; what have you
> said to show that I can reach my own
> spiritual possibilities through such a
> door as this? How can the laborious
> study of a dry and technical system,
> the greedy watch for clients and
> practice of shopkeepers' arts, the
> mannerless conflicts over often sor-
> did interests, make out a life?
> —O.W. Holmes, Jr., *The Profession
> of the Law*

A.   THE NEED TO SEARCH

Leo Tolstoy, *A Confession,* Bayley, ed., *The Portable Tolstoy*
pp.676-680 (Penguin 1978).

I wrote: teaching what was for me the only truth—namely,
that one should live so as to have the best for oneself and one's
family.

So I lived; but five years ago something very strange began
to happen to me. At first I experienced moments of perplexity
and arrest of life, as though I did not know what to do or how to
live; and I felt lost and became dejected. But this passed, and I
went on living as before. Then these moments of perplexity
began to recur oftener and oftener, and always in the same form.
They were always expressed by the questions: What is it for?
What does it lead to?

At first it seemed to me that these were aimless and irrelevant questions. I thought that it was all well known, and that if I
should ever wish to deal with the solution it would not cost me
much effort: just at present I had no time for it, but when I

47

wanted to I should be able to find the answer. The questions however began to repeat themselves frequently, and to demand replies more and more insistently; and like drops of ink always falling on one place they ran together into one black blot. . . .

I understood that . . . if these questions constantly repeated themselves they would have to be answered. And I tried to answer them. The questions seemed such stupid, simple, childish ones; but as soon as I touched them and tried to solve them I at once became convinced, first, that they are not childish and stupid but the most important and profound of life's questions; and secondly that, try as I would, I could not solve them. Before occupying myself with my Samára estate, the education of my son, or the writing of a book, I had to know *why* I was doing it. As long as I did not know why, I could do nothing and could not live. Amid the thoughts of estate management which greatly occupied me at that time, the question would suddenly occur: "Well, you will have 6,000 *desyatinas* of land in Samára Government and 300 horses, and what then?" . . . And I was quite disconcerted and did not know what to think. Or when considering plans for the education of my children, I would say to myself: "What for?" Or when considering how the peasants might become prosperous, I would suddenly say to myself: "But what does it matter to me?" Or when thinking of the fame my works would bring me, I would say to myself, "Very well; you will be more famous than Gógol or Púshkin or Shakespeare or Molière, or than all the writers in the world—and what of it?" And I could find no reply at all. The questions would not wait, they had to be answered at once, and if I did not answer them it was impossible to live. But there was no answer.

I felt that what I had been standing on had collapsed and that I had nothing left under my feet. What I had lived on no longer existed, and there was nothing left. . . . My life came to a standstill. I could breathe, eat, drink, and sleep, and I could not help doing these things; but there was no life, for there were no wishes the fulfilment of which I could consider reasonable. If I desired anything, I knew in advance that whether I satisfied my desire or not, nothing would come of it. Had a fairy come and offered to fulfil my desires I should not have known what to ask. If in moments of intoxication I felt something which, though not a wish, was a habit left by former wishes, in sober moments I knew this to be a delusion and that there was really nothing to wish for. I could not even wish to know the truth, for I guessed of what it consisted. The truth was that life is meaningless. I had as it were lived, lived, and walked, walked, till I had come to a precipice and saw clearly that there was nothing ahead of me but destruction. It was impossible to stop, impossible to go back, and impossible to close my eyes or avoid seeing that there was nothing ahead but suffering and real death—complete annihilation. . . .

And all this befell me at a time when all around me I had what is considered complete good fortune. I was not yet fifty; I had a good wife who loved me and whom I loved, good children, and a large estate which without much effort on my part improved and increased. I was respected by my relations and acquaintances more than at any previous time. I was praised by others and without much self-deception could consider that my name was famous. And far from being insane or mentally diseased, I enjoyed on the contrary a strength of mind and body such as I have seldom met with among men of my kind; physically I could keep up with the peasants at mowing, and mentally I could work for eight and ten hours at a stretch without experiencing any ill results from such exertion. And in this situation I came to this—that I could not live, and, fearing death, had to employ cunning with myself to avoid taking my own life. . . .

Involuntarily it appeared to me that there, somewhere, was someone who amused himself by watching how I lived for thirty or forty years: learning, developing, maturing in body and mind; and how, having with matured mental powers reached the summit of life from which it all lay before me, I stood on that summit —like an arch-fool—seeing clearly that there is nothing in life, and that there has been and will be nothing. And *he* was amused. . . .

But whether that "someone" laughing at me existed or not, I was none the better off. I could give no reasonable meaning to any single action or to my whole life. I was only surprised that I could have avoided understanding this from the very beginning —it has been so long known to all. To-day or To-morrow sickness and death will come (they had come already) to those I love or to me; nothing will remain but stench and worms. Sooner or later my affairs, whatever they may be, will be forgotten, and I shall not exist. Then why go on making any effort? . . . How can man fail to see this? And how go on living? That is what is surprising! One can only live while one is intoxicated with life; as soon as one is sober it is impossible not to see that it is all a mere fraud and a stupid fraud! That is precisely what it is: there is nothing either amusing or witty about it, it is simply cruel and stupid.

There is an Eastern fable, told long ago, of a traveller overtaken on a plain by an enraged beast. Escaping from the beast he gets into a dry well and sees at the bottom of the well a dragon that has opened its jaws to swallow him. And the unfortunate man, not daring to climb out lest he should be destroyed by the enraged beast, and not daring to leap to the bottom of the well lest he should be eaten by the dragon, seizes a twig growing in a crack in the well and clings to it. His hands are growing weaker and he feels he will soon have to resign himself to the destruction that awaits him above or below, but still he clings on. Then he sees that two mice, a black and a white one, go regularly round and round the stem of the twig to which he is clinging and gnaw at it. And soon the twig itself will snap and he will fall into the dragon's jaws. The traveller sees this and knows that he will inevitably perish; but while still hanging he looks around, sees some drops of honey on the leaves of the twig, reaches them with his tongue, and licks them. So I too clung to the twig of life, knowing that the dragon of death was inevitably awaiting me, ready to tear me to pieces, and I could not understand why I had fallen into such torment. I tried to lick the honey which formerly consoled me, but the honey no longer gave me pleasure, and the white and black mice of day and night gnawed at the branch by which I hung. I saw the dragon clearly and the honey no longer tasted sweet. I only saw the unescapable dragon and the mice, and I could not tear my gaze from them. And this is not a fable but the real unanswerable truth intelligible to all. . . .

Comment

Prior to my participating in the project on humanistic education in the law, my approach to teaching, and perhaps to life, could have been summarized in the single word, "control." In class this meant that I had to be in absolute command of the material, of myself and of the students. The hour was prestructured with incredible detail including questions and observations designed to elicit each nuance (from my perspective) of the material assigned. With a much more than adequate background preparation of the material and with the construction and rehearsal of an intricate script, I was then ready to appear stage center and perform. And perform I did. The students uniformly gave my courses high marks and indicated that they thought they had learned a lot. Random and chance follow-ups with them in practice indicate that this is so. They seemed to develop both a firm grasp of the substantive material covered and the ability to lawyer effectively in the lacunae between various opinions and statutes. The foregoing was, and is, a source of immense satisfaction to me and in large part confirms my choice of career.

The quest for the rationally relevant dominated my classroom. The personal experience, the curiosity about what happened on remand after the appellate opinion we were studying—these and like concerns were rewarded with the demeaning phrase, "that's irrelevant," and sometimes with the condescending explanation that we were there to master principles of law and to develop dexterity in manipulating them.

My approach to teaching was but a manifestation of my most orderly approach to life, an approach characterized by intellect and rationality. Decisions, whether great or small, were rarely spontaneous; they reflected a careful weighing of alternatives and consequences. Each action had to be predicated on deliberate choice capable of articulation. An idea, option or concern unsusceptible to explicit expression, if not rejected out of hand, was viewed with much suspicion. A hunch was rarely pursued. Considerable energy was expended in determining what was relevant to the particular issue at hand. The discounting of the feeling or emotional approach to problem-solving represented, at least in part, a shorthand manifestation of the conclusion that the underpinnings of such feelings, once they could be identified, probably would be irrelevant to the appropriate resolution of the issue.

Steeled with this orientation and armed with massive preparation and careful rehearsal I was equipped to control, indeed to dominate, the class hour. I would use it efficiently and effectively. There would very rarely be an issue I had not foreseen, a question I could not answer, a cite I could not give; should such a situation occur, it would occasion a feeling of acute discomfort but would be acknowledged honestly and remedied at the start of the next hour—an embarrassing chink in the armor turned to pedagogical advantage by reinforcing the role model of industry and thoroughness.

I sometimes fancied myself as the successful conductor of an orchestra. With a meticulous score I could elicit all the needed notes, develop the thematic material and lead it to appropriate conclusion. The students in this scenario were really more instruments than players, and I played them all. Yet it should be noted that the conductor was not ruthless. The student who was struggling, whether by reason of lack of ability or from marginal preparation, was not made to look ridiculous. Indeed a couple of ridiculous performances and the entire symphony would be demeaned. Instead I would reward each student for whatever slight contribution was offered and then select a more finely tuned instrument. The student was aware, having been passed over so quickly, of my perception of his inadequacy, yet was encouraged to try again. This technique of positive rather than negative reinforcement had evolved during my first years of teaching and seemed to have a most salutary impact on student preparation and participation.

I conducted and collectively we performed. The enterprise was working. They were learning law and how to lawyer, precisely the aim of my teaching. Yet I could not deny a slight hint of personal disquiet. As a hunch or feeling it was easily ignored; still its recurrence was enough to give pause. With hindsight I can rationalize the germination of this uneasiness but am not confident of the accuracy of any of the possible explanations.

It may have been occasioned by a fear of becoming stale and repetitious with too tightly organized a script to follow. This seems a legitimate concern and one that is not remedied simply by refining the score each year. The most effective solution I have found for this particular malady has been to switch courses fairly frequently and rarely teach one more than three or four years. However, for one who is manic about preparation, this solution has obvious dire consequences for other spheres of professional and private life.

Another source of my unease may have been the gradually dawning realization that the brilliance of *my* performance was not necessarily correlated with the success of the particular class hour. To the contrary, I sometimes suspected that the more brilliantly I performed, the less investment the student had to make. The more responsibility that I took for each segment of class time, the less the student had to take. Sometimes I would be certain that I had done extremely well yet sensed that from an overall perspective the class had been rather flat.

On the other hand, even when classes were going well, I may have begun to suspect that nonetheless something was missing, at least for me. This could certainly have been a function of a standard mid-thirties passage: "Is this all there is?" I had been devoting an extraordinary amount of energy to developing an expertise in knowledge and technique, and, on achieving it, found it a bit hollow. Not only did my success feel lean; that realization itself made me pause and wonder about how fulfilling the next thirty years might be. Notwithstanding the pride I took in the knowledge and abilities of my students, undeniably I began to feel that teaching was not as personally rewarding as I wanted it to be. I could not articulate what it was that seemed to be missing. I now suspect that in part it may have been a fear that life, in terms of human interaction, was slipping by unappreciated.

Finally (and though I wish this were the primary reason, I strongly suspect that it was least important at the time), I may have started to develop a skepticism about the net worth to society of my endeavors. Even now I could hardly quarrel with my then operative assumption that a competent lawyer is preferable to an incompetent one. The difficulty had to do with the narrowness of my definition of competence. My requirements of task orientation, strict relevance, and dismissal of all feeling, if closely followed, culminate in the tunnel vision of the hired gun. One could pay lip service to important values but readily dismiss them as unrelated to the immediate problem at hand. This syndrome may help to explain why so many of those involved in Watergate were attorneys.

For whatever complex of these and other motivations I found myself drawn into a re-examination of my approach to law teaching.

                                                                   W.M.

Viktor Frankl, *Man's Search for Meaning*
pp.76-80 (Beacon 1962).

> [S]omething . . . was drawn to my attention by the chief doctor of our concentration camp. The death rate in the week between Christmas, 1944, and New Year's, 1945, increased in camp beyond all previous experience. In his opinion, the explanation for this increase did not lie in the harder working conditions or

the deterioration of our food supplies or a change of weather or new epidemics. It was simply that the majority of the prisoners had lived in the naive hope that they would be home again by Christmas. As the time drew near and there was no encouraging news, the prisoners lost courage and disappointment overcame them. This had a dangerous influence on their powers of resistance and a great number of them died.

As we said before, any attempt to restore a man's inner strength in the camp had first to succeed in showing him some future goal. Nietzsche's words, "He who has a *why* to live for can bear with almost any *how*," could be the guiding motto for all psychotherapeutic and psychohygienic efforts regarding prisoners. Whenever there was an opportunity for it, one had to give them a *why*—an aim—for their lives, in order to strengthen them to bear the terrible *how* of their existence. Woe to him who saw no more sense in his life, no aim, no purpose, and therefore no point in carrying on. He was soon lost. The typical reply with which such a man rejected all encouraging arguments was, "I have nothing to expect from life any more." What sort of answer can one give to that?

What was really needed was a fundamental change in our attitude toward life. We had to learn ourselves and, furthermore, we had to teach the despairing men, that it did not really matter what we expected from life, but rather what life expected from us. We needed to stop asking about the meaning of life, and instead to think of ourselves as those who were being questioned by life—daily and hourly. Our answer must consist, not in talk and meditation, but in right action and in right conduct. Life ultimately means taking the responsibility to find the right answer to its problems and to fulfill the tasks which it constantly sets for each individual.

These tasks, and therefore the meaning of life, differ from man to man, and from moment to moment. Thus it is impossible to define the meaning of life in a general way. Questions about the meaning of life can never be answered by sweeping statements. "Life" does not mean something vague, but something very real and concrete, just as life's tasks are also very real and concrete. They form man's destiny, which is different and unique for each individual. No man and no destiny can be compared with any other man or any other destiny. No situation repeats itself, and each situation calls for a different response. Sometimes the situation in which a man finds himself may require him to shape his own fate by action. At other times it is more advantageous for him to make use of an opportunity for contemplation and to realize assets in this way. Sometimes man may be required simply to accept fate, to bear his cross. . . .

When a man finds that it is his destiny to suffer, he will have to accept his suffering as his task; his single and unique task. He will have to acknowledge the fact that even in suffering he is unique and alone in the universe. No one can relieve him of his suffering or suffer in his place. His unique opportunity lies in the way in which he bears his burden.

For us, as prisoners, these thoughts were not speculations far removed from reality. They were the only thoughts that could be of help to us. They kept us from despair, even when there seemed to be no chance of coming out of it alive. Long ago we had passed the stage of asking what was the meaning of life, a naive query which understands life as the attaining of some aim through the active creation of something of value. For us, the meaning of life embraced the wider cycles of life and death, of suffering and of dying.

Once the meaning of suffering had been revealed to us, we refused to minimize or alleviate the camp's tortures by ignoring them or harboring false illusions and entertaining artificial optimism. Suffering had become a task on which we did not want to turn our backs. We had realized its hidden opportunities for achievement, the opportunities which caused the poet Rilke to write, *"Wie viel ist aufzuleiden!"* (How much suffering there is to get through!) Rilke spoke of "getting through suffering" as others would talk of "getting through work." There was plenty of suffering for us to get through. Therefore, it was necessary to face up to the full amount of suffering, trying to keep moments of weakness and furtive tears to a minimum. But there was no need to be ashamed of tears, for tears bore witness that a man had the greatest of courage, the courage to suffer. Only very few realized that. Shamefacedly some confessed occasionally that they had wept, like the comrade who answered my question of how he had gotten over his edema, by confessing, "I have wept it out of my system."

The tender beginnings of a psychotherapy or psychohygiene were, when they were possible at all in the camp, either individual or collective in nature. The individual psychotherapeutic attempts were often a kind of "life-saving procedure." These efforts were usually concerned with the prevention of suicides. A very strict camp ruling forbade any efforts to save a man who attempted suicide. It was forbidden, for example, to cut down a man who was trying to hang himself. Therefore, it was all important to prevent these attempts from occurring.

I remember two cases of would-be suicide, which bore a striking similarity to each other. Both men had talked of their intentions to commit suicide. Both used the typical argument—they had nothing more to expect from life. In both cases it was a question of getting them to realize that life was still expecting something from them; something in the future was expected of them. We found, in fact, that for the one it was his child whom he adored and who was waiting for him in a foreign country. For the other it was a thing, not a person. This man was a scientist and had written a series of books which still needed to be finished. His work could not be done by anyone else, any more than another person could ever take the place of the father in his child's affections.

This uniqueness and singleness which distinguishes each individual and gives a meaning to his existence has a bearing on creative work as much as it does on human love. When the impossibility of replacing a person is realized, it allows the responsibility which a man has for his existence and its continuance to appear in all its magnitude. A man who becomes conscious of the responsibility he bears toward a human being who affectionately waits for him, or to an unfinished work, will never be able to throw away his life. He knows the "why" for his existence, and will be able to bear almost any "how."

Comment

Many law students and lawyers whom I know are not sure why they are in law, go through the motions without direction, are bitter about their careers. They disdain idealists. Their cynicism is infectious and it topples others who are still undirected but have hope.

Frankl says the life we are responsible for living, the meaning we alone can give to it, and the goals we can reach in life are all out there, waiting for us to accept their reality. It is our responsibility to live the life, to accept that it has a meaning and give it that meaning in the way we live our lives. He says that even when we don't know what we want, something is wanted from us. I find it very difficult to accept that each person alone is responsible for his or her life and it is up to each of us to give meaning to our lives. This is not a message that offers much superficial comfort. To bring it down to the mundane, I find it a lot easier to get mad at the law school for the way things are than to hold myself responsible for making changes. But the message offers great possibilities. By expecting myself to make changes, I am admitting the possibility of my own power and giving an exciting direction to my life. I find that to believe that I can be responsible in these respects, I have to accept that I, too, have my importance in the scheme of things.

I have often felt, after reading this passage, that meaning in life and meaning in career are linked in an odd fashion for law students. Most students I know, myself included, came to law school with poorly defined career goals. We wanted something amorphous—to do good, to be powerful, or just to make a comfortable living. But the need to decide what we will be doing is always near. It is necessary to establish goals even if they can't be phrased in terms of a particular field of law or type of practice.

At Columbia the first decision-point for many comes at the start of the second year when the corporate law firms come to the campus to interview and make offers. It is in part just because those employers are present that many Columbia law students end up working for them. Perhaps because the idea that there might be no meaning in life is too scary to cope with, some students expect their professional lives to lack meaning. Then they vent all their anger at the possibility that their life has no meaning by inflicting the cynicism and disaffection—the fruits of their imagined betrayal—on the legal profession. It is difficult to accept responsibility for finding meaning in our lives. It is much more difficult to ask what life expects from us than to see what life is doing to us. It is more difficult to ask what we expect from ourselves as a lawyer than to see how the perfect employer will not offer us a position.

If we students could accept that we really want a meaning for our lives and accept that we can discover the meaning for ourselves, we could begin to sort out our true feelings about a legal career. Does being a lawyer satisfy something important inside of me? What sort of work is consistent with my vision of what is most important to my life?

Most law students are at the threshold of the age when it is no longer socially acceptable to puzzle over such things as the search for meaning in life. The entry into the job market with its emphasis on external standards encourages us to leave such questions behind. But for me, the lesson of Frankl is to take seriously the craving I feel for a meaning to my life, to expect that desire to last my whole life and not subside with adolescence. That means taking stock, looking over my past, finding what intrigues me there, what I see as valuable experience, what filled my life with love, what I have to feel proud of, what I would change if I could, and then not dropping these thoughts. Instead I could take them into my life, try to apply what I have learned about myself, knowing that I live my life, I am responsible for it as I am responsible for its meaning, and knowing that these questions apply to my professional as well as my personal life, and that a large part of my life is the work I do.

It means looking at where I am and what is being asked of me. Frankl says "it did not really matter what we expected from life, but rather what life expected from us."

E.D.

Comment

Three years after writing the preceding comment and now a teacher rather than a law student, I see more to the relationship between career choices and meaning in the profession and in life. I still believe that it is the responsibility of a law student to find the meaning for his or her life. I also believe that much in legal education encourages, whether by design or inadvertance, evasion of the struggle to find meaning in the profession.

What I find most disturbing is the extent of rationalization and its easy acceptance in the law school. For example, students quickly learn the premise that in our legal system everyone deserves representation. In discussing career choices, they often go on to say that since any person has a valid claim on the services of a lawyer, it does not matter whose ends a lawyer furthers; all ends are legitimate and therefore of equal weight. Since no legal work is more compelling than any other, why not work for those clients who can pay the most? The premise that justifies the representation of unpopular groups or of those who lack needed legal services is transformed into a justification for believing, in effect, that legal representation is a meaningless business.

Such illogic affords us all real comfort. The world of legal practice is confusing, particularly for law students with no defined career goals. The external pressures of the market-place encourage the students' belief that they are in a dependent and powerless position; they can only respond to what exists rather than develop their own sense of the right choices to make. Under such circumstances, adopting the standards and rationale of one's peers at least carries the consolation of knowing that one is not alone, and makes it seem possible to avoid or postpone questions of morality and the meaning of one's work in our world.

I do not believe that these students are evil or that all would be well if lawyers truly adopted and acted on the belief that everyone deserves representation. I am not discussing that belief here, only the way it is so commonly used to support the conclusion that the lawyer's decision to work in a particular field or represent certain clients is of little importance, to the lawyer and to society. And it is not only the students who take this easy way out. The indoctrination into the adversary system itself contributes to this wholly relativist view of law practice. Seeing themselves as advocates for the causes of others, students develop increasing skill in presenting rational arguments for any point of view. I have no quarrel with developing students' abilities as advocates. It is again the accompanying estrangement from their own beliefs and the lack of focus on the relation between a lawyer's work and underlying principles and beliefs, those of the legal system and the students' own, that I find troubling.

There is something wrong when students do not perceive the lawyer's choice of work as critical to the validity of the adversary system. By failing to ask serious questions seeking to develop students' ability to make responsible choices for their own lives and for the profession, we as law teachers reinforce the tendency not to see such fundamental responsibility as a crucial part of the lawyer's identity. To me, this silence serves to legitimate a view of professional work as amoral, remote from the world of meaning.

E.D.

Archibald MacLeish, *Riders on the Earth*
pp.3-26 (Houghton Mifflin 1978).

Saul Bellow . . . called on his fellow writers to "return from
the peripheries." To tell the writers of the world to return from
the peripheries to the center, to "the main human enterprise," is,
in effect, to tell them that they are not at the center now. Indeed,
Saul Bellow told them so precisely in so many words: "We do
not, we writers, represent mankind adequately." We do not
satisfy the "immense painful longing" of mankind. . . . It would
be difficult, I think, to put the accusation more comprehensively.
But Bellow's words not only draw the indictment; they also identify the suspect. . . .

I refer, of course, to the proposition which drove the art of
letters from the human center to the peripheral islands, the
peninsulas of ice, some thirty years ago: the notion propagated,
largely in France, after the Second World War, that Aristotle
had somehow died in that great disaster, and that truth to life
was no longer the criterion of art because life was no longer the
criterion of anything—life had been found out at last—life was
absurd.

For decades after the Second World War this tremendous
discovery was paraded up and down to the applause of undergraduates, American and other, and not a voice was raised to call
it naked, not a finger pointed. Even the most intelligent critics
held their tongues. . . .

Not so Saul Bellow at Stockholm. Saul Bellow, though he did
not mention Aristotle's name or recall his words—only those of
Conrad and of Proust—refused to walk across the corpse as
though it were not there. He reminded his fellow writers that the
human center still existed and was still the center and that the
peripheries were what they always had been: peripheries; fog-
banks off at sea. . . . [T]he greatest propagator of the Absurd,
that admirable man and enchanting writer, Camus, never believed in it. . . .

"Absurdity is king but love saves us." Life is absurd—and
therefore we must live our own lives—find our own meanings in
life—love's meanings. As one reads the *Notebooks* one sees that
it is not life which is absurd to Camus but the *idea* of life—the
idea of life ending in death—the idea of life with all its happiness
and death beyond for answer. Life, life *as* life, is as dear to Camus
as it was to Sappho herself to whom "the bright and the beautiful" belonged "to the desire of the sunlight." . . .

No one doubts that, in the world of ideas, the inevitability of
death makes human effort as pointless as the labor of Sisyphus.
But it is not in the world of ideas that life is *lived*. Life is lived for

better or worse *in* life, and to a man *in* life his life can no more be absurd than it can be the opposite of absurd, whatever that opposite may be. It *is*. And *he* is, in it. Buckminster Fuller following Whitehead who knew that "the process is the reality," once remarked that "truth is a verb." Life is a verb also. It may be ridiculous to a god observing it but to ourselves who live it, who *are* the verb, the process, the becoming, it cannot be ridiculous. Hateful, yes. Brutal, often. Painful, frequently. Tragic, without doubt. But ridiculous? Only in words. Only on a printed page....

[The succeeding chapter opens by turning to a discussion of students in the 1960's.] Here, suddenly and almost without warning, was a generation of undergraduates that reversed everything that had gone before, rejected the traditional undergraduate isolation, refused the conventional segregation of the university from the troubled world, and not only accepted for itself but demanded for itself a measure of responsibility for both—for university *and* world, for life as well as for education.

And the question, if we wish to understand this famous crisis, is: Why? Why has this transformation of ideas—metamorphosis more precisely—taken place? . . . [I]s it open to us to consider that the crisis in the university may actually have been what we called it: a crisis *in* the university— a crisis in education itself precipitated by a revolution in ideas, a revolution in the ideas of a new generation of mankind? . . .

The "relevance" these students spoke of was not relevance to the newspapers. It was relevance to their own lives, to the living of their lives, to themselves as men and women living. And their resentment, their very real resentment and distress, rose not only from the tragedies and mischances of the sixties but from a human situation, a total human situation, involving human life as human life, which had been three generations in the making.

At the time of the Sorbonne riots, a French politician spoke in terms of apocalypse: We had come to a time like the fall of Rome when civilizations collapse because belief is dead. What was actually happening in Paris and elsewhere was, of course, the precise opposite. Belief, passionate belief, had come alive for the first time in the century and, with it, rage and violence. The long diminishment, the progressive diminution, of value put upon man, upon the idea of man, in modern society had met the revulsion of a generation of the young who condemned it in all its aspects, left as well as right, Communist as well as capitalist, the indifference of the Marxist bureaucracies as well as the bureaucratic indifference of the industrial West.

This diminishment of the idea of man has been a long time in the making. . . .

Without the belief in man, the university is a contradiction in terms. The business of the university is education at its highest level, and the business of education at its highest level is the relation of men to their lives. But how is the university to concern itself with the relation of men to their lives, to the living of their lives, to the world in which their lives are lived, without the bold assumption, the brave, improbable hypothesis, that these lives matter, that these men count—that Odysseus on his battered, drifting raft still stands for a reality we take for real?

And how can a generation of the young, born into the world of the diminished man and in revolt against it—in revolt against its indifference to humanity in its cities and in its wars and in the weapons of its wars—how can a generation of the young help but demand some teaching from the universities which will interpret all this horror and make cause against it?

Centuries ago in a world of gods and mysteries and monsters when man's creativity, his immense creative powers, had been, as Berdyaev put it "paralyzed by the Middle Ages"—when men had been diminished in their own eyes by the demeaning dogma of the Fall—centuries ago the university conceived an intellectual and spiritual position which released mankind into a new beginning, a rebirth, a Renaissance. What is demanded of us now in a new age of gods and mysteries and monsters—not without dogmas and superstitions of its own—is a second humanism that will free us from our new paralysis of soul, as the earlier humanism freed us from that other. . . .

[A] conscious and determined effort to conceive a new humanism . . . is not only a present dream but a present possibility . . . not despite the generation of the sixties—but because of it.

That generation was not perhaps as sophisticated politically as it—or its activist spokesmen—would have had us think. Its moral superiority to earlier generations may not have been in every instance as great as it believed. But one virtue it did possess to a degree not equaled by any generation in this century: It believed in man.

It was an angry generation, yes, but its resentment was not the disgust of the generation for which Beckett spoke. Its resentment was not a resentment of our human life but a resentment *on behalf* of human life; not an indignation that we exist on the earth but that we *permit* ourselves to exist in a selfishness and wretchedness and squalor which we have the means to abolish. Resentment of this kind is founded, can only be founded, on belief in man. And belief in man—a return to the belief in man—is the reality on which a new age can be built.

Thus far, that new belief has been used by the young largely as a weapon—as a justification of an indictment of earlier generations for their exploitation and debasement of human life and earth. When it is allowed to become itself—when the belief in man becomes an affirmative effort to re-create the life of man—the crisis in the university may well become the triumph of the university.

For it is only the university in this technological age which can save us from ourselves. And the university, as we now know, can only function effectively when it functions as a common labor of all its generations dedicated to the highest purpose of them all.

Comment

The themes MacLeish writes about are significantly interrelated for me as a legal educator; I believe that they underlie the current state of legal education and the experience of teachers and students in law schools. The themes are: the dynamic tension between the two apparently irreconcilable perceptions of human life as absurd and as having meaning; and the developmental process of our culture, in particular in the university.

Although often presented in the form of seemingly unrelated dialogues about substantive matters, questions that reflect the tension between absurdity and meaning—whether the role of lawyers is a wholly instrumental one, devoid of meaning, and the purpose of law school simply the attainment of facility in a craft, or whether there is a higher human purpose to law and our life in law—constantly reverberate in the halls, the classrooms, the lounges and in our minds. I hear the dialogue in my own mind, some days one set of responses holding sway, sometimes the other. I imagine that students, including those who argue most vociferously for one side or the other, are carrying on a similar dialogue with themselves.

Is it then all just a question of opinion, of the tides of the 60's, 70's, or 80's, or is there some greater sense in all this? MacLeish helps us to see a bigger pattern by refusing to see things statically, in the moment; he looks at them developmentally, over time. The doctrine of the absurd has been the culmination of the scientific and technological age—a product of the faith that everything can be reduced to formula. Uncompromising relativism was the step, perhaps the logical one, that our culture needed to take before we could go farther on, to cry out, "there must be more." If that developmental view makes sense for our culture, may it not also make sense for us individually? The experience of life as important and meaningful so often follows the opposite experience that the latter seems to be a necessary prerequisite to the former. The relation between the two perceptions is something more than that of simple diametric opposition; it is more akin to a developmental or sequential relation.

For those of us looking for an emerging humanistic value base to law teaching, the apparent moral relativism of many law students is understandably frustrating. We variously interpret it as simply another conservative trend, or a sensible, however fearful, response to market pressures and realities. MacLeish's view, in the sense I am discussing it here, supports another interpretation: Moral relativism can be seen as a step along the way, perhaps a necessary step, to a sense of human meaning within the profession. A rejection of the values that we have learned from outside sources is often a necessary step to our acceptance of an intrinsic set of values. Values derived from social norms or other external sources of morality often yield to a pragmatic and relativist view. And this view can in turn yield to the questioning that seeks to find something more in life—to discover ways of bringing the poles of pragmatism and humanism, relativism and fundamental beliefs, into a complementary relationship which will embolden us to seek meaningful change in the world.

I can see that happening with students, slowly, however, for when we are looking developmentally it is time that is relative. The tension may be resolved in a moment or stay unresolved for a lifetime. If I see reality as static, without past or future, this perspective may seem totally irrelevant. But if it is true, it will remain so whether or not I acknowledge it and it will influence me, my students' lives and the institution of legal education nonetheless.

It has become increasingly important for me to see legal education developmentally—I mean by that my own development as a teacher, students' development in becoming lawyers, and the development of legal education itself within the broader trends of our culture. As I do that, my frustration merges with hope, and I believe I see some sense to it all.

J.H.

Karl Llewellyn, "Beyond Bread and Butter," in *The Bramble Bush* pp.119-127 (Oceana 1960).

[F]or too much law, more law will be the cure. If law makes blind, more law will make you see.

But more law of what kind? More of the bread and butter kind, of the straight trade dope? That turns, I fancy, on how you conceive your trade. There is a bony structure of technique without which you will be a feckless artisan—worthless, and unsuccessful. Those hard bones you must have. You must assemble them into a whole, each in its place, each one articulated with the rest. When that is done you can refine somewhat on the articulation, get joints to working neatly. But I do not know that extra bones will bring much vision to the eye-sockets of a skull.

It all depends on what you want of law, what law can offer you. That turns, in turn, on what you want of life.

There is a brand of lawyer for whom law is the making of a livelihood, a competence, a fortune. Law offers means to live, to get ahead. It is so viewed. Such men give their whole selves to it, in this aspect. Coin is their reward. Coin makes it possible to live. Coin is success, coin is prestige, and coin is power. . . .

I have no quarrel to fight out with this way of life. No quarrel to fight out with it, even as a way of *life*. It is as satisfactory, doubtless, as any; it may be more so. Single-heartedness simplifies choices; choices are most uncomfortable business. And if the coin-chaser does achieve his goal at forty-five, he has achieved a happiness that few can rival. Happiness after all is a balance between desires and fulfillment. He whose desires have shrunk to meat and drink and income tax evasion, to bowing butlers and the bejewelling of his wife—he has his happiness if he can gain the coin. I would not say that "more law" had brought him vision. But neither do I see that he desires vision, or could use it.

One thing does trouble me about a man like this, and about you, if you make this your ideal of the law. I shall say nothing here of service to society. As society stands, its own institutions warrant any man in holding that he best serves the whole who gathers purchasing power to himself. I shall say nothing, either, of any ethical duty to make those institutions work out a bit more decently. As things stand I perceive no basis for assuming such a duty, *except as to men who can themselves perceive it.* . . .

What troubles me about a man like this is something else. It may seem far-fetched to you—a matter of a foolish distant future. To me, an educator, it seems pressing to you even now. What troubles me about this man is his children. How is this single-minded lawyer to get the resiliency without which he will stand blank and helpless before the new generation that he raises up—on which, in keeping with his way of life, he pins more hopes and more ambitions than on his own career? I have watched many of these simple, hard-headed, single-hearted men, with those grown sons and daughters who were *never* like themselves. I have watched the complete satisfaction of achievement fade and give place to hopeless emptiness. If this is your aim, you may do better not to marry. It seems to be possible to be a husband, comfortably, along these lines; although it is not easy on the wife. But being a father calls for human qualities which will get in your way. It will destroy the virtue of the single heart.

There are men to whom this choice of life is barred by an eager, uneasy temperament. We find them making another current in the bar. They have ideals of another sort; they, like academicians, are prey to queer feelings that a profession—or even a trade—should carry an obligation of some weight to a community it purports (they think it does purport) to serve. . . . They have, too, restless desires. The grind of the law they accept. A man must keep alive. Indeed, a man must get ahead—to keep in with the intellectual set, to follow the theatre, to be abreast of music and art, to have the adequate residence address and freedom of movement that metropolitan living requires. . . .

[O]bserving the facts of life, they see that the road to coin is the road to freedom. Freedom is their desire.

Neither with these men have I any quarrel. Their work I welcome. They find time and interest, again and again, to do things which the others will not do, and which need doing. They give service to new causes, whether popular or not. They have, as I said, ideals. And they are good companions.

Yet happy they are not. A good way of life they have not found. The cartoons in the New Yorker give them a pleasant moment; a lovely distortion by Brancusi in the living room brings comfort for a while; there is a fine superior feeling at spreading abroad the inside dope on this and that, at being one of the first to take up the tabloids, tom thumb golf, what have you next; at wisecracking over the Yahoos in the sticks. But it is a nervous, a sickish business, to be disgusted at your work. Calm cynicism counsels: you need the money; you can do this as well as the next man, and better; at times you give some service that he would not give. Yet of two things one: either the man finds himself not man enough to carry his two lives separately, either he goes under in the surge of the law-factory, to be thrown up after five years upon the beach, a dry, smooth, shining pebble with the others of our first, our hard-boiled group; so with the vast bulk of the men who try this road.—Or else, or else, carrying on—as so few can—after ten years of it or twenty the man looks out on the world with the sensation: part of my soul, though it has shrunk and warped, I still have saved, but at the cost of all my working hours. It is more than a feeling of wastage in his work; it is a feeling of unremittent compromising and soiling of the very ideals that the coin was meant to salvage.

As to this course of life at the bar I have only this to say: do not fool yourselves into thinking it is easy. Most who try it fail. And those who succeed are far from finding ease.

As at the bar, so in your schooling. You can do nothing but the law, and of that content yourself with bones. Grubbing of rules today, grubbing of dollars tomorrow. Or you can divide your time into the dirt and the delight; do what you must with law, and do it well, but leave the real hours of living for your reading, for social contacts, and for Toscanini.

There is a third course I would put before you: to wed the unity of the one way with the perspective of the other. To make of your law a study of the way and the working and the wonder of this curious higher primate known as Man. That will not hamper your learning of the trade. On the contrary, if you know anything of Man you will know that only perfect mastery of the details of his institutions will give you any key to what he is or how he works; but, you will know also that only study of his ways and drives will give you insight into these his institutions. . . .

So, too, and so only, if you are one of those queer souls who dream dreams of something, somehow, sometime better, you can be proof against disgust. There can be no disgust at what you understand. Each one of us is what his life has made him. See that, and look to the causes. That will leave regrets. But it will remove the sticky, queasy feeling. It will leave you free to observe, and understand, and act, and learn. Of course, if you grow jaded, this is no help for long: If this "is just another case of an injured workman" your contact with living life will have been lost.

Nor do I know how to forestall the jading. I can say only this. That human drama, for all that it runs in types, is never twice the same. Our typification, our setting up of types—and so our jading—I take to be chiefly due to a pair of factors. The first, intellectual. To cope with situations one must think. To get out of them their common elements, and thus to arrange one's thinking, one's tools for dealing with new situations like them, is, while the work goes on, a pleasant process. So, for a while, is the check-up process which follows, the testing of one's prior thinking, the trying out of one's tools and skill. When that is over, when one is sure that he is right, this stimulus ceases. There comes no further titillation of the wish for novelty.

The second factor I take to be emotional. Life is so full of pain, so instinct with trouble, that in a mere effort to keep going we have either to shut ourselves in from suffering, to keep from seeing it, or else to dull our sensitivity. The latter is the rule when we are called upon to do our work with social pain. To give oneself wholly to one's case is to burn oneself up. But to condition oneself against the burning is to set the ruts for jading.

These tendencies are present and eternal. Nor does one man know the answer, for another's temperament. But it should be possible to retain as live an interest in the *differences* of situations as in their similarities. It should be possible to see in types of situation not merely a technical tool, but a device for ordering, arranging, deepening his knowledge of his fellows, a device whereby the similarities of situations are employed to throw their unfailing differences into relief. And on the emotional side, it should be possible to dampen burning, consuming, useless sympathy, to dampen down expectation of results as well, without destroying all one's urge to learn and do—or help. . . .

The problem . . . touches me closely. It cuts into the marrow of my work. . . .

If nature is ineluctable, then we are beaten. Then you go forth, hard-eyed, hard-minded, with one end in life. If we are beaten, then since life is bunk, and law is bunk, and ideals of the softer sort are folly, a single-mindedness for the bank account will be in order, and God help any who are in the way! . . . I have seen this result in many and I have beat my breast to have contributed to the schooling of the wolves.

But I cannot believe that nature has us thus in the stranglehold. I cannot believe that analysis and observation leave us helpless. There is a will to do, *apart* from expectation of result, a will to do that gives heart even to the disillusioned. There is in Gaugin's painting an expression of what I am trying to say that dwarfs poor words. . . . Look on the faces of his South Sea women. There is no expectation there, from life. Desire is empty, effort is illusion. Do what one will, there will come disappointment. Yet look again, and see the power of living, the vigor, the exuberance of life, driving on gloriously—while expecting nothing. There is the answer to our disillusion, in that old truth that neither rainbow nor the pot of gold can be attained, nor would be worth the having if it were. But the search is good.

If I knew ways of making this seem real I should be troubled at your disillusion not at all. Nay, I should welcome it. Freedom from butted aching heads, freedom from sacrifices to the empty idols, freedom for action fitted to your ends, straight-cut, hard-hitting. These, if you grasp them, are the fruits of shattered dreams. These—if you grasp them.

For I see in disillusion no dampening of interest. Rather I see all interest gaining height and depth. All that is lost is expectation of the unattainable. And the attainable becomes the more worth while, the more enthralling. Two things, and two things only, are the need: a will to understand, and a certain patience.

No, gentlemen, for the disillusioned there are three roads, unless they are to rack themselves to bits. The first, a whole-souled selfishness, in any form: self-seeking, self-consistent, self-contained. The second, mysticism—which your very turning to the law well nigh negates, for you.—The third, an act of faith in the worthwhileness of doing, accepting in advance a failure to achieve the ultimate end.

Such faith in the worthwhileness of doing as such, and grounds for such faith, I personally can conceive only in terms of interest in people, in Man, in men; and for a lawyer I can conceive them only in terms of grafting upon his law that interest, of working out a unity between law and his living life. . . .

Comment

I came to Columbia Law School as a beginning law student a few years after Karl Llewellyn left. It is fair to say that, his physical departure notwithstanding, he was one of the most influential voices in the first-year faculty. He stood for the ideas contained in the above excerpt—a vision of the potential of a legal career for providing a meaningful life, as an expression of our connection to fellow humans—and he stood as well for a commitment to the highest level of craft-proficiency and analytic rigor. I do not perceive that I, or my classroom teachers, would have found any inconsistencies between these two sets of objectives.

It is striking to me that the above was written nearly 50 years ago, when it has been so hard for me to bring to my own consciousness many thoughts, priorities and feelings that are expressed there so strongly. I think that one reason for this is that in an important way legal education has retrogressed during the last generation. The ideas that Llewellyn expresses above are now more often seen as at war with others, to which he was also committed, and which dominate much of legal education today. We, all of us, have lost a lot of the confidence our predecessors had in the utility of our own work. I believe that this inevitably produces a narrowness, that is, an eagerness to see differing priorities as conflicting. This in turn produces a diminished view of what an excellent legal education includes. I am glad to be able to invoke Llewellyn as an ally, not only because of the credentials he lends, but because his own career illustrated so ably that his concern with the values expressed in the excerpt above did not denigrate the importance of others, which legal education can also serve.

H.L.

B. THE REPRESSION OF THE SEARCH

Frank Haronian, "The Repression of the Sublime,"
in *The Proper Study of Man,* James Fadiman, ed.
p.239 (Macmillan 1971).

I do not think it is necessary to define the concept of repression but I do want to go into the question of what is meant in this instance by the sublime. We could be orthodox-psychoanalytic about it and consider all higher artistic, social and spiritually oriented activities as sublimations of primitive, erotic and aggressive drives. These would be sublime activities, but as sublimations of lower drives. But we can also consider that these same higher impulses, desires or motives exist in their own right, and that they develop whether or not the sexual and aggressive drives are satisfied. In fact, one might go so far as to claim that the higher and more sublime needs of the person are more likely to be awakened and developed if the so-called lower, more carnal drives are satisfied rather than if these are frustrated and 'sublimated.' For it is often out of a sense of boredom and dissatisfaction with the gratification of the senses, that we begin to look for higher meanings to our life.

There are still other ways of looking at the term *sublime*. In its broadest sense it covers all of man's impulses, instincts, drives and urges to be something more, better, greater than he is. Personal growth and differentiation is part of the picture, to be sure, but beyond that the concept of the sublime involves several other general areas. It refers to the true, the good, the beautiful. We orient ourselves towards the sublime when we disinterestedly seek to know things as they are; when we nurture others for the pleasure of seeing them grow; when we arrange physical events so that they are seen as beautiful or artistic.

Then there is the tendency towards community, brotherliness, and caring. It is based on the feeling, the belief, the conviction that we all share the same destiny, ultimately. According to Robert Desoille, in whose writings I first came across the idea of the repression of the sublime, the impulse towards the sublime demands that we be concerned with others, that we feel the need to communicate with others with the best of ourselves, and that we find our deepest satisfaction in service to others. He says: "There are many forms of service, and among them the disinterested efforts of the scientist and the artist are among the

68

highest." The impulse to act in such ways is the expression of a profound urge to trust life, to give freely of oneself, and to forget one's selfish concerns. These are among the traits of the sublime.

There is another aspect of the sublime which can be called spiritual, in the broadest sense of the word. This is the inescapable need of every person to answer the existential questions for himself and to dedicate himself to a purpose, a goal, an ideal that he sees as greater and more important, more durable than his own transient existence and powers. When we sense the sublime as the feeling of communion with, and dedication to something that is greater than ourselves, then we are experiencing this basic spiritual impulse. It may be religious, agnostic or atheistic; it does not require a belief in God, but it is consonant with such a belief. . . .

I would like to demonstrate that to feel the pull of the sublime in the several ways that I have described is an essential part of being fully human. And it is typically neurotic for us to repress the urge of trying to answer this call. However, we often do repress it.

There are many ways in which we evade the call of the sublime. Why do we evade, for example, the challenge of personal growth? We fear growth because it means abandoning the familiar for the unknown. And that involves risks. I recently came across the same idea in the works of Andras Angyal where he says

> Abandoning the familiar for the unknown always involves risks. When the changes are far-reaching or precipitous they are bound to arouse anxiety. The view that growth is inseparable from anxiety is shared by practically all thinkers who have substantially contributed to our understanding of anxiety. . . .The anxiety felt at the prospect of dissolution of one's current mode of being has been related by some to the fear of final dissolution . . . since growth requires the breaking of old patterns, willingness "to die" is a precondition of living. . . . Excessive fear of death is often a correlate of the neurotic fear of growth and change.

Why do we evade the expression of care and concern for others? Often it is because we fear that we won't know where to draw the line and that we will find ourselves used and exploited by others. In the popular parlance, if you give a person an inch, he'll take a mile. Somehow we lack the stable sense of self which would permit us to have our "yes" and our "no" in such situations. I think that this fear is also related to the fact that as a part of the pattern of modern life, we know too many people too superficially—and we experience too little responsibility for each other.

I suspect that the loss of a sense of community with others, of the sense of sharing a common destiny, has led us to a state in which we are no longer able to commit ourselves to an ideal whose value, in our eyes, transcends that of our personal existence. This is the opposite of the situation that normally exists in primitive tribes. Today, the old tribal claims for loyalty in return for status and security are weak. We too seldom experience a close relatedness to others for whose lives we are responsible and on whom we, in turn, can call for aid when we are distressed or threatened. Because of this loss, the motive for commitment to something greater than oneself must nowadays attach itself to something more abstract than one's tribe, something harder to define and to hold in mind and heart as a goal. . . .

Comment

The phenomenon Haronian calls the repression of the sublime sheds light on why there are so few lawyers who are able to find the "unity between law and [their] living life" that Karl Llewellyn discusses, p. 66 above. Such a lawyer is one for whom an interest in people is paramount and whose work embodies that interest, who sees law and legal institutions as a reflection of the noble and base needs, desires, and strivings of people, and who sees the lawyer's life in the law as intimately connected with his or her needs, values and ideals.

The concept of the repression of the sublime amplifies the dynamic Llewellyn calls the emotional factor: "Life is so full of pain, . . . that in a mere effort to keep going we have either to shut ourselves in from suffering, to keep from seeing it, or else to dull our sensitivity." What I take Llewellyn to be saying is described in this excerpt from Bertrand Russell's obituary*:

"Three passions, simple but overwhelmingly strong, have governed my life: the longing for love, the search for knowledge and unbearable pity for the suffering of mankind."

In those words Bertrand Arthur William Russell, the third Earl Russell, described the motive forces of his extraordinarily long, provocative and complex life. But only one yearning, that for love, was fully satisfied, he said, and only when he was 80 and married his fourth wife, Edith Finch, then a 52-year-old American.

Of his search for knowledge, he reflected, "a little of this, but not much, I have achieved." And as for pity:

"Echoes of cries of pain reverberate in my heart. Children in famines, victims tortured by oppressors, helpless old people a

---

* New York Times, Feb. 3, 1970, by Alden Whitman.

hated burden for their sons, and a whole world of loneliness, poverty and pain make a mockery of what human life should be. I long to alleviate this evil, but I cannot, and I too suffer."

What feels so true for me is the dilemma Llewellyn poses. It does my work, my clients and my students no good for me to be so overwhelmed with the reality of the world, with the gap between the ideal society and the society we live in, that I just sit and feel bad. I do need to be able to act, to use my skills, to be able to move and not be paralyzed with sadness. Yet if I close myself off to the sadness of others, in me, the sadness that is reflected in our laws, if I close myself off to what can paralyze me, I also close myself off to what draws me to this work, to my values and ideals, and I can become more closed off to the others I work with.

These are very hard things to talk about, especially in a law school classroom. They make me feel uncomfortable, edgy; the students often don't see the relevance to their practical interests, and it is easier to brush these sorts of questions aside. They are "personal" matters and ones we all have to work out for ourselves. They can't be taught. And so these sorts of questions are often set aside, not to be considered in conjunction with our study of law. And we learn that our lives as lawyers will be different and separate from our living lives.

If we want to work out a unity between a life in the law and our living life, we will need to be able to see the human reality in the law, a reality that includes human suffering. If we want to bring our ideals and values into our work, we will also bring with them a heightened awareness of how far we must develop before we personally and as a society will be able to implement our ideals and values.

E.D.

James R. Elkins, *The Paradox of a Life in Law*
40 U. Pitt. L. Rev. 129, 130, 139-143 (1979).

> While the paradoxical nature of our existence as lawyers can be traced to a number of contradictory aspects in legal education and lawyering, the paradox at the very core of our lives as students, law teachers and lawyers is the reconciliation of the "real" and the "ideal." Students confront the dichotomy of the real and ideal as they chart a difficult course in learning law and as they determine whether a life in law offers opportunity for expression of deeply held values. Law school is often experienced as a place that limits imagination and creativity and stifles ideals. Law teachers are frustrated by students who have "given in" to learning for grades, and yet teachers often reinforce the belief that personal values and social ideals are obstacles to learning the law and becoming a skilled lawyer. Students, in turn, see little utility in innovation or in creative efforts to improve learning. Both law students and law teachers seem to be part of a system in which each acts to destroy the efforts of the other toward

achieving his ideal. Students emerge from such a learning environment only to find themselves in a similar position in the legal system. The practicing lawyer struggles with real clients and real legal problems while often seeking an expression of self that being a legal technician does not allow.

I have chosen the real and the ideal as the polar elements of the paradox for one who chooses law as a career. . . .

First year law students face the unsettling prospect of three years of legal study and a saturated employment market. Many students have struggled to gain admission and once enrolled are faced with financial pressures which are forcing larger numbers of students to work and those students already working to increase their work load. It is not surprising, then, to find students today concerned not with the "ultimate," but frustrated and fighting for survival. To survive is to obtain a law degree and pass a bar examination, mere stops along the way. Law school is simply a place to put in time, and there are some who avoid even that minimal requirement. Many law students today have little time for subjects or instructors who are not attuned to the student's work world.

Today's pragmaticism and concern for "relevance" should be distinguished from the relevance in legal education demanded by the activist student in the late 1960's and early 1970's. Relevance then expressed concern for social responsibility of law and lawyer and the role of legal education in promoting a new ethic. Today relevance means little more than an illusory relationship between teaching material, course coverage, and the work the student expects to perform after graduation. The fear of today's law student is that he will join a law firm and be asked to research a client problem involving a "secured interest," not having had a course in the subject in law school.

Therefore, there is renewed student concern for practical skills. Students are increasingly pragmatically oriented and expect to learn "how to do it" as opposed to learning the theoretical structure and philosophy underlying legal rules.[29] A

---

29. One of the most scathing attacks on the how-to-do-it approach to legal education was delivered by Robert Hutchins. See Hutchins, The University Law School, in The Law School of Tomorrow 5 (1968). Hutchins declares that "[t]he best practical education is a theoretical one" and declares "war" on the how-to-do-it law school. Id. at 15. Hutchins regards the law as a "great intellectual discipline." He argues that:

> [t]o have the university and the law school dedicated to training technicians is so far from the potentialities

of either as to be a scandal, and too flagrant to continue.

> The responsibilities and opportunities of the university and the law school are now greater than ever. Society needs centers of independent thought and criticism as never before. The law faces new problems that must be solved if civilization is to survive. The university is the place where wisdom can be generated. The law needs that wisdom and must contribute to it. Other civilizations have fallen because of the barbarians with-

rejection of theory and a lack of concern for the subtle nuances of the style, art, and craft of lawyering alienate the students from both law and law teachers. . . .

Getting a career ticket punched is the work of a practical man. With an eye to the real world of lawyering one can guard against illusions of grand possibilities in the world. The practical man suffers from an illusion that he engages the world only through practice and that theory and ideals are of little value. With the denouncement of theory comes the masking of ideals. Listen to the voice of the practical man in law school: "I want courses which tell me what the law is so that I can use it when I get out into legal practice. Courses should be more practical. Teachers should spend less time talking about theory and more time showing students how to draft documents, file papers, and deal with the real problems which I will face in legal practice. I like courses which help me become a competent lawyer."

Robert Pirsig in *Zen and the Art of Motorcycle Maintenance* has described this as a classical view of the world. It is a view which is concerned with how to fix things, how to solve practical problems. Again listen to the voice of the student: "Look here. Clients will be coming into my office with all kinds of problems. They want answers, not theories. You don't get paid by a client for the theories you know. My clients will want to believe that I know the law and can suggest an answer to their problem. I've got to have the legal tools which will allow me to serve my clients." . . .

Legal educators forget that we present to students the possibility that they will fail to meet required standards, and many of them accept the real possibility of failure. Before he can direct any effort toward the ideals that he hopes to express in a life in law, the student must become convinced of his ability to survive. Abraham Maslow has argued persuasively that our basic needs must be met before higher ideals can be pursued. . . .

out. That may happen to us. But it seems more likely that we may fall prey to the barbarians within, from which the university and the law might save us.

Id. at 17. Robert Redmount, a longtime student of legal education, adds:

Legal education does not serve the lawyer who is consulted on a variety of personal, social, and institutional problems nearly as well as it serves the lawyer who is appointed to operate the traditional mechanism of authority of law. The need is for excellence in delving into and ordering the properties of experience, as well as excellence in defining and advocating some of the properties of authority that guide end results.

Redmount, Humanistic Law through Legal Education, 1 Conn. L. Rev. 201, 215 (1968).

Many in legal education will welcome the new pragmatism, the concerns of which permit legal educators and students to get on with being lawyers as opposed to social critics. Thus, we will undoubtedly see a strong coalition of survival-oriented law students and a faculty component which has never given up rule-structured legalism as its raison d'être.

Whatever the ideals that accompany the student to law school, the initial task is simply to learn how to learn law. Law teaching is substantially different from most undergraduate teaching. It requires a major effort for students to learn how to do basic things, such as briefing cases and taking final examinations. Admittedly learning how to learn is a pre-eminent concern only of first year law students; yet even second and third year students must deal with the anxiety that comes from dealing with unknown teachers and a new approach to yet another complex area of law.

[The work] of the law student entails the mastery of numerous fields of substantive law, the ability to do legal research, draft legal documents, and attain skills in trial and appellate advocacy. We indeed ask a great deal of law students. The law student is deeply enmeshed in the "reality work" of becoming a lawyer.

To be a lawyer is to be able to perform the role of lawyer by pursuing legal strategies for solving a particular type of human problem. As Karl Llewellyn has observed, "any man who proposes to *practice* a liberal art [like law] must be *technically competent.*"[34] Clearly one must learn the method of law, the major outlines of the substance of law, and the traditional concerns and values of those who live a life in law. The value of this "reality work" is unquestioned. The problem lies in the way that the reality work of the student comes to obscure the ideals that he had on entering law school.

Rather than exacerbating student anxieties about employment and bar examination results, legal educators should face the problem. Given an awareness of the problem on the part of law school administrators, faculty and students, we can proceed to structure a legal and academic environment which produces competent and skilled lawyers and reduces the anxieties of the student. This goal should not, however, obscure the tragedy of a legal education which successfully indoctrinates students into "thinking like a lawyer" but stifles idealism, social consciousness and creativity.

Benjamin Cardozo once commented in a lecture to Yale law students:

You think perhaps of philosophy as dwelling in the clouds. I hope you may see that she is able to descend to earth. You think that in stopping to pay court to her, when you should be hastening forward on your journey, you are loitering in

34. K. Llewellyn, Jurisprudence: Realism in Theory and Practice 380 (1962) (emphasis in original).

bypaths and wasting precious hours. I hope you may share my faith that you are on the highway to the goal. Here you will find the key for the unlocking of bolts and combinations that shall never be pried open by clumsier or grosser tools. You think there is nothing practical in a theory that is concerned with ultimate conceptions. That is true perhaps while you are doing the journeyman's work of your profession. You may find in the end . . . that instead of its being true that the study of the ultimate is profitless, there is little that is profitable in the study of anything else.

Abraham Maslow, "The Jonah Complex," in
The Farther Reaches of Human Nature pp.35-40 (Viking 1974).

I would like to turn to one of the many reasons for what Angyal called the evasion of growth. We have, all of us, an impulse to improve ourselves, an impulse toward actualizing more of our potentialities, toward self-actualization, or full humanness or human fulfillment, or whatever term you like. Granted this, then what holds us up? What blocks us?

One such defense against growth that I'd like to speak about specially—because it hasn't been noticed much—I shall call the Jonah complex.

In my own notes I had at first labeled this defense the "fear of one's own greatness" or the "evasion of one's destiny" or the "running away from one's own best talents." I had wanted to stress as bluntly and sharply as I could the non-Freudian point that we fear our best as well as our worst, even though in different ways. It is certainly possible for most of us to be greater than we are in actuality. We all have unused potentialities or not fully developed ones. It is certainly true that many of us evade our constitutionally suggested vocations (call, destiny, task in life, mission). So often we run away from the responsibilities dictated (or rather suggested) by nature, by fate, even sometimes by accident, just as Jonah tried—in vain—to run away from *his* fate.

We fear our highest possibilities (as well as our lowest ones). We are generally afraid to become that which we can glimpse in our most perfect moments, under the most perfect conditions, under conditions of greatest courage. We enjoy and even thrill to the godlike possibilities we see in ourselves in such peak moments. And yet we simultaneously shiver with weakness, awe, and fear before these very same possibilities.

I have found it easy enough to demonstrate this to my students simply by asking, "Which of you in this class hopes to write the great American novel, or to be a Senator, or Governor, or President? Who wants to be Secretary-General of the United

Nations? Or a great composer? Who aspires to be a saint, like Schweitzer, perhaps? Who among you will be a great leader?" Generally everybody starts giggling, blushing, and squirming until I ask, "If not you, then who else?" Which of course is the truth. And in this same way, as I push my graduate students toward these higher levels of aspiration, I'll say, "What great book are you now secretly planning to write?" And then they often blush and stammer and push me off in some way. But why should I not ask that question? Who else will write the books on psychology except psychologists? So I can ask, "Do you not plan to be a psychologist?" "Well, yes." "Are you in training to be a mute or an inactive psychologist? What's the advantage of that? That's not a good path to self-actualization. No, you must want to be a first-class psychologist, meaning the best, the very best you are capable of becoming. If you deliberately plan to be less than you are capable of being, then I warn you that you'll be deeply unhappy for the rest of your life. You will be evading your own capacities, your own possibilities."

Not only are we ambivalent about our own highest possibilities, we are also in a perpetual and I think universal—perhaps even *necessary*—conflict and ambivalence over these same highest possibilities in other people, and in human nature in general. Certainly we love and admire good men, saints, honest, virtuous, clean men. But could anybody who has looked into the depths of human nature fail to be aware of our mixed and often hostile feelings toward saintly men? Or toward very beautiful women or men? Or toward great creators? Or toward our intellectual geniuses? It is not necessary to be a psychotherapist to see this phenomenon—let us call it "Counter-valuing." Any reading of history will turn up plenty of examples, or perhaps even I could say that any such historical search might fail to turn up a single exception throughout the whole history of mankind. We surely love and admire all the persons who have incarnated the true, the good, the beautiful, the just, the perfect, the ultimately successful. And yet they also make us uneasy, anxious, confused, perhaps a little jealous or envious, a little inferior, clumsy. They usually make us lose our aplomb, our self-possession, and self-regard. (Nietzsche is still our best teacher here.)

Here we have a first clue. My impression so far is that the greatest people, simply by their presence and by being what they are, make us feel aware of our lesser worth, whether or not they intend to. If this is an unconscious effect, and we are not aware of why we feel stupid or ugly or inferior whenever such a person turns up, we are apt to respond with projection, i.e., we react as if he were *trying* to make us feel inferior, as if we were the target. Hostility is then an understandable consequence. It looks to me so far as if conscious awareness tends to fend off this hostility.

That is, if you are willing to attempt self-awareness and self-analysis of your *own* counter-valuing, i.e., of your unconscious fear and hatred of true, good, beautiful, etc., people, you will very likely be less nasty to them. And I am willing also to extrapolate to the guess that if you can learn to love more purely the highest values in others, this might make you love these qualities in yourself in a less frightened way.

Allied to this dynamic is the awe before the highest . . . the universal . . . fear of direct confrontation with a god or with the godlike. In some religions death is the inevitable consequence. Most preliterate societies also have places or objects that are taboo because they are too sacred and *therefore too danger-ous*. . . . (I want to stress that this awe is intrinsic, justified, *right*, suitable, rather than some sickness or failing to get "cured of.")

But here again my feeling is that this awe and fear need not be negative alone, something to make us flee or cower. These are also desirable and enjoyable feelings capable of bringing us even to the point of highest ecstasy and rapture. Conscious aware-ness, insight, and "working through," à la Freud, is the answer here too I think. This is the best path I know to the acceptance of our highest powers, and whatever elements of greatness or good-ness or wisdom or talent we may have concealed or evaded. . . .

There is still another psychological process that I have run across in my explorations of failure to actualize the self. This evasion of growth can also be set in motion by a fear of paranoia. Of course this has been said in more universal ways. Promethean and Faustian legends are found in practically any culture. For in-stance, the Greeks called it the fear of *hubris*. It has been called "sinful pride," which is of course a permanent human problem. The person who says to himself, "Yes, I will be a great philosopher and I will rewrite Plato and do it better," must sooner or later be struck dumb by his grandiosity, his arrogance. And especially in his weaker moments, will say to himself, "Who? Me?" and think of it as a crazy fantasy or even fear it as a delusion. He compares his knowledge of his inner private self, with all its weakness, vacillation, and shortcomings, with the bright, shining, perfect, and faultless image he has of Plato. Then, of course, he'll feel presumptuous and grandiose. (What he doesn't realize is that Plato, introspecting, must have felt just the same way about himself, but went ahead anyway, overriding his doubts about himself.)

For some people this evasion of one's own growth, setting low levels of aspiration, the fear of doing what one is capable of doing, voluntary self-crippling, pseudostupidity, mock-humility are in fact defenses against grandiosity, arrogance, sinful pride, hubris. There are people who cannot manage that graceful integration between the humility and the pride which is absolutely necessary for creative work. To invent or create you must have the "arrogance of creativeness" which so many investigators have noticed. But, of course, if you have *only* the arrogance without the humility, then you are in fact paranoid. You *must* be aware not only of the godlike possibilities within, but also of the existential human limitations. You must be able simultaneously to laugh at yourself and at all human pretensions. If you can be amused by the worm trying to be a god then in fact you may be able to go on trying and being arrogant without fearing paranoia or bringing down upon yourself the evil eye. . . . Aldous Huxley . . . was able to accept his talents and use them to the full. He managed it by perpetually marveling at how interesting and fascinating everything was, by wondering like a youngster at how miraculous things are, by saying frequently, "Extraordinary! Extraordinary!" He could look out at the world with wide eyes, with unabashed innocence, awe, and fascination, which is a kind of admission of smallness, a form of humility, and then proceed calmly and unafraid to the great tasks he set for himself.

Finally . . . it is certainly demonstrable that we need the truth and love it and seek it. And yet it is just as easy to demonstrate that we are also simultaneously *afraid* to know the truth. For instance, certain truths carry automatic responsibilities which may be anxiety-producing. One way to evade the responsibility and the anxiety is simply to evade consciousness of the truth.

I predict that we will find a similar dialectic for each of the intrinsic Values of Being,* and I have vaguely thought of doing a series of papers on e.g., "The love of beauty and our uneasiness with it." "Our love of the good man and our irritation with him." "Our search for excellence and our tendency to destroy it," etc., etc. Of course, these counter-values are stronger in neurotic people, but it looks to me as if all of us must make our peace with these mean impulses within ourselves. And my impression so far is that the best way to do this is to transmute envy, jealousy, presentiment, and nastiness into humble admiration, gratitude, appreciation, adoration, and even worship via conscious insight and working through. . . . This is the road to feeling small and weak and unworthy and *accepting* these feelings instead of needing to protect a spuriously high self-esteem by striking out.

And again I think it is obvious that understanding of this basic existential problem should help us to embrace the B-Values

---

* [In his work, Maslow has developed his view that people have a hierarchy of needs. The Values of Being, or B-Values, refer to the expression of the higher needs—for justice, beauty, courage, truth and meaning in life, as contrasted with the more basic security needs for food and shelter, and for recognition and love.]

not only in others, but also in ourselves, thereby helping to resolve the Jonah complex.

Comment

I am always pulling back, afraid to commit myself to producing something, afraid to stretch myself, afraid to use the capabilities I know I possess. My first reaction is almost always "I can't." Of course, I have reasons, peculiar to me, for deciding "I can't." "I can't, I'm still a child; I can't, I'm not a real lawyer; I can't, I don't understand; I can't, I'm confused; I can't. . . ." Maslow believes that most people have similar voices. Although the message will differ, some part of us prefers that we fail to accomplish whatever we most want to be doing in our lives.

A thought that helps me go on, despite all the doubts clattering around in my head, is one from this article: If I don't do the work, who will? Why am I here if not to act? Sometimes I still feel too weak to act on these questions. At such times, I say "I won't" instead of "I can't" to be more honest and to leave open the possibility of change. When I feel a bit stronger I do act. I still have the fear; I still doubt myself and I manage to act while feeling these things. This poem expresses that for me:

> Come to the edge.
> We might fall.
> Come to the edge.
> It's too high. . . .
> COME TO THE EDGE!
> And they came
> And he pushed
> And they flew.*

                                                                    E.D.

Robert Bolt, *A Man for all Seasons*
(Vintage 1962).

(Lights rise to show MORE, seated, and ROPER, standing. . . .
      ROPER is dressed in black and wears a cross. . . .)

MORE   Must you wear those clothes, Will?

ROPER   Yes, I must.

MORE   Why?

ROPER   The time has come for decent men to declare their allegiance!

MORE   And what allegiance are those designed to express?

ROPER   My allegiance to the Church.

---

* Christopher Logue, in New Numbers,
p. 83 (Knopf 1970).

MORE   Well, you *look* like a Spaniard.

ROPER   All credit to Spain then!

MORE   You wouldn't last six months in Spain. You'd have been burned alive in Spain, during your heretic period.

ROPER   I suppose you have the right to remind me of it. (Points accusingly) That chain of office that *you* wear is a degradation!

MORE   I've told you. If the bishops in Convocation submitted this morning, I'll take it off. . . . It's no degradation. Great men have worn this.

ROPER   When d'you expect to hear from the bishops?

MORE   About now. I was promised an immediate message.

ROPER   I don't see what difference Convocation can make. The Church is already a wing of the Palace, is it not? The King is already its "Supreme Head"! Is he not?

MORE   No.

ROPER   (Startled) You are denying the Act of Supremacy!

MORE   No, I'm not; the Act states that the King—

ROPER   —is Supreme Head of the Church in England.

MORE   Supreme Head of the Church in England—(Underlining the words) "so far as the law of God allows." How far the law of God does allow it remains a matter of opinion, since the Act doesn't state it.

ROPER   A legal quibble.

MORE   Call it what you like, it's there, thank God.

ROPER   Very well; in your opinion how far does the law of God allow this?

MORE   I'll keep my opinion to myself, Will.

ROPER   Yes? I'll tell you mine—

MORE   Don't! If your opinion's what I think it is, it's High Treason, Roper! (Enter MARGARET above, unseen) Will you remember you've a wife now! And may have children!

MARGARET   Why must he remember that?

ROPER   To keep myself "discreet."

MARGARET   Then I'd rather you forgot it.

MORE   You are either idiots, or children. (Enter CHAPUYS [the Spanish Ambassador], above)

CHAPUYS   (Very sonorously) Or saints, my lord!

MARGARET   Oh, Father, Signor Chapuys has come to see you.

MORE   (Rising) Your Excellency.

CHAPUYS   Or saints, my lord; or saints.

MORE   (Grins maliciously at ROPER) That's it of course— saints! Roper—turn your head a bit—yes, I think I do detect a faint radiance. (Reproachfully) You should have told us, Will.

CHAPUYS   Come come, my lord; you too at this time are not free from some suspicion of saintliness.

MORE   (Quietly) I don't like the sound of that, Your Excellency. What do you require of *me*? What, Your Excellency?

CHAPUYS   May I not come simply to pay my respects to the English Socrates—as I see your angelic friend Erasmus calls you.

MORE   (Wrinkles nose) Yes, I'll think of something presently to call Erasmus. (Checks) Socrates! I've no taste for hemlock, Your Excellency, if that's what you require.

CHAPUYS   Heaven forbid!

MORE   (Dryly) Amen.

CHAPUYS   Must I require anything? After all, we are brothers in Christ, you and I!

MORE   A characteristic we share with the rest of humanity. You live in Cheapside, Signor? To make contact with a brother in Christ you have only to open your window and empty a chamberpot. There was no need to come to Chelsea.
                                                                (pp.47-49)

[MORE learns that the Bishops have acknowledged the King as head of the Church, and resigns his office as Chancellor.]

ALICE   So there's an end of you. What will you do now—sit by the fire and make goslings in the ash?

MORE   Not at all, Alice, I expect I'll write a bit. I'll write, I'll read, I'll think. I think I'll learn to fish! I'll play with my grandchildren—when son Roper's done his duty. Alice, shall I teach you to read?

ALICE   No, by God!

MORE   Son Roper, *you're* pleased with me I hope?

ROPER   (Goes to him; moved) Sire, you've made a noble gesture.

MORE   (Blankly) A gesture? (Eagerly) It wasn't possible to
       continue, Will. I was not *able* to continue. I would have if I
       could! I make no gesture! My God, I hope it's understood I
       make no gesture! Alice, you don't think I would do this to
       you for a gesture! *That's* a gesture! (Thumbs his nose)
       That's a gesture (Jerks up two fingers) I'm no street acrobat
       to make gestures! I'm practical!

ROPER You belittle yourself, sir, this was not practical; this
       was moral!

MORE   Oh, now I understand you, Will. Morality's *not* practi-
       cal. Morality's a gesture. A complicated gesture learned
       from books—that's what you say, Alice, isn't it? . . . And
       you, Meg?

MARGARET   It *is,* for most of us, Father.   (pp.54-55)

[Sometime later.]

ROPER There's to be a new Act through Parliament, sir!

MORE   Act?

ROPER Yes, sir—about the marriage!

MORE   (Indifferently) Oh.

MARGARET   Father, by this Act, they're going to administer
       an oath.

MORE   (With instantaneous attention) An oath! On what com-
       pulsion?

ROPER It's expected to be treason!

MORE   (Very still) What is the oath?

ROPER (Puzzled) It's about the marriage, sir.

MORE   But what is the wording?

ROPER We don't need to know the (Contemptuously) wording
       —we know what it will mean!

MORE   It will mean what the words say! An oath is *made*
       of words! It may be possible to take it. Or avoid it. Have we
       a copy of the Bill?

MARGARET   There's one coming out from the City.

MORE   Then let's get home and look at it. . . .

ROPER But sir—

MORE   Now listen, Will. And, Meg, you listen, too, you know I
       know you well. God made the *angels* to show him splendor—
       as he made animals for innocence and plants for their

simplicity. But Man he made to serve him wittily, in the tangle of his mind! If he suffers us to fall to such a case that there is no escaping, then we may stand to our tackle as best we can, and yes, Will, then we may clamor like champions . . . if we have the spittle for it. And no doubt it delights God to see splendor where He only looked for complexity. But it's God's part, not our own, to bring ourselves to that extremity! Our natural business lies in escaping—so let's get home and study this Bill.   (pp.72-73)

[Again, later.]

NORFOLK   (Leaping to his feet; all rise save MORE) Prisoner at the bar, you have been found guilty of High Treason. The sentence of the Court—

MORE   My lord! (NORFOLK breaks off. MORE has a sly smile. From this point to end of play his manner is of one who has fulfilled all his obligations and will now consult no interests but his own) My lord, when I was practicing the law, the manner was to ask the prisoner *before* pronouncing sentence, if he had anything to say.

NORFOLK   (Flummoxed) Have you anything to say?

MORE   Yes. (He rises; all others sit) To avoid this I have taken every path my winding wits would find. Now that the Court has determined to condemn me, God knoweth how, I will discharge my mind . . . concerning my indictment and the King's title. The indictment is grounded in an Act of Parliament which is directly repugnant to the Law of God. The King in Parliament cannot bestow the Supremacy of the Church because it is a Spiritual Supremacy! And more to this the immunity of the Church is promised both in Magna Carta and the King's own Coronation Oath!

CROMWELL   Now we plainly see that you *are* malicious!

MORE   Not so, Master Secretary! I am the King's true subject, and pray for him and all the realm . . . I do none harm, I say none harm, I think none harm. And if this be not enough to keep a man alive, in good faith I long not to live. . . .
                                                          (pp.92-93)

Comment

Bolt portrays so graphically here a most reluctant saint. More is vigilant to detect, in himself no less than others, "a faint radiance"; scornful of his act if it is viewed as a "gesture"; profoundly committed to "escaping" through a "legal quibble": He honestly can say, at the end, "To avoid this I have taken every path my winding wits would find." Neither his son-in-law, William Roper, nor his prosecutor, Thomas Cromwell, can see any of this. Roper speaks of "a noble gesture," and Cromwell furiously derides More at his trial as a "shrill incessant pedagogue about his own salvation" (p. 89), invoking his conscience to "provide a noble motive for his frivolous self-conceit." Today, in canonizing Sir Thomas More—whether we do so literally or not—we all tend, I think, to fall into Cromwell's and Roper's way of looking at him, and one quality which traitors and saints have in common is that we find in their lives very little real guidance for our own.

I believe that all of this is centrally connected to important aspects of "the repression of the sublime." More did all he could to assure himself that he was in fact innocent of Cromwell's hostile charge (and Roper's admiring charge) of self-conceit. Yet he could not prevent its being made. For myself, and I suspect for many others too, it is so difficult to know when I would be truly innocent of that charge that I find it difficult even to run the risk. More (like Jonah) is a very distant model; Roper, basking in his "faint radiance," lies close to hand for all of us, and the sure, safe way to keep *him* out of our mirror is to see him in every assertion of our will to find meaning, of our commitment to values that make us feel out of step with our peers. Norfolk's appeal—come with us, "for fellowship" (p. 18, above)—offers a powerful refuge, for it offers with fellowship the assurance that one is not playing Roper.

H.L.

Robert Pirsig, *Zen and the Art of Motorcycle Maintenance*
p.114 (Bantam 1975).

> His early failure had released him from any felt obligation to think along institutional lines and his thoughts were already independent to a degree few people are familiar with. He felt that institutions such as schools, churches, governments and political organizations of every sort all tended to direct thought for ends other than truth, for the perpetuation of their own functions, and for the control of individuals in the service of these functions. He came to see his early failure as a lucky break, an accidental escape from a trap that had been set for him, and he was very trapwary about institutional truths for the remainder of his time. He didn't see these things and think this way at first, however, only later on. . . .

Comment

Pirsig writes here of the trap that "success" can be, and so very often is. As I read this passage, I immediately reflected upon how I and, I suppose, others can become so readily and subtly prisoners of our own success. I have never enjoyed, it is strange to say, the luxury of failure. According to most objective criteria, my career has been marked by a series of successes, from grade through law school, as a practicing attorney, as a teacher in a law school. Escaping failure, I have never been thrown back totally on myself, at least not academically. Discovering myself apart from my successes is a privilege I have to fight for, fighting against the security my successes have brought me.

This struggle has been most obvious for me in the tension I have had around teaching. For the first two years after I became aware of the desire to bring a humanistic educational orientation into my own teaching, I felt I had to do it secretly. I don't just mean carefully, for that indeed was warranted by my own inexperience, the newness of the field, the elusiveness of the issues. I mean that to "protect" my identity as a law teacher gained through my success, I hesitated to share openly my concerns and experiences—with my colleagues, with my students, and at times even with myself. Each time I walked into the law school (it still happens easily) I became a little different. I pulled the mantle of success a little tighter, and I became careful in what I said, sometimes in what I thought. And it was not just that "they" might have difficulty understanding. It was somehow that "I" would be threatened. The first time I spoke openly with my students about my interests and pursuits—I had prepared my way very carefully—it was I who was surprised. The students evidenced neither shock nor dismay, rather a quiet appreciation and regard, and that was more for my honesty than the "revelation."

In accepting an institutional identification, born of my successes in many different academic settings, I had accepted an array of premises about life, about people, and about law. I questioned them only occasionally, when I felt so deeply unsettled that the questions could not be ignored. At times I even needed to deny that I had any questions at all. I somehow sacrificed my own truth, and a common shared truth as well, for an institutional truth. As Pirsig writes, institutions, even those created to serve good and noble causes, can quickly turn into monuments to their own survival. Welfare systems, courts, schools become edifices of bureaucracy. The persons serving in them often experience themselves in terms of the institutional concerns of self-perpetuation. I don't mean this as just a sociological statement of fact about institutions and those working in them. It is a fact of human nature—we tend to "institutionalize" internally our successes and gains in ways that deny the urge that gave life to them. I wonder whether we have the courage to change all this before we have all failed, the courage to see our current failures as a lucky break, enabling us to do differently in the future.

What is most difficult for me to capture and hold to is that independence of thinking, free of institutional restraints, of which Pirsig writes. My own thinking, including my original thinking, is often a response to institutions around me; even my rebellion has been a reaction. And I am so sorely tempted to take any live creative expression and turn it into another success, robbing it of its vitality and institutionalizing it within my own pride. One of the greatest traps in my own teaching arises when I suddenly realize in a class that what I have been trying to do has "worked," and instantly I make it something different, a testimony to my achievement rather than to the meaning that the students and I had shared. I pay the price of success dearly.

J.H.

Casner & Leach, *Cases and Text on Property*
pp.275-278, 382-384 (Little, Brown 1951).

In old England the ancestral estate, not commerce, was normally the basis of the family fortune. It was also the focus of family pride. These factors provided the motivation for attempts to keep the land in the family as long as the family lasted; and the estate tail was the basic instrumentality designed for that purpose. . . . Before 1285 it was common for O, an owner in fee simple, to convey "to A and the heirs of his body." [T]he form of conveyance was designed to require that upon A's death the property should pass to his lineal descendants or, if there were no descendents, revert to O. In passing upon such conveyances the courts seem to have held that . . . if A had issue born alive, he could then convey a fee simple, thus cutting off the inheritance of his issue and O's reversion. . . .

The estate with these characteristics was called a fee simple conditional. . . . A Petition of the Barons in 1258 called attention to the manner in which the intention of grantors was being frustrated by allowing tenants in fee simple conditional to convey a fee simple absolute after birth of issue. But it was not until 1285 that a statute was passed on the matter. [It] provided:

> The will of the giver according to the form in the deed of gift manifestly expressed shall be from henceforth observed, so that they to whom the land was given under such condition shall have no power to alien the land so given, but that it shall remain unto the issue of them to whom it was given after their death, or shall revert unto the giver or his heirs if issue fail. . . . (Many words omitted.)

The estate given to one "and the heirs of his body" came to be known as a fee tail—from the French "tailler," meaning "to carve," the thought being that the grantor has carved an estate precisely to his liking. . . .

Disentailing conveyances. From 1285 until 1472 the estate tail seems to have functioned as planned . . . and 187 years is well above the life expectancy of legal institutions. In 1472 Taltarum's Case, Y.B. 12 Edw. IV, 19, decided that a tenant in tail in possession could convey a fee simple by suffering a common recovery. A common recovery was a type of conveyance by means of a collusive law suit. It represented an all-time high in legalistic hocus-pocus. . . .

The Strict Settlement. We are now in a position to appreciate the deftness of the Strict Settlement, the method by which the estates of the landed families were so tied up in legal meshes, over the period roughly from 1650 to 1925, that it was quite unlikely that they would stray out of the family circle. . . . Let us assume that F, a father, has a son, S, who is about to marry and for whom he wants to set up an estate. He conveys the property to S for life, remainder to Trustees for the life of S to preserve contingent remainders, remainder in tail male to the first son of S, with successive remainders in tail male to the other sons of S. [T]he estate in the Trustees effectively blocks any attempt on the part of S to break up the settlement by destroying the contingent remainders in his sons. When a son is born, whom we will call G, his remainder in tail vests. When G reaches 21, S has reached his forties or fifties and feels himself the guardian of the family honor, tradition and estates. G may be rebellious and undisciplined, but he cannot disentail and thereby acquire a fee simple in remainder, because disentailment is possible only for a tenant in tail in possession; so, no matter what wild and radical ideas G may have at the age of 21, he can do the family estates no damage. It was at this point that, traditionally, S called G in for a chat. He explained to him that, having arrived at manhood's threshold, G would be wanting to make the Grand Tour of the continent, and present himself at the London season; this would take money, but there were family funds, controlled by S, available for members of the family who showed that they had the family interests at heart. S further explained that one of the important interests of the family was the continuation of the family estates and that there were a few papers to be signed to that end, now and at once. Thus gently nudged, it was traditional for G to sign as requested and thus make available to himself those advantages which flow from a generous parental allowance. The resettlement which would be created at this point comprised the following steps:

(a) S, the life tenant, and the Trustees surrendered their estates to G, the remainderman in tail. This made him a tenant in tail in possession.

(b) G suffered a recovery in favor of the family solicitor, thus making the solicitor owner of the fee simple.

(c) The family solicitor conveyed to S for life, remainder to G for life, remainder to Trustees for the lives of S and G to preserve contingent remainders, remainders to the first and other sons of G in tail male, remainders to the second and other sons of S in tail male.

Thus the basic pattern was pushed forward one generation. S could now rest easy in the confident belief that G would have no power to put the estates out of the family until he had a son 21 years old; and by that time G in his turn would be settled down, devoted to a shire life of farming and fox hunting, and determined to see that the family estates were preserved. . . . By this method thousands of estates . . . were kept substantially intact for centuries. . . .

Comment

Casner and Leach surely had other purposes in mind, but their discussion of the Strict Settlement gives graphic, if exotic, testimony in support of the proposition that it is only the young who need be pressured to surrender immediate goals for long-range ones: As we grow older, we learn to do that without prompting. This excerpt summarizes the constant tension, reflected in the law, between the compelling immediate needs of large landowners for freedom of alienation and their dynastic interests in preventing it. It is no exaggeration to say that the success of the latter force during a period of three centuries, to the extent it rested on the legal device of the Strict Settlement, rested as well on the strength of the psychological insight that a commitment to surrender an option, though "temporary," may well outlast the will to exercise it.

Today's law students have in common with G their age bracket—and the notion that they are not yet living their real life but only preparing for it. Whether that preparation consists of the Grand Tour, sowing wild oats, or gathering "A's" where one may, is not central. Indeed, today's young adult has a longer past and a longer future of embryonic existence. Having reached law school, he or she has already put off a lot—and, often, long ago internalized the pressure to do so—in order to do well in high school, get into a good college, do well there, score high on standardized tests, and get into a "good" law school—there to continue on, seeking to make law review if possible, buck for Officer, work at a large firm in the summer "for experience," interview for a firm or a clerkship. The future is no different: Whether the next step is to make partner, establish a practice, or earn academic tenure, our lives are structured so that what we "really" want to do is always for the moment not feasible, and must responsibly be postponed until one more bit of preparation can be laid carefully in place. Tenured professors yearn for named Chairs, prestigious offers, governmental assignments; senior partners aspire for an opportunity for government service, important Bar Association assignments, or the bench; district judges calculate their chances for promotion; Supreme Court justices speculate (do they?) on the longevity of their Chief or ponder the near-miss of Charles Evans Hughes.

It seems that the only reality not viewed as a preparation for the next stage is retirement. I was walking with a friend down the corridor of the law school he had attended several years earlier. The school had the practice of hanging portraits of its faculty as they retired, and as we passed that of one of his first-year teachers, he said: "Oh, I see that _____ made the wall." _____ is now presumably free to follow his own present priorities, provided he can remember them.

We vainly romanticize about a free future life, and dismiss as impractical and romantic any who attempt to live their present lives according to their true values and priorities. That seems to me the only cold-eyed *practical* thing I can do, given the eloquent testimony of the wrecks of so many plans deferred in search of that elusive next "something" that will make true freedom to live possible.

H.L.

Comment

> You look at where you're going and where you are and it never makes sense, but then you look back at where you've been and a pattern seems to emerge. And if you project forward from that pattern, then sometimes you can come up with something.
> Robert Pirsig, *Zen and the Art of Motorcycle Maintenance* 162.

Sometime around the middle of my third year at law school I was musing over my feelings about law, law school, and job choices. I thought back to what had attracted me to law in the first place and realized it had been the possibility of power and control: Power to be able to do things for myself and others and control over my own life by not being dependent on anyone else to interpret the laws that affected me and my concerns. I had lost track of these personally held, vaguely social-activist ideas in the last two years.

I've recognized two factors that played an important role in my losing touch with why I came to law school. One is the constant emphasis among students on the jobs we'll hold or would like to hold when we leave. The focus is always on the jobs that exist out there and whether we'll be judged suitable for them. In that atmosphere it is easy to forget to look inside ourselves, decide what we want, and then look for a job to match. The other factor is the message I received from my first year professors: Wipe your slate clean; we are here to make you into lawyers. I did wipe my slate clean and in the process I lost my own goals.

I had been distressed because no legal career seemed to really interest me—public or private litigation, test cases, appellate work, etc. I'd known for some time that I was not interested in litigation and said as much, knowing intellectually that it was fine to feel that way but still feeling as though I were making an excuse. Having no interest in litigation seemed to leave me with commercial law, which was interesting because I like counseling but nothing seemed to really touch me. I felt very negative about the whole issue of choosing a job.

When I began remembering and focusing on what had attracted me to law in the first place, I finally realized how positive my feelings were and became very excited. I realized there was something I was very interested in doing—community projects. If that included a law suit, fine, but my major concern has been with "grass roots" quality of life changes. When I looked at how I had been living my life, I realized I have always worked for changes in whatever school community I have been in from high school to law school. I became excited about broadening my view of "community." I could use my legal and non-legal talents to help others and myself gain more control over our lives, using law in a broader context than a particular law suit. By focusing on why I had been attracted to law in the first place I realized why I had been dissatisfied with most public interest jobs—they were too specialized, fragmented and litigation-based for my tastes.

For the first time since I started job-hunting, I feel focused and the focus is positive. I had been eliminating jobs based on my negative views and was left feeling directionless. Now I can choose, based on what I know I want. The good feelings and positive energy that have been with me since these musings are fantastic. I feel much more in control, and I am excited knowing that I can do something with my skills that will be useful and satisfying for me. Not only can I do it in the future, but I've been doing this work for some time, only not from a conscious choice. Now I've got a handle on how important it is to me to work for and live within a community, how much I like it, and how it ties together many of my interests that before seemed so disparate. I think I can do the work better now that I recognize that this is what I want to do, that it is the work I like to do, and it is the work I have always done.

M.E.

3. ASSUMING RESPONSIBILITY

A. RESPONSIBILITY, AUTHORITY AND CHOICE

Felix S. Cohen & Morris R. Cohen, *Readings on Jurisprudence and Legal Philosophy* (2d ed. by Philip Shuchman, Little, Brown, 1979)
Preface to 1st Edition, by F.S. Cohen, p. xv.

A distinguished teacher once gave a series of lectures on law and ethics that made so deep an impression that the notes taken by his students are still being widely circulated. In his final lecture, this teacher commented on the prevailing notion of practical men that legal ideals are other-worldly or utopian, and made this ever-pertinent observation on the nature of ethical doctrine:

It is not in heaven, that thou shouldest say, Who shall go up for us to heaven, and bring it unto us, and make us to hear it, that we may do it? Neither is it beyond the sea, that thou shouldest say, Who shall go over the sea for us, and bring it unto us, and make us to hear it, that we may do it? But the word is very nigh unto thee, in thy mouth, and in thy heart, that thou mayest do it.

Note

The quoted passage is from Deuteronomy (XXX:12), Moses' final charge to the Israelites. It strikes me as compellingly pertinent to the question of the assumption of personal responsibility for one's acts and statements. I do not feel comfortable commenting on this passage and, happily, can set forth here a traditional comment of others. The *Babylonian Talmud* recounts a legend centering on this excerpt:

If he cut it into separate tiles, placing sand between each tile: Rabbi Eliezer declared it clean, and the Sages declared it unclean. . . .[5] Rabbi Eliezer brought forward every imaginable argument but they did not accept them.

Said he to them: "If the law agrees with me, let this carob-tree prove it!" Thereupon the carob-tree was torn a hundred cubits out of

---

5. This refers to an oven, which instead of being made in one piece, was made in a series of separate portions with a layer of sand between each. Rabbi Eliezer maintains that since each portion in itself is not a utensil, the sand between prevents the whole structure from being regarded as a single utensil, and therefore it is not liable to uncleanness. The Sages however hold that the outer coating of mortar or cement unifies the whole, and it is therefore liable to uncleanness.

its place. . . . "One cannot bring proof from a carob-tree," they retorted. Again he said to them: "If the law agrees with me, let the stream of water prove it!" Whereupon the stream of water flowed backwards. "One cannot bring proof from a stream of water," they rejoined.

Again he said to them: "If the law agrees with me, let it be proved from Heaven!" Whereupon a Heavenly Voice cried out: "Why do ye dispute with Rabbi Eliezer, seeing that in all matter the law agrees with him!" But Rabbi Joshua arose and exclaimed: " 'It is not in heaven.' " What did he mean by this?—Said Rabbi Jeremiah: "That the Law had already been given at Mount Sinai; we pay no attention to a Heavenly Voice. It is for man and not God to interpret and decide. One cannot bring proof from God."

Rabbi Nathan met Elijah [the Prophet, who was said to be immortal and to appear frequently to the Rabbis,] and asked him: "What did the Holy One, Blessed be He, do in that hour?"—"He smiled," he replied, "saying, 'My children have prevailed, My children have prevailed.' "

(Order Nezikin, Tractate Mezia, 59a-59b).

The editors of the Soncino edition of the *Talmud* describe this legend as "a remarkable assertion of the independence of human reasoning" (*id.* at 59b n.2 (1935)). It is clear that there is being asserted not only the freedom of humankind "to interpret and decide," but an obligation as well to exercise this freedom, and not to fall back on the supposed authority of Heavenly Voices. Earthly voices, it hardly need be added, carry no greater authority. Indeed, the *Talmud* itself contains, in another reference to Deuteronomy XXX:12, an eloquent reminder that we are not to abdicate our judgment to those learned in the law—a reminder presumably applicable to the authority of erudite law professors, prestigious judges, respected attorneys, etc., etc.:

What is the significance of the text, *It is not in heaven. . .* ? Rabbi Johanan expounded, "It is not in heaven," it is not to be found with him who, because he possesses some knowledge of it, towers in his pride as high as the heavens, ["*neither is it beyond the sea*"] it is not found with him who, because of some knowledge of it, is as expansive in his self-esteem as the sea.

(Order Moed, Tractate Erubin, 55a).*

                                                                   H.L.

*   I am indebted to Aaron Kriegel, a member of the Class of 1979 at the University of Pennsylvania Law School and a Conservative Rabbi, for these Talmudic references, and for valuable help in arriving at an appropriate rendition in English.

Comment

The first semester of law school the teachers told us to clear our slates for a new experience: Nothing in the past or outside counted anymore—just their own unknowable measuring sticks of what was right, good and intelligent. They had set down the rules for learning this mysterious skill and for becoming successful, and I did not question them. I just wanted to learn the correct way so I, too, could be a lawyer and be powerful.

Learning law was a puzzle; I wanted help and needed help to get past the hurdles. I got the help and became passive in the process. I trusted my teachers instead of myself. I let their view of an area of law channel my thinking. The teachers' opinions of my intellectual worth and the value of my ideas became more important to me than what I thought. I censored everything I said. I was quiet, unless spoken to. I wanted to learn and I let them take over, let them decide what I needed to learn and how to learn it.

It was the exams and grades that changed all this for me. I had liked studying for the first-semester exams. Things became clearer and I felt I was definitely getting the hang of becoming a lawyer. The exams themselves upset me deeply. I could do them, but they were boring. I left them feeling empty and I realized they existed only to help someone judge me—not for me to learn. My trust was shaken. I had turned over my life, hopes and dreams to the law school and I received in return some grades that had little meaning to me and no connection to the four months I had lived through. I had done well in the law school grading system and for the first time some teachers recognized my existence. That recognition only made me feel angry. I was the same person I had been before and when I looked at the exam answers—my own, others' and the model answers—the whole system seemed arbitrary.

At least the arbitrariness gave me a push. I saw what was happening, knew that it was not valuable for me, and withdrew my blind trust. I started listening to myself more.

M.E.

John Steinbeck, *The Grapes of Wrath*
pp.42-53 (Viking 1939).

The owners of the land came onto the land, or more often a spokesman for the owners came. They came in closed cars, and they felt the dry earth with their fingers, and sometimes they drove big earth augers into the ground for soil tests. The tenants, from their sun-beaten dooryards, watched uneasily when the closed cars drove along the fields. And at last the owner men drove into the dooryards and sat in their cars to talk out of the windows. The tenant men stood beside the cars for a while, and then squatted on their hams and found sticks with which to mark the dust.

Some of the owner men were kind because they hated what they had to do, and some of them were angry because they hated to be cruel, and some of them were cold because they had long ago found that one could not be an owner unless one were cold. And all of them were caught in something larger than themselves. Some of them hated the mathematics that drove them, and some were afraid, and some worshiped the mathematics because it provided a refuge from thought and from feeling. If a bank or a finance company owned the land, the owner man said, The Bank—or the Company—needs—wants—insists—must have —as though the Bank or the Company were a monster, with thought and feeling, which had ensnared them. These last would take no responsibility for the banks or the companies because they were men and slaves, while the banks were machines and masters all at the same time. Some of the owner men were a little proud to be slaves to such cold and powerful masters. The owner men sat in the cars and explained. You know the land is poor. You've scrabbled at it long enough, God knows.

The squatting tenant men nodded and wondered and drew figures in the dust, and yes, they knew, God knows. . . .

And at last the owner men came to the point. The tenant system won't work any more. One man on a tractor can take the place of twelve or fourteen families. Pay him a wage and take all the crop. We have to do it. We don't like to do it. But the monster's sick. Something's happened to the monster. . . .

The tenant men looked up alarmed. But what'll happen to us? How'll we eat?

You'll have to get off the land. The plows'll go through the dooryard.

And now the squatting men stood up angrily. Grampa took up the land, and he had to kill the Indians and drive them away. And Pa was born here, and he killed weeds and snakes. Then a bad year came and he had to borrow a little money. And we was born here. There in the door—our children born here. And Pa had to borrow money. The bank owned the land then, but we stayed and we got a little bit of what we raised.

We know that—all that. It's not us, it's the bank. A bank isn't like a man. Or an owner with fifty thousand acres, he isn't like a man either. That's the monster.

Sure, cried the tenant men, but it's our land. We measured it and broke it up. We were born on it, and we got killed on it, died on it. Even if it's no good, it's still ours. That's what makes it ours—being born on it, working it, dying on it. That makes ownership, not a paper with numbers on it.

We're sorry. It's not us. It's the monster. The bank isn't like a man.

Yes, but the bank is only made of men.

No, you're wrong there—quite wrong there. The bank is something else than men. It happens that every man in a bank hates what the bank does, and yet the bank does it. The bank is something more than men, I tell you. It's the monster. Men made it, but they can't control it.

The tenants cried, Grampa killed Indians, Pa killed snakes for the land. Maybe we can kill banks—they're worse than Indians and snakes. Maybe we got to fight to keep our land, like Pa and Grampa did.

And now the owner men grew angry. You'll have to go.

But it's ours, the tenant men cried. We—

No. The bank, the monster owns it. You'll have to go.

We'll get our guns, like Grampa when the Indians came. What then?

Well—first the sheriff, and then the troops. You'll be stealing if you try to stay, you'll be murderers if you kill to stay. The monster isn't men, but it can make men do what it wants.

But if we go, where'll we go? How'll we go? We got no money.

We're sorry, said the owner men. The bank, the fifty-thousand-acre owner can't be responsible. You're on land that isn't yours. Once over the line maybe you can pick cotton in the fall. Maybe you can go on relief. Why don't you go on west to California? There's work there, and it never gets cold. Why, you can reach out anywhere and pick an orange. Why, there's always some kind of crop to work in. Why don't you go there? And the owner men started their cars and rolled away. . . .

At noon the tractor driver stopped . . . near a tenant house and opened his lunch. . . . After a while the tenant who could not leave the place came out and squatted in the shade beside the tractor.

"Why, you're Joe Davis's boy!"

"Sure," the driver said.

"Well, what you doing this kind of work for—against your own people?"

"Three dollars a day. I got damn sick of creeping for my dinner—and not getting it. I got a wife and kids. We got to eat. Three dollars a day, and it comes every day."

"That's right," the tenant said. "But for your three dollars a day fifteen or twenty families can't eat at all. Nearly a hundred people have to go out and wander on the roads for your three dollars a day. Is that right?"

And the driver said, "Can't think of that. Got to think of my own kids. Three dollars a day, and it comes every day. Times are changing, mister, don't you know? Can't make a living on the land unless you've got two, five, ten thousand acres and a tractor. Crop land isn't for little guys like us any more. You don't kick up a howl because you can't make Fords, or because you're not the telephone company. Well, crops are like that now. Nothing to do about it. You try to get three dollars a day someplace. That's the only way."

The tenant pondered. "Funny thing how it is. If a man owns a little property, that property is him, it's part of him, and it's like him. If he owns property only so he can walk on it and handle it and be sad when it isn't doing well, and feel fine when the rain falls on it, that property is him, and some way he's bigger because he owns it. Even if he isn't successful he's big with his property. That is so."

And the tenant pondered more. "But let a man get property he doesn't see, or can't take time to get his fingers in, or can't be there to walk on it—why, then the property is the man. He can't do what he wants, he can't think what he wants. The property is the man, stronger than he is. And he is small, not big. Only his possessions are big—and he's the servant of his property. That is so, too."

The driver munched the branded pie and threw the crust away. "Times are changed, don't you know? Thinking about stuff like that don't feed the kids. Get your three dollars a day, feed your kids. You got no call to worry about anybody's kids but your own. You get a reputation for talking like that, and you'll never get three dollars a day. Big shots won't give you three dollars a day if you worry about anything but your three dollars a day."

"Nearly a hundred people on the road for your three dollars. Where will we go?"

"And that reminds me," the driver said, "you better get out soon. I'm going through the dooryard after dinner."

"You filled in the well this morning."

"I know. Had to keep the line straight. But I'm going through the dooryard after dinner. Got to keep the lines straight. And—well, you know Joe Davis, my old man, so I'll tell you this. I got orders wherever there's a family not moved out—if I have

an accident—you know, get too close and cave the house in a little—well, I might get a couple of dollars. And my youngest kid
never had no shoes yet.''

"I built it with my hands. Straightened old nails to put the
sheathing on. Rafters are wired to the stringers with baling wire.
It's mine. I built it. You bump it down—I'll be in the window
with a rifle. You even come too close and I'll pot you like a
rabbit.''

"It's not me. There's nothing I can do. I'll lose my job if I
don't do it. And look—suppose you kill me? They'll just hang
you, but long before you're hung there'll be another guy on the
tractor, and he'll bump the house down. You're not killing the
right guy.''

"That's so," the tenant said. "Who gave you orders? I'll go
after him. He's the one to kill.''

"You're wrong. He got his orders from the bank. The bank
told him, 'Clear those people out or it's your job.' "

"Well, there's a president of the bank. There's a board of
directors. I'll fill up the magazine of the rifle and go into the
bank.''

The driver said, "Fellow was telling me the bank gets orders
from the East. The orders were, 'Make the land show profit or
we'll close you up.' "

"But where does it stop? Who can we shoot? I don't aim to
starve to death before I kill the man that's starving me.''

Comment

There is much in the concerns of the legal system, and in the study of
law, which encourages our inclination to accept the division of individual
responsibility. Judge Jon Newman, of the federal court in Connecticut,
has called to mind a "horrifying aspect" of the execution of Private Eddie
Slovik in 1944 (the only American executed for desertion since the Civil
War): "No member of the court-martial [which sentenced him to death]
believed the sentence would be carried out." (*Foreword* to *Parole Release
Decisionmaking and the Sentencing Process*, 84 Yale L.J. 810, 812 (1975).)
A more far-reaching and dramatic example of the division of responsibility is the American bombing of Vietnam and Cambodia during the
Johnson and Nixon administrations: From presidential advisor to
employee for a Defense Department contractor, each actor played only a
limited role, dependent on the others for its lethal force, and all removed
from direct confrontation with the consequences.

Alongside such examples, and Steinbeck's, the harms done in legal
education by the division of responsibility are truly pale. Yet, if the Battle
of Waterloo was won on the playing fields of Eton, the foundations for the

participation of honorable and humane people in dislocation and death are laid in school. The particular basis for disclaiming responsibility—the belief that (as in *The Grapes of Wrath*) the harm will occur in any event; that (as in the Slovik case) the harm will not occur in any event; or that, as is the case with much that we do in law school, the results will be harmful only because of the actions of others—is for me not controlling.

As law teachers, we teach in an effort to engage and develop our students' critical faculties and their capacity to make the law better serve human needs; we disclaim responsibility for the societal and other pressures which often bring students to us so obsessed by the need for approval and security that they can see in the study of law little more than a test of their prospects for achieving them. We want to educate students whose work choices will span the full range of society's needs for legal representation; we do not accept responsibility for what has happened to the cost of higher education, and to the rate and distribution of attorney compensation, which combine to channel more and more graduates into the representation of the most powerful segments of society. We take seriously (somewhat) our function as gatekeeper for the profession, to screen out those whose acts evidence serious lack of ability or character; we are not, we assert, responsible for aspects of the lives of individual students that contribute to their acting in ways that are academically or morally unacceptable.

The acceptance of responsibility—the refusal to disclaim responsibility by dividing it and assigning the critical portion to others—is not an act of "guilt-tripping" or masochistic self-indulgence. The frenzy to repudiate guilt, so prevalent today, seeks to stigmatize the acceptance of responsibility as merely the reflection of some unworthy psychiatric quirk, and serves to legitimate the most extreme forms of individualistic acquisitiveness. There is a critical difference between responsibility and guilt. Many actors and many forces influence society, and to say that the responsibility for a bad result is not ours alone, and that our individual action is not morally blameworthy, does not end the matter of responsibility. Nor is it to say that our responsibility is to right the world's wrongs. In each case, we need as law teachers to decide what course of conduct we want to follow, neither accepting the "blame" for someone else's choice nor seeking refuge from the need to make a fully advertent choice in the acts or omissions of other people or institutions.

All of this is said with admirable clarity and concreteness by Douglas Phelps, in a brief discussion of the question of law school responsibility for the placement process—surely a prime illustration of long-standing refusal to accept responsibility on the ground that any perceived problem is the product of the actions of outside forces. What Phelps says has relevance and validity far beyond the law school's role in the placement process, and is worth reading with its broader message in mind.

H.L.

Douglas Phelps, *Law Placement and Social Justice*
53 N.Y.U.L. Rev. 663-665 (1978).

The passage from law student to lawyer, a transition mediated by the law school placement office, is immensely important to both the student and society. Personal decisions are made during this period, sometimes unconsciously, that shape the student's future career, as well as his or her professional identity. Taken collectively, these decisions determine the distribution of lawyers in our society and the character of the legal profession. Since law schools are deeply involved with this transitional process and necessarily concerned about its impact, law placement deserves a good deal more attention than it receives.

For the individual law student, this life transition is one during which conflicting personal values that have heretofore coexisted easily must now be confronted. Which values will be actualized and which abandoned? At the same time, all career options can no longer be kept alive. Which will be chosen? Since a tension often exists between values and options, questions about vocation and its place in one's own life take on tremendous significance. Out of the struggle with these questions must come a more concrete sense of identity, replacing the inchoate self-images that have sufficed through twenty years of schooling. The personal and vocational priorities that emerge tend to endure far into an individual's life.

This process of law student passage into the legal profession, and the decisions it entails, are also of fundamental concern to the larger society. It profoundly influences which populations and interests will be represented and have access to law, the legal system, and democratic processes, and which will not. The involvement of lawyers with particular communities and causes, and their involvement, or lack thereof, with solutions to pressing social problems, is initially a product of this transitional process.

Given an awareness of this process, the way law schools structure and facilitate the transition from law student to lawyer might be expected to reflect three elements: sensitivity to the difficult emergence of the new lawyer's self-concept and professional identity; conscious regard for the social outcomes of the transition process in terms of the allocation of legal services and the character of the legal profession; and careful analysis of the nature of the law school placement program's influence on both the student's identity and these aforementioned social outcomes.

The influence of the placement service may manifest itself in quite subtle ways. Consider, for example, the term "placement."

This characterization of the passage from the educational to the professional community seems, by virtue of its familiarity, innocuous enough. Yet "placement" implies one particular view of this life transition; it is not synonymous with it. Moreover, this view may not be one we want to encourage.

The term "placement" assumes and reinforces a static world view, a view of the world as "given," as a fixed reality within which one finds a "place." It underemphasizes the extent to which the world should be seen as an evolving environment that the individual acts upon, changes, and is responsible for. "Placement" rivets attention on jobs to be obtained, as opposed to social needs to be met. It accents ambition and downplays obligation. It suggests a passive posture by the student who wants to be "placed." Fundamentally, it implies a future to which one is going, alone, rather than a future that we are creating, together.

The term "career" carries a similar bias, inherently diminishing a fully human notion of an individual's future life work. It tends to reduce vocation, the process by which one seeks to actualize oneself in history and thereby contribute to society and humanity, to merely a prospective succession of jobs. "Career" creates an illusion of isolation, while in reality a person's life work is intricately bound to all other lives.

The use of such terminology is significant for two reasons. Thinking about the future *structures* the future, and the terms in which we think prefigure our thoughts. If students consider their futures in inadequate terms, this will tend to result in an inadequate future—in this case one for which no one feels responsible.

More importantly, this terminology reflects a more general tendency in our current approach to facilitating students' transition into the legal profession—a tendency to treat work as though it is socially purposeless activity. Through the placement office lens, focused narrowly on jobs, vocation appears disembodied from the social and historical content that gives it meaning. Work, a social activity that brings about particular social ends, is treated as an end in itself. History, in turn, seems reduced to a spectacle, which we may choose to watch or ignore, but in which we do not participate.

In such a context, is it any wonder that law students' idealism and sense of larger purpose wane? If law school placement processes serve to emphasize the material aspects of particular work, while ignoring or mystifying the social ends inherent in that work, then they reduce a profound life choice to the dimensions of a commodity exchange.

This result is reinforced in the most prestigious law schools by the fact that certain employment choices are, in a purely mechanical sense, made to seem more tangible than others. Law placement at these schools typically revolves around on-campus interviewing by employers in the early fall, followed by invitations to interview further at the employers' offices. The economic costs of participating in this process are prohibitive for all but the largest corporate law firms and corporate legal departments. Moreover, job offers made in the fall expire before most other employers even know their hiring requirements. And since these same employers that interview in the fall are able to offer the highest salaries and greatest professional status by traditional standards, students confront a choice between two birds in the hand and one in the bush. The consequence, again, is to discourage serious reflection about one's values and vocation, in this case by limiting the otherwise wide range of career options that would make such reflection rich and meaningful.

If we assume that the law school's role in assisting students to enter the legal profession should be value-neutral and should maximize informed consideration of career options, the situation thus far described is clearly troublesome. Existing placement processes tend to structure this transition in ways both narrow and value-laden.

Moreover, an alternative criterion for assessing law placement can be imagined—one that posits some larger notion of justice as the proper standard for evaluation. A law school might find it appropriate to focus the institution's placement role on facilitating its graduates' involvement with combating social injustice. The latter could be defined in purely procedural terms, such that emphasis is placed on servicing unmet legal needs, or in substantive terms, such that law students are helped to find employment that contributes to the resolution of widely-acknowledged social problems. With either approach, the ultimate choice of job would remain the student's, as is currently the case. The change would involve only a shift in the law school's point of departure with respect to law placement, from existing jobs toward legal needs.

Edwin Greenebaum, *Attorney's Problems in Making Ethical Decisions* 52 Ind. L.J. 627, 629-632 (1977).

The profession draws to it persons who want [the law] to ... be clear, predictable and just and show the clear road to proper ethical choices. The disappointing fact is that the law is in many respects unclear and unpredictable and is sometimes the engine of injustice. Further, law is a helping profession in which practitioners are faced with subtle and difficult conflicts of interest between themselves, their clients and society, frequently involving distressing human circumstances. The ethical choices facing the legal practitioner are a challenge to anyone's maturity. The reality of the law, then, is unsatisfactory, and students and practitioners will be motivated to avoid seeing it.

The traditions of the profession do provide rationalizations for those who would abandon their own judgment to that of the group, although practitioners may have to choose between discrepancies in role behaviors acceptable to subgroups of the profession: the ABA or the local bar, firms representing substantial business interests, the personal injury bar or legal services groups and so forth. Whatever rationalizations lawyers accept, however, there will remain that portion of their personalities which holds to notions of goodness which were learned as children growing up in a family and in the general community. Coping with the resulting internal conflicts is a part of every attorney's personal agenda.

The alternative to abandoning one's judgment to that of the group is to learn to acknowledge one's conflicting personal motivations and to make judgments on explicit recognition and weighing of facts and values influencing decisions. If this is the path of greater responsibility, however, it is also potentially one of greater distress, requiring as it does living with insoluable dilemmas, with concern for the suffering of clients and others, and with never having certain knowledge that one's decisions are right or wrong. Attorneys can never be certain of the moral correctness of their decisions because of the uncertainty of values and because of uncertain knowledge of the likely consequences. Training in ethical behavior cannot responsibly content itself with extinguishing inappropriate defenses to practitioners' anxieties, but must help in learning new behaviors, which while consonant with professional values, will also make possible living with the stresses of professional work.

I believe that ethics commentators share with law students the wistful hope that reasoned discussion can result in the resolution of dilemmas and that a code of professional responsibility can and ought to provide clear and generally acceptable guidance to attorney conduct. The ethical problems facing attorneys, however, are true dilemmas, and action decisions will not be generally acceptable. The extent to which decisions should be governed by authorities and the extent to which they should be left to the consciences of individual attorneys is itself a value question. An attorney with appropriate humility will frequently defer in his judgment to colleagues or to the mores of the legal community. The extent to which the profession pre-empts the individual attorney's judgment by rules with enforcible sanctions is a decision made through political processes. The legal profession will not become more "ethical" until allocation of authority and acceptance of responsibility are more realistically faced.

Just as it is difficult for parents with children and for doctors with patients, it will always be difficult for lawyers to deny their dependent clients something they want or something an attorney feels a client needs. And it will always remain difficult for attorneys to know when they are being appropriately humble in giving deference to group norms and when they are merely avoiding responsibility or being personally prudential. . . .

Practitioners, coming from a posture of not wanting responsibility, are plunged into contexts where their freedom of choice is very limited. Discussion in much of the literature seems to proceed from the premise that attorneys are free to make their own ethical decisions. Especially for attorneys just starting out, this is just not the case. The most extreme situation occurs when attorneys are instructed by their employers—senior partners in their firms, not their clients—to do something which the attorney considers improper. . . .

Even without such direct coercion, attorneys motivated to maintain, not to mention advance, their economic positions and social status are under intense pressures to conform to the approved conduct of the groups or individuals which maintain them, which include clients, employers and the local bar. Wherein do the canons of professional conduct weigh in the economic security of one's spouse and children and one's aspirations for position in the community? Being a lawyer will have different meaning for different people, but it will have important meaning both to individual attorneys and their families as well as to others important to them. Sacrificing status for the sake of ethical conduct is not easily done.

The emotional pressures to view oneself as honest and honorable cause practitioners to rationalize what they are compelled to do as ethical conduct, or they are likely to find a new context in which to earn a livelihood. It is no wonder that, however rationalized, the action ethic of the profession is most client-oriented in those areas of practice wherein clients are best situated to hire and fire their attorneys, and that client-oriented ethics are on shakier ground where attorneys' economic security depends on relations to institutions other than the client. Effective discussion of ethical conduct of the profession must go beyond the advancement of rationalizations to enhancing attorneys' effective choice. . . .

Comment

Greenebaum is discussing some of the blocks to attorneys' assuming responsibility for the ethical decisions they make. I imagine that the most effective impediment to taking responsibility is being unaware and, for me, in particular a lack of awareness of the uncertainty in life. By not seeing (a client's bitterness, suffering, fear or confusion, the implications of a decision, our own ambivalence about a course of action) we can avoid facing the existence of a problem in the first place. It all seems clear and a great deal of distress is avoided. That distress is very real, and avoiding it often appears to be the wise thing to do.

Yet there is a cost. Nothing illustrates this better for me than a bad class on professional responsibility. The teacher asks: What are the conflicts here? What sections of the Code are relevant? What should the lawyer do? Some students trot out the answers—the competing considerations on both sides—stew for a few minutes in the unanswerable questions, and dismiss the experience as another fruitless academic search. To me, feeling that there is nothing to a particular subject matter unless there is some complexity to be mastered, finding the injunctions of the ethical code clear-cut and the hypotheticals easy to answer or to push away, it really feels as if there is very little to teach. I sit in class, feeling bored and empty, wondering: What is all the fuss about? Why doesn't this seem real?

For me with my reasons, for others with theirs, we are going through the motions. We are paying the cost, I think, of protecting ourselves, teacher and students, from the distress and the richness of reality.

E.D.

Thomas Shaffer, *Christian Theories of Professional Responsibility*
48 So. Cal. L. Rev. 721, 752-759 (1975).

> I choose, as Sartre said, even when I seem not to choose. I choose by not choosing. In either event, I choose what I am to be. In this life of inevitable choice I make myself into a person who is or is not able to respond to God.

> The purpose of Canon Nine[100] is example. . . . The codifiers quote the Illinois Supreme Court. . . .

> The lawyer assumes high duties, and has imposed on him grave responsibilities. He may be the means of much good or much mischief. Interests of vast magnitude are entrusted to him; confidence is reposed in him; life, liberty, character, and property should be protected by him. He should guard, with watchfulness, his own reputation, as well as that of his profession.

---

100. "A lawyer should avoid even the appearance of professional impropriety."

Aspirations of that sort imply a strong, trusted personal reputation and a respected profession, and they imply that the reason to guard this position is to assure that the community will be able to grow. But fulfillment of these aspirations is left to the individual abilities of lawyers to make the choices of behavior which will make strength and growth possible. . . . A person's morality—his efforts to make himself and his profession honorable and open to change—defines his existence. In a person's life as a lawyer he can easily enter upon a course of conduct which seems to involve no significant moral choices by simply walking down the street and not looking. He can live unwillingly, as others seem to expect him to live, and his oblivious, undiscovering conduct will define everything that is important about him. He will be destroyed by his moral blindness and will have made himself blind without noticing. It will never have occurred to him to see.

The social side of this ethic of choosing a life of discovery is that decisions which change society are individual and even eccentric. They are not objectively self-evident. Jesus could have chosen not to be murdered, Thomas More could have found his way out of the Act of Supremacy, and Dr. Thomas Dooley could have gone on practicing middle-class, domestic medicine. No one could have demanded of these individuals the life-defining decisions they made, but they were compelled by the nature of the person each of these men chose to be[117]. . . . These choices have in common an import for society (and for professions) and a unique individuality; that is, they are not decisions of time and mores, but decisions a person makes in the solitude of his own conscience. They are decisions taken by one who "cannot expect society around him to be virtuous, so that his integrity may come easily."

More's life, in this respect, can be contrasted to the life of his successor, Francis Bacon. Bacon was probably a brighter man; he had certainly a better education, more money, and more power. More is a saint, though, and a model unlike any other for lawyers. Bacon is remembered in our profession as a judge who took bribes. "The tragedy," I wrote several years ago, "is that Bacon, as the legal profession sometimes does, fell short of a realizable ideal." Today, a similar shortcoming to that of Bacon can be observed in a legal profession whose best men are "exclusively in the defense of the powerful, to the detriment of individuals less powerful and, ultimately, to the detriment of the entire society."

---

117. "All I mean by truth," Holmes said, "is the road I can't help travelling." 1   Holmes-Pollock Letters 100 (M. Howe ed. 1941).

What seems to bind together these instances of failure at example— . . . Bacon, and the modern American lawyers I think of as Bacon's heirs—is that they did what everyone else was doing. In every instance the plea in defense is *vitia temporis* (everybody's doing it). And in every instance the moral destination of these undistinguished, unchosen professional lives is loss of responsibility and even of the ability to respond. This is the estate which is evil. These were the men whom Jesus judged— who seemed to have condemned themselves, rather than to have been condemned. They were unable to respond to God when God chose to seek response among men, and they were therefore unable to respond to God in more ethereal garb, when he proposed to welcome them to immortality.[121]

What seems to bind together the instances of success at example—Jesus, More, those who saw God in the poor, and those in our profession today who choose to lead us out of blindness—is the moral habit of unique choice. These examples of good example are imitable only in their courage. Their decisions are not imitable because each of them chose to be somebody whom his society and his times could not have produced. Robert Bolt said of More that he was "a man with an adamantine sense of his own self." And of those who would, in the present historical and social context, decline the opportunity to be examples—i.e., decline to notice something worth bearing witness over—he says:

> [W]e fly from the idea of an individual to the professional describers, the classifiers, the men with the categories. . . . Both socially and individually it is with us as it is with our cities—an accelerating flight to the periphery, leaving a center which is empty when the hours of business are over.

Bolt's More "knew where he began and left off . . . and . . . at length he was asked to retreat from that final area where he located his self . . . and could no more be budged than a cliff."

We can, in Bolt's view, yearn for More's sense of selfhood, but we can hardly yearn for More's self, which was his own. Each of us has the harder choice of his own self, and each of us is free to choose against his self. We tend to choose better when we choose with advertence, and to choose poorer professional lives, and a

---

121. Bolt's More seems to sense the ordinariness of evil in this sense. . . .
JAILER (Reasonably): You understand my position, sir, there's nothing I can do; I'm a plain, simple man, and just want to keep out of trouble. MORE cries out passionately: Oh, Sweet Jesus! These plain simple men!
The point seems almost as banal as the human lives it despairs of, but ordinariness explains a great deal about dead Jews in Nazi concentration camps and about starving Irishmen in 1850—more than any amount of calculation or ominous rhetoric.

worse profession, when we choose by not choosing. The important thing about Canon Nine is that our choices define ourselves and all that is defined in America by the legal profession.

Comment

Shaffer evokes the insight of existentialism that the capacity and responsibility to choose and so make oneself is the essential defining characteristic of a human being. Man chooses to be who he wants to be and how he wants to be and by such choices makes himself; the ultimate moral moment is to choose one's own self. Never making a choice is a choice in itself and man is judged by who he chooses to be.

Shaffer presents his message as a Christian one; he emphasizes choosing to see God in all people and thus to love one's brothers. These thoughts stir me. I have chosen a life in the law that is impelled by sympathy for the suffering. I started my legal career as a Wall Street lawyer and quit that practice because it did not serve all people. I am now a law school administrator and my interest in legal education arose from my belief that changes in legal education would produce lawyers moved by a vision similar to Shaffer's. Long periods of time go by, however, during which I forget to see the suffering and I am timid to promote my version of Shaffer's message. I frequently choose by inadvertence not to promote my vision while at the same time I don't notice that I have chosen not to choose. At other times I remember and engage in a small meditation on my purposes and resolve to do more. Sometimes I even do more. And through all this I still worry about the larger societal problem of the suffering the justice system inflicts on so many and my failure to take any direct steps to alleviate these problems. One of the hardest choices now necessary for me to make is to choose not to wallow in self-recrimination for not doing more. For I find that I can choose a life of guilt, without consciously choosing, as easily as a life of not seeing suffering.

Recently I have come to view my work differently than I used to. Rather than seeing my work as so many jobs to be struggled through, I now see it as an opportunity to help people whom I care about. This shift gives me energy and a sense of rightness. The good feelings that result from this change in attitude toward my immediate world of law school administration have made me feel much stronger about my broader goals for life in the law. My experience of things working well close to home makes my aspirations for the broader reaches seem much more real and attainable. Originally I did not experience the shift as an active choice: "I will now decide to see things this way," but rather felt pulled into it by the apparent correctness of the stance. Now I do actually choose this attitude; and it is a hard one to hold, requiring constant recall.

It is hard to care for those who are indifferent to me. It is hard to care for those who criticize me because of my inevitable mistakes or because of some job I haven't been able to complete on time. It is hard to maintain love for those who react angrily toward me after I have refused some request of theirs. Any one of these instances, and similar ones, can operate to knock me down and, for a time, I can go along without noticing that I have chosen to be less than the person I want to be. For me, now, returning to my purpose in my immediate environment is a necessary part of the larger search for these goals among us all.

P.S.

Comment

Today I am in the process of choosing a career. I'm in the process because being in law school hasn't led me to the career I want to choose. The law school offers me a straight line. This gatekeeper of the legal profession has not been useful to my thinking about what I want to do as a lawyer. The model of a legal career that I have felt the school dangled before me from the first day would have landed me in work I distinctly do not want to do. I still feel hostile toward the school for this. I object to having to hustle to discover for myself the alternative ways to practice, because the school makes it so very easy to follow its straight line and I feel as though I just barely escaped falling into step.

Of course, it was not a question of falling into anything. The choice and responsibility would have been mine even if I had accepted the offered option. Some parts of me wanted to respond to the school's model of lawyering, while other parts sensed that it didn't fit. The battle was within me, not really between me and "them," the law school. The battle in me raged for quite some time before I was aware of it, before I could articulate some of my contending concerns. Security (money) hadn't been on my agenda. It was something I assumed would flow from the good fortune that's always attended my life. But after a while I began to have very serious questions about whether I would be employed. What risk of that grim prospect was I willing to take in order to do work I felt a particular kind of commitment to? Commitment, personal goals, social conscience, a huge debt were (and still are) spinning in my head as I tried to keep my goals current. The danger in the dangling of the model, for me, was that if I accepted it, everything could be so much easier: easier to know what a lawyer is, without figuring out much about who I, as a lawyer, could be.

I am not entirely certain why I didn't take that easier way, other than that that was not what I had come to law school for. Not having gone along with it makes me feel that in this respect I am acting in accord with my own direction-finder. I'm not giving over to the law school the power to make decisions that so greatly affect me. Knowing that gives me a greater sense of self-knowledge, and eases my fears that the work I do may shape me into someone I will not want to be. The choices are more clearly mine. Struggling to stay on my own path, I feel satisfaction and a sense of sure-footedness that persists even when the going is not so smooth.

My process of choosing a career is circular. The key is to keep returning to beginnings. I never wanted to be a law student. I wanted and still want, with passion, to be a lawyer, a believer in justice, an idealist, a maker of happenings. It was my heart that brought me here, and that, I found, doesn't make for a linear approach to my life and lawyering. And it is through my heart that I will find work that is consistent with what I value in lawyering.

B.B.

Carl Rogers, "Toward a Modern Approach to Values: The Valuing Process in the Mature Person," in *Person to Person* pp.4-20 (Pocket 1971).

There is a great deal of concern today with the problem of values. . . . The world culture, in all its aspects, seems increasingly scientific and relativistic, and the rigid, absolute views on values which come to us from the past appear anachronistic. . . . [T]he modern individual is assailed from every angle by divergent and contradictory value claims. It is no longer possible, as it was in the not too distant historical past, to settle comfortably into the value system of one's forebears or one's community and live out one's life without ever examining the nature and the assumptions of that system.

In this situation it is not surprising that value orientations from the past appear to be in a state of disintegration or collapse. Men question whether there are, or can be, any universal values. It is often felt that we may have lost, in our modern world, all possibility of any general or cross-cultural basis for values. One natural result of this uncertainty and confusion is that there is an increasing concern about, interest in, and a searching for, a sound or meaningful value approach which can hold its own in today's world. I share this general concern. . . .

Let me first speak about the infant. The living human being has, at the outset, a clear approach to values. He prefers some things and experiences, and rejects others. We can infer from studying his behavior that he prefers those experiences which maintain, enhance, or actualize his organism, and rejects those which do not serve this end. . . . [T]he infant's approach to values . . . is first of all a flexible, changing, valuing *process,* not a fixed system. He likes food and dislikes the same food. He values security and rest, and rejects it for new experience. What is going on seems best described as an organismic valuing process, in which each element, each moment of what he is experiencing is somehow weighed, and selected or rejected, depending on whether, at this moment, it tends to actualize the organism or not. This complicated weighing of experience is clearly an organismic, not a conscious or symbolic function. These are operative, not conceived values. But this process can none the less deal with complex value problems. I would remind you of the experiment in which young infants had spread in front of them a score or more of dishes of natural (that is, unflavored) foods.

Over a period of time they clearly tended to value the foods which enhanced their own survival, growth, and development. If for a time a child gorged himself on starches, this would soon be balanced by a protein "binge." If at times he chose a diet deficient in some vitamin, he would later seek out foods rich in this very vitamin. He was utilizing the wisdom of the body in his value choices, or perhaps more accurately, the physiological wisdom of his body guided his behavioral movements, resulting in what we might think of as objectively sound value choices.

Another aspect of the infant's approach to value is that the source or locus of the evaluating process is clearly within himself. Unlike many of us, he *knows* what he likes and dislikes, and the origin of these value choices lies strictly within himself. He is the center of the valuing process, the evidence for his choices being supplied by his own senses. He is not at this point influenced by what his parents think he should prefer, or by what the church says, or by the opinion of the latest "expert" in the field, or by the persuasive talents of an advertising firm. It is from within his own experiencing that his organism is saying in non-verbal terms, "This is good for me." "That is bad for me." "I like this." "I strongly dislike that." . . .

What happens to this highly efficient, soundly based valuing process? By what sequence of events do we exchange it for the more rigid, uncertain, inefficient approach to values which characterizes most of us as adults? Let me try to state briefly one of the major ways in which I think this happens.

The infant needs love, wants it, tends to behave in ways which will bring a repetition of this wanted experience. But this brings complications. He pulls baby sister's hair, and finds it satisfying to hear her wails and protests. He then hears that he is "a naughty, bad boy," and this may be reinforced by a slap on the hand. He is cut off from affection. As this experience is repeated, and many, many others like it, he gradually learns that what "feels good" is often "bad" in the eyes of others. Then the next step occurs, in which he comes to take the same attitude toward himself which these others have taken. Now, as he pulls his sister's hair, he solemnly intones, "Bad, bad boy." He is introjecting the value judgment of another, taking it as his own. He has deserted the wisdom of his organism, giving up the locus of evaluation, and is trying to behave in terms of values set by another, in order to hold love.

Or take another example at an older level. A boy senses, though perhaps not consciously, that he is more loved and prized by his parents when he thinks of being a doctor than when he thinks of being an artist. Gradually he introjects the values attached to being a doctor. He comes to want, above all, to be a doctor. Then in college he is baffled by the fact that he repeatedly fails in chemistry, which is absolutely necessary to becoming a physician, in spite of the fact that the guidance counselor assures him he has the ability to pass the course. . . .

Perhaps these . . . illustrations will indicate that in an attempt to gain or hold love, approval, esteem, the individual relinquishes the locus of evaluation which was his in infancy, and places it in others. He learns to have a basic distrust for his own experiencing as a guide to his behavior. He learns from others a large number of conceived values, and adopts them as his own, even though they may be widely discrepant from what he is experiencing. Because these concepts are not based on his own valuing, they tend to be fixed and rigid, rather than fluid and changing. . . .

Because these conceptions are not open to testing in experience, he must hold them in rigid and unchanging fashion. The alternative would be a collapse of his values. Hence his values are "right"—like the law of the Medes and the Persians, which changeth not.

Because they are untestable, there is no ready way of solving contradictions. If he has taken in from the community the conception that money is the summum bonum and from the church the conception that love of one's neighbor is the highest value, he has no way of discovering which has more value for *him*. Hence a common aspect of modern life is living with absolutely contradictory values. We calmly discuss the possibility of dropping a hydrogen bomb on Russia, but then find tears in our eyes when we see headlines about the suffering of one small child.

Because he has relinquished the locus of evaluation to others, and has lost touch with his own valuing process, he feels profoundly insecure and easily threatened in his values. If some of these conceptions were destroyed, what would take their place? This threatening possibility makes him hold his value conceptions more rigidly or more confusedly, or both. . . .

The valuing process which seems to develop in [the] mature person is in some ways very much like that in the infant, and in some ways quite different. It is fluid, flexible, based on this particular moment, and the degree to which this moment is experienced as enhancing and actualizing. Values are not held rigidly, but are continually changing. The painting which last year seemed meaningful now appears uninteresting, the way of working with individuals which was formerly experienced as good now seems inadequate, the belief which then seemed true is now experienced as only partly true, or perhaps false. . . .

It has been a striking fact of my experience that in therapy, where individuals are valued, where there is greater freedom to feel and to be, certain value directions seem to emerge. These are not chaotic directions but instead have a surprising commonality. This commonality is not dependent on the personality of the therapist, for I have seen these trends emerge in the clients of therapists sharply different in personality. This commonality does not seem to be due to the influences of any one culture, for I have found evidence of these directions in cultures as divergent as those of the United States, Holland, France, and Japan. I like to think that this commonality of value directions is due to the fact that we all belong to the same species—that just as a human infant tends, individually, to select a diet similar to that selected by other human infants, so a client in therapy tends, individually, to choose value directions similar to those chosen by other clients. As a species there may be certain elements of experience which tend to make for inner development and which would be chosen by all individuals if they were genuinely free to choose.

Let me indicate a few of these value directions as I see them in my clients as they move in the direction of personal growth and maturity.

> They tend to move away from facades. Pretense, defensiveness, putting up a front, tend to be negatively valued.

> They tend to move away from "oughts." The compelling feeling of "I ought to do or be thus and so" is negatively valued. The client moves away from being what he "ought to be," no matter who has set that imperative.

> They tend to move away from meeting the expectations of others. Pleasing others, as a goal in itself, is negatively valued.

> Being real is positively valued. The client tends to move toward being himself, being his real feelings, being what he is. This seems to be a very deep preference.

> Self-direction is positively valued. The client discovers an increasing pride and confidence in making his own choices, guiding his own life.

> One's self, one's own feelings come to be positively valued. From a point where he looks upon himself with contempt and despair, the client comes to value himself and his reactions as being of worth.

> Being a process is positively valued. From desiring some fixed goal, clients come to prefer the excitement of being a process of potentialities being born.

Perhaps more than all else, the client comes to value an openness to all of his inner and outer experience. . . .

Sensitivity to others and acceptance of others is positively valued. The client comes to appreciate others for what they are, just as he has come to appreciate himself for what he is.

Finally, deep relationships are positively valued. To achieve a close, intimate, real, fully communicative relationship with another person seems to meet a deep need in every individual, and is very highly valued. . . .

I find it significant that when individuals are prized as persons, the values they select do not run the full gamut of possibilities. I do not find, in such a climate of freedom, that one person comes to value fraud and murder and thievery, while another values a life of self-sacrifice, and another values only money. Instead there seems to be a deep and underlying thread of commonality. I dare to believe that when the human being is inwardly free to choose whatever he deeply values, he tends to value those objects, experiences and goals which make for his own survival, growth, and development, and for the survival and development of others. I hypothesize that it is characteristic of the human organism to prefer such actualizing and socialized goals when he is exposed to a growth-promoting climate. . . .

[I]t appears that we have returned to the issue of universality of values, but by a different route. Instead of universal values "out there," or a universal value system imposed by some group—philosophers, rulers, or priests—we have the possibility of universal human value directions emerging from the experiencing of the human organism. Evidence from therapy indicates that both personal and social values emerge as natural, and experienced, when the individual is close to his own organismic valuing process. The suggestion is that though modern man no longer trusts religion or science or philosophy nor any system of beliefs to *give* him his values, he may find an organismic valuing base within himself which, if he can learn again to be in touch with it, will prove to be an organized, adaptive and social approach to the perplexing value issues which face all of us. . . .

Comment

Rogers is writing about something that calls forth a resounding yes from inside me. Many of the values I have held and do hold came from the outside. I feel that I've distorted myself by accepting without question as my values those held by the worlds I move in.

Many of the thoughts that I formerly accepted when deeply involved with religion are the same as some of the thoughts I now preach about law. Some of them are no longer introjected guides to correct living, but are preferences, choices, values that are the truth as I see it from inside myself. It has taken a long time to make some of these connections, between the "Thou Shalt" from the outside and the inner "Yes, I will."

The quality of my action is different, depending on the locus of the value signal on which I am acting—for example, preparation for a class because I ought to, or because I value the preparation. That inner yes seems to be the way to my will, my power and my honesty.

It is easy for me to confuse my own evaluation with my use of rules I've picked up from around me, because I will state the rule as if it were my own: "I had better get that reading done." I'm not really telling myself what I think so I have to look hard, in different ways and look repeatedly, if I want to discover a particularly entrenched given rule and compare that with what I truly think is right.

When I don't try to discover such given rules, I have abdicated my decision-making power over the aspects of my life that they govern. Then, by definition, it seems to me, I am only pretending to know or to believe something. I haven't done the work, the internal process of discovering my values, that would qualify me as a believer or a knower. It is in this way that I distort myself.

I see this happening on a mass scale in my class at law school. People come, not knowing what they want or what their options might be. Many come without using their inner means for answering their questions. The school shows principally one answer so that becomes The Answer, and many people try to believe it is their own.

The hardest part of doing the work of valuing, for me, is to trust myself, especially when I hear so many tell me that I'm wrong. It doesn't even take many, often it takes no one other than myself to start me doubting. An example is my work for this book—"the good stuff" turned out to be the thoughts and writings I wanted to throw away. It has helped me to learn to do the work of valuing, to work with people who create the type of environment Rogers writes about: an environment in which an individual has worth, separate from the rest.

I've come to believe that my feelings and intuitions are sometimes wiser than my mind, which is something I did not know before. I keep and use them, because I have found this to be true. This is not to say that I value intellectual skills less; rather, I have moved from regarding my mind as the one "real" tool with which to do my work. So, I put aside the rule of the professors that feelings will only interfere with legal analysis, and instead I use my judgment as to what combination of all my powers are needed in each situation. This is a freedom I allow myself. It's a struggle to do it continuously, and I often fail. Still, it is clear to me that people can help each other to do their own valuing and follow what is right for them, in lawyering as in life.

B.B.

Comment

When I am with those of my colleague law school administrators who are traditionally oriented, I tend to respond with what I think they would like to hear. And when I am with law teachers and students who are more "humanistically" oriented, I tend to respond another way, moved by what I think *they* would like to hear. That is, I have difficulty being true to myself. Having written this, I feel somewhat guilty about being confessional and running myself down. And I am aware of some of my friends who would jump on me for judging myself too severely.

Then there is part of me that would like to be the critic, scolding and lecturing others for not being honest, particularly those of us who are or will become committed to this work. If I am asking myself to be honest, then, damn it, the people I deal with should too. But if judging myself harshly is bad, judging others is anathema. Is there a way of being honest without this incessant judging?

I try to be honest. Sometimes I think I am really quite honest. Sometimes I don't know and suspect I may be deluding myself. Frequently, as in the examples I gave above, I block my immediate response out of deference to the persons I am talking to, and sensitivity to the prospect that they will reject me. I can be so concerned with promoting my own self-esteem and so occupied with showing myself off to advantage that I hardly know in these circumstances what the truth is for me, much less express it. If we are all doing this, what happens to honesty?

I do know that the truth for me, and the way out of such morasses, often involves expressing my own personal thoughts and feelings as best I can. So, in spite of some fear, I can say "That's wonderful what you just said. It excites me, and I feel so very good about you." Or, "Why don't you just once try to listen to what I am saying from my perspective and not worry about always responding in a way which seems designed to show what a novice I am and how wise you are. It hurts me and makes me feel small. I don't like you much when I see you as an authority figure." When I reach this level, the relationship with the other becomes very real and true; sometimes painful, intense, charged, without pretense or vanity, dramatic, totally absorbing and honest.

P.S.

Scott Turow, *One L*
pp.74-75, 284-287 (Putnam 1977).

[September]

. . . I felt ambivalent about volunteering. . . . For one thing, it seemed a crazy feistiness, if I was scared of Perini and uncom-

fortable at the idea of being called on, to willingly expose myself
to the same kind of interrogation. More important, I'd begun to
realize how complicated the personal politics of speaking in class
had become.

By the second week, a mood of disapproval had grown up in
the section toward any sign of aggressiveness or competitive
spirit displayed by a fellow student. Some of that is generational.
To want to do better than others is out of keeping with the
egalitarian ethic on which most of us who came of age after the
1960s cut our teeth. But part of it too, I thought, had to do with a
widespread effort by classmates to suppress their own ambitions. We had all been extremely successful students in the past,
but a desire to repeat that success here was not only an
unrealistic hope amid so talented a group, but even a dangerous
one when you considered the extent to which it could be
frustrated. At the end of the term, the professors would examine
and then grade us. Given our present incompetence with the law,
that was a frightening idea. During the first weeks most people
had been struck with the seeming equality of everyone's abilities, and that became an impression many of us were eager to
cling to. If everyone was the same, you couldn't come out ahead,
as you always had before, but you wouldn't end up behind,
either, which would be crushing and which, at the moment,
seemed the more real possibility. Parity, then, became a kind of
appealing psychic bargain everybody swore with himself, re-
nouncing competitiveness in the process.

I remember a conversation I had with a classmate, Helen
Kirchner, late in the second week. She told me she already hated
law school.

When I asked her why, she said, "Because the people are so
aggressive."

I knew she had been through Exeter and Princeton at the top
of each class and I asked if she wasn't aggressive herself.

"I am," she answered, "but I try not to show it."

Trying not to show it became a dominant style of behavior in
class. Some people seemed to withdraw almost from the initial
sessions. . . .

The other means of containing competitive feelings was
simply to deny them. Many people said they didn't care how
they did, what their grades might be, how they were perceived.
That was what I often said. Like Helen, those people tended to
blame others for the feeling of a competitive atmosphere.

But with the great majority of us, that competitiveness was
simply part of our nature. It was what had gotten us through the

door of the joint in the first place. There was something, some faith in distinction, which had led us to *Harvard* Law rather than to a less revered school. And we were all gladly training now for an intensely competitive profession in which there are winners and losers every time the jury returns, or the judge speaks. Nor was it unreasonable that we were competitive. Competitiveness had led to recognition and pleasure for many of us in the past; it was an old and rewarding habit.

But we carried those feelings with us at all times. In many ostensibly informal conversations with classmates—in the hallways, the gym, at lunch—I had the feeling that I was being sized up, that people were looking for an angle, an edge on me; I caught myself doing that to others now and then. And especially within the classroom, where the professors' questions acted to pit the 140 of us against each other, our aggressions were bound to be excited, whether they were acknowledged or not.

[May]

People were skipping classes now to outline. Everytime I passed the copy center under Langdell, I saw another member of Section 2 in line there with a sheaf of papers and a distrustful look—people whom I'd felt close to. We were in warring camps now, different study groups.

Late Thursday afternoon, following classes, Stephen and Terry and I stood in one of the Pound classrooms talking about how bizarre it had all become.

"Man," Terry said, "I've been thinking. We should give everybody who wants it a copy of our outline."

"With a quid pro quo," Stephen added.

"Screw the quid pro quo," Terry said. "I mean, hey, I asked myself why we did this. To review, right? To learn. That's all we have to worry about." He looked at me. " Right?"

"I don't know," I answered. I was still overwrought. It had been a miserable week.

"Man, you're the one who was sayin' give it away."

"But look at the situation," I said. "Kyle's trying to screw everybody. Half the people in the section think we're crazy."

"Hey, listen, what do you care about Kyle?" Terry asked.

"What's the difference, if we can help some folks out?"

I thought a second. Then suddenly I was speaking from the frenzied center of everything that had gripped me in the last week.

"I want the advantage," I said. "I want the competitive advantage. I don't give a damn about anybody else. I want to do better than they."

My tone was ugly, and Stephen and Terry both stared at me an instant. Then we quietly broke apart to find our separate ways home.

It took me a while to believe I had actually said that. I told myself I was kidding. I told myself that I had said that to shock Terry and Stephen. But I knew better. What had been suppressed all year was in the open now. All along there had been a tension between looking out for ourselves and helping each other; in the end, I did not expect anybody—not myself, either—to renounce a wish to prosper, to succeed. But I could not believe how *extreme* I had let things become, the kind of grasping creature I had been reduced to. I had not been talking about gentlemanly competition to Stephen and Terry. I had not been talking about any innocent striving to achieve. There had been murder in my voice. And what were the stakes? The difference between a B-plus and a B? This was supposed to be education—a humane cooperative enterprise.

That night I sat in my study and counseled myself. It had been a tumultuous year, I decided. I had been up. And I had been down. I had lost track of myself at moments, but because of whatever generosity I'd extended my own spirit, I had not lost my self-respect. But it would not stretch much further. I knew that if I gave in again to that welling, frightened avarice as I had this afternoon, I would pay for a long time in the way I thought about myself.

It's a tough place, I told myself. Bad things are happening. Work hard. Do your best. Learn the law. But don't suffer, I thought. Don't fear. And for God's sake, don't give up your decency.

The madness in the atmosphere, the battle between the study groups, persisted. People continued to surreptitiously hand each other outlines in brown-paper bags. Jack Weiss kept making insulting remarks. Our study group met one afternoon to go over one of Perini's former exams and we soon discovered that none of us could even begin to answer it; for a day Stephen fretted that we would all fail Contracts. In Kyle's group, Gina reported, there had been an insurrection because no one could understand Kyle's remarks on collateral estoppel, a crucial subject for the exam. Karen Sondergard cried one day when she decided she preferred to be in our group rather than another. Fearful rumors spread that a group had stolen a copy of one of the exams. At another point, Stephen became convinced that

Aubrey and Stan had made a backstage deal with Kyle's group and were receiving information which they were not sharing with the rest of us. And all along our own group continued to swell. Stephen always found ways to employ the new members. By the last week of classes the group had grown to eleven or twelve.

"John Yolan has changed his mind," Stephen told me one day in the library.

"Fine," I said, "give him the outline."

"With a quid pro quo?" Stephen asked.

"With or without," I said. "Just give it to whoever wants it. Terry is right."

After that Thursday afternoon in that classroom, I tried not to let myself fall into that tangle of fears again. There were times I felt it happening and would work hard to resist. One day I found myself pacing back and forth in the law school gym, muttering, "I'm okay, I'm okay," trying to keep in mind that I had some worth which would outlast exams. But I felt it was important not to give in. I knew where I stood now. I knew what I was against.

I had finally met my enemy, I figured, face to face.

Comment

Turow illustrates graphically the process by which the fearful and unexpected breaking-into-consciousness of uncensored, unrestrained competitiveness enabled him to begin to find the place for it that expressed his own chosen values and priorities. We do not change by denying what we are, but by acknowledging what we are. We do not change by insisting that we feel no internal struggle when parts of ourselves are in conflict. The very act of acknowledging that there are impulses within us that we do not like is the beginning of coming to terms with them. The very act of acknowledging the legitimacy of aspects of us that we do not like is the beginning of ending their tyranny over us.

A statement of the theoretical basis for the operation of this process is contained in the following excerpt:

[Frederick Perl's change theory] underlies much of his work and is implied in the practice of Gestalt techniques. I will call it the *paradoxical theory of change,* for reasons that shall become obvious. Briefly stated, it is this: *that change occurs when one becomes what he is, not when he tries to become what he is not.* Change does not take place through a coercive attempt by the individual or by another person to change him, but it does take place if one takes the time and effort to be what he is—to be fully invested in his current positions. By rejecting the role of change agent, we make meaningful and orderly change possible.

[C]hange does not take place by "trying," coercion, or persuasion, or by insight, interpretation, or any other such means. Rather, change can occur when the patient abandons, at least for the moment, what he would like to become and attempts to be what he is. The premise is that one must stand in one place in order to have firm footing to move and that it is difficult or impossible to move without that footing.

The person seeking change by coming to therapy is in conflict with at least two warring intrapsychic factions. He is constantly moving between what he "should be" and what he thinks he "is," never fully identifying with either. The Gestalt therapist asks the person to invest himself fully in his roles, one at a time. . . .

The Gestalt therapist believes in encouraging the patient to enter and become whatever he is experiencing at the moment. He believes with Proust, "To heal a suffering one must experience it to the full."

Arnold Beisser, "The Paradoxical Theory of Change," in Fagan & Shepherd, eds., *Gestalt Therapy Now* pp.77-78 (Science and Behavior Books, 1970).

H.L.

William Stringfellow, *My People Is the Enemy*
pp.24-28 (Holt, Rinehart and Winston 1964).

In the days that immediately followed, I spent a lot of time just trying to make my new household habitable. I remember using over thirty pounds of putty just to seal the spaces between the floor and the walls, and making innumerable other repairs in the apartment. My first few months in East Harlem made me a household handyman, with experience in wiring, plastering, elementary carpentry, and other such skills. It was during those days, when I was trying to make a place to live in, against the odds which prevail in such a building, that I began to realize and appreciate the extremity of the attrition which they suffer whose daily life is in such apartments, in such tenements, in such neighborhoods—they who, what with families and all, had every day much more to contend with than I did. I remember my exhaustion from trying to maintain my own one life there. How much more exacting and costly it must be for a parent of a family of five or six children, and particularly one who did not have the option, as I did, to return to the outer city.

Finally, a place to live was wrought, though I was promptly and aptly reminded that for me to make a place to live in, in the midst of the Harlem slums, still meant something quite different from what it would be for someone—a Negro or a Puerto Rican—indigenous to these same slums. One symbol of that, in my own experience, is contained in a conversation I had with a Negro from the neighborhood whom I had come to know and whom I bumped into on the street one morning. He stopped me and suggested that we have a cup of coffee, which we did. During the conversation he mentioned that he had noticed that I shined my shoes every day—a custom in which I had been indoctrinated five years before while serving with the Second Armored Division in Germany. He said he knew that this represented the continuation, in my new life in Harlem, of the life that I had formerly lived; and he added that he was glad of it, because it meant that I had remained myself and had not contrived to change, just because I had moved into a different environment. In order, in other words, as I heard him, to be a person in Harlem, in order that my life and work there should have integrity, I had to be and to remain whoever I had become as a person before coming there. To be accepted by others, a man must first of all know himself and accept himself and be himself wherever he happens to be. In that way, others are also freed to be themselves.

To come to Harlem involved, thus, no renunciation of my own past or of any part of it. There was no occasion in Harlem to repudiate anything in my own history and heritage as a white Anglo-Saxon Protestant, nor to seek to identify with the people of Harlem, either by attempting to imitate any of them or by urging any of them to imitate me. What was necessary was just to be myself. I had learned something about that long before moving to Harlem. I learned it, as I suppose others have, in the military service. I recall feeling somewhat resentful about military service when I first entered the Army after college. It seemed an interruption in my education and career, not wholly a waste of time, given the conditions in the world then, but a sort of void which would not further me personally in any significant way. Most other guys felt about the same, I think. I soon discovered that I was dead wrong. I found that I could be, and was, fulfilled as a person just as much in the service as in school or work—that where I happen to be and what I happen to be doing does not determine the issue of who I am as a human being, or how my own person may be expressed and fulfilled. I learned the meaning of vocation in the Army. It was an emancipating discovery, for then it became possible to go anywhere and to do any sort of work—in full knowledge of my own identity and integrity.

So, moving to Harlem, for all its differences in empirical ways from other places where I had lived, was really an easy thing to do. And as my friend pointed out, when he noticed that my shoes were shined, coming to Harlem did not mean desertion of my past; it meant bringing it with me into a new situation. There was no need for any psychological disassociation, nor was there any practical disassociation, either. I am a lawyer, and I continued, all the years I was in Harlem, to remain in contact with colleagues in the downtown law firms and in the law schools in New York and elsewhere. I found my own practice of the law in Harlem intellectually provocative, and therefore I continued to write and speak about some of the issues of the law and the philosophy of the law with faculty and students from the law schools and with fellow lawyers. I am an Episcopalian, and I had long been active in the affairs of the Episcopal Church. This continued during the time in Harlem, in participation in the congregation to which I belonged and in many other ways as well. I am a white man, and to live in Harlem did not mean that I need be separated from white society. . . . I crossed a lot of boundaries in the course of a day. That in itself is not so important. What is *very* important is that in crossing boundaries of class and race and education and all the rest, a man remain himself. What is important is not where a man is, but who a man is, and that he be the same man wherever he is.

I recall one day in the tenement when a young curate from my parish stopped by to call. A boy from the neighborhood was there; we had just been talking about one of the gangs. The curate happened to be a graduate of Union Theological Seminary in New York. The previous day I had received an invitation to give a lecture at the seminary. The invitation pleased me, partly because I have a continuing disagreement with some of the faculty there, and I welcomed the opportunity to state my own views publicly at the seminary. In the conversation with the curate, in the presence of the boy, I remarked facetiously, "I have an invitation from the seminary to give a lecture—now I will have a chance to speak in the heart of the enemy camp!"

Subsequently, on the day of the lecture, just as it was about to begin, the boy who had heard this remark entered the classroom, walked down the aisle, and seated himself in the front row. After I had delivered the lecture—about the relationship of Christ and law as described in the Letter to the Colossians— there were several questions from the seminarians, many of whom were manifestly antagonistic to the views I had presented. Two or three times during this discussion, after hostile questions had been asked, the boy passed me notes to reassure me, by charming if obscene comments about those who asked the questions. I thought to myself that the boy had taken seriously my crack about being in the "enemy camp" and had come to the lecture to be a sort of bodyguard. That was a great comfort.

Later, the boy and I returned together on the bus to Harlem. On the way, he talked about the lecture and the seminary, and he said: "That was nice—you talked to them the same way you talk to me."

That was an even greater comfort.

The issue for any man, in any place, is to be the same man he is in every place. It was that issue which I joined in a conclusive way while I was in the Army. It was the resolution of that issue which made simple and, so to speak, natural, the years in Harlem and which authorized the crossing of many boundaries.

Comment

I thought part of becoming a lawyer would involve confronting myself with who I really am and finding out what I really wanted to do. I find self-confrontation frightening and hide a great deal from myself. I successfully avoided it over the past few years and law school helped me do that avoiding. I kept myself frenetically busy with highly regarded activities such as mounds of school work and extra-curricular school-related organizations. At the same time I relaxed and became lazy about self-confrontation because I was presented with many clear examples of how to achieve and be successful in the legal world. I didn't have to confront myself; I assumed that the school and teachers knew the answers not only to how to think like a lawyer, but also to what was good for me in terms of career and behavior. I left these heavy uncomfortable thoughts, decisions, and questions to them. My faith cracked on their ideas of how I should behave as a lawyer and finally broke over careers.

I have known much of this intellectually for some time, but it has taken me longer to really feel it and think about the implications for myself. I'm scared. It was so much easier when I thought that they had the answers about how to become the best lawyer I could be—just follow them or at least their advice. It isn't a bad path as far as I can see; they do have what I'd like to have—power and influence. Sure, I fuss and chafe within the confines of their path, but to go to the uncharted outside makes me cringe and want to return to their path. All I see is an unknown future.

The way I coax myself out again is by reminding myself that I've gotten this far by myself. This particular present life of mine was an unthought-of future when I was a 22-year-old college graduate, staring at the abyss of a future yawning in front of me. I followed my own path then and survived. I think about how I feel and know that I'm a decidedly different individual than most law school teachers. Their choices, dreams, and aspirations are not the same motivating forces as mine. I will have to deal with my own fears of the unknown in my own way. I will have to take—need to take—my own risks, make my own choices, or I will spend a good deal more of my life and energy chafing inside someone else's dream, deriding myself for not measuring up to their standards. This view is becoming more clear to me, which means it is becoming less and less comfortable to get back on anyone else's path. Realizing I have to make the choices for my life, I have been focusing on myself and rediscovering what my wants and needs are. I've gained a sense of my own priorities and am less distracted by what other people are saying or doing. I am gearing myself up for some important choices. I will be taking some more risks. I'm still scared and I'm still going.

M.E.

B. EXERCISING RESPONSIBILITY

Scott Turow, *One L*
pp.55-56, 131 (Putnam 1977).

Why did I bother? Why did I care? Why didn't I write Perini off as a bully or a showman? Why was I afraid?

Imagine, is all that I can answer.

You are twenty-six or twenty-two, it makes little difference. Either way you have a stake. You have given up a job, a career, to do this. Or you have wanted to be a lawyer all your life.

All your life you've been good in school. All your life it's been something you could count on. You know that it's a privilege to be here. You've studied hours on a case that is a half page long. You couldn't understand most of what you read at first, but you have turned the passage inside out, drawn diagrams, written briefs. You could not be more prepared.

And when you get to class that demigod who knows all the answers finds another student to say things you never could have. Clearer statements, more precise. And worse—far worse— notions, concepts, whole constellations of ideas that never turned inside your head.

Yes, there are achievements in the past. They're nice to bandage up your wounded self-esteem. But "I graduated college *magna cum laude*" is not the proper answer when the professor has just posed a question and awaits your response with the 140 other persons in the class.

The feeling aroused by all of that was something near to panic, a ferocious, grasping sense of uncertainty, and it held me, and I believe most of my classmates, often during that first week and for a long while after. On many occasions I discovered that I didn't even understand what I didn't know until I was halfway through a class. Nor could I ever see how anyone else seemed to arrive at the right answer. Maybe they were all geniuses. Maybe I was the dumbest guy around.

. . . .

I made *mistakes,* in fact, silly blunders. If lucky, I was mediocre. And my conviction of my mediocrity was sour and unhappy. I had given up a good career, some security and distinction, to be swallowed in the horde, to confront intelligence which overshadowed my own. The shame at what I'd lost and was incapable of doing had become acute; and the day I embarrassed myself by making that mistake in Mann's class, I was low enough that my feelings worsened into something harrowing.

Walking out of that session, I was as close to tears as I had been in a decade. I wanted to explain to Mann, to all my classmates, that I really wasn't dumb or indiscreet, that I was able to accomplish many things worth doing. But there was no way to prove that, to them or even to myself.

When I had recovered somewhat, I vowed that I wouldn't let that feeling overcome me again. But that didn't mean taking a more balanced view of my feelings or a broader perspective on what was going on in general. I was too caught up in all of it by then. I promised instead that I would not talk in class. That meant feeling distant and frustrated while I sat in each meeting; it meant that I was giving in to fear. But I suffered it all, rather than face that horrible shame again, and for weeks I did not let myself be heard.

Comment

Turow demonstrates how the need to be right and the fear of making mistakes or appearing foolish can easily block our attempts to keep our eyes set on what is most important to us. He narrows his vision to the single goal of not appearing stupid. Because he wants to protect himself, he doesn't do anything but protect himself. He establishes his guidelines: He won't participate in class, he'll feel distant and frustrated but at least he won't make a fool of himself.

It is so easy to do what Turow did. As a new teacher I have had my own experience of the problem. The answer for students, it seems to me, has little to do with the teacher's creating a safe environment. Situations will inevitably arise in school, practice, or life where the instinctive reaction will be to do whatever is necessary to feel safe, sacrificing other goals in the process. If we are dependent on others to make us feel protected enough to begin to satisfy goals other than that of security, we will never feel protected enough and never satisfy those other goals.

The answer for me involves learning how to take care of my need to feel safe in a way that doesn't prevent my accomplishing other goals I hold in life. That might mean over-preparing for a class, it might mean getting a hug from a friend before I walk into a scary situation, it might mean feeling frightened and proceeding with what I have to do anyway, and it might mean deciding that today, this week, this semester, or this year will be devoted to building up my experience until I feel more competent and not taking a risk until then. Even then I will need to be willing to make mistakes.

The only solution I do not want to reach is that of so narrowing my vision that I forget there is something more I want from my career besides feeling safe.

E.D.

Karl Llewellyn, *The Bramble Bush*
pp.124-126 (Oceana 1960).

And we? These fabrics we seize and tear as idle cobweb. These mirrors of old dear-held truth we shatter. The law itself dissolves before our acids. Right and justice come to figure as pretty names for very human acts done on often the less human of human motivations. I have said before that this tendency of our teaching has caused me worry, in its aspect as developing the technician at the cost of the whole man. It gives me double pause in this connection—in its effect on young men already disillusioned beyond the portion of young men.

In the first place, iconoclasm can be a sport as well as a condition; even when not so viewed, the fact of smashing calls disproportionate attention to the broken pieces; revolt is seldom characterized by balanced judgment. We of the teaching world are still as full of our discovery as once was tortured Galileo: move, move it *does*, the law. And if to make you see the movement we must shout down the pious words with which courts have pretended that no change occurred—then we must shout, shout disbelief. We must blaspheme the legal oracles. Well, then, we do. We strip the trappings, verbal and other, off the courts. We turn the spotlight on the places where the tinsel gaps, where you see cheap cotton, or see sweaty skin beneath. These are the crucial cases for the argument—but are they type or caricature of the run of legal work? The tendency of the teaching has its worry. To get across a vital lesson one must risk distortion.

The sight of falling tinsel, too, may seem to argue falling dignity. It is a vicious seeming. It is as false as the ill superstition that the tinsel is the measure of a man. Rather are measures and dignity of man and office to be found when folderol and claptrap are stripped off; when, free of pomp, on the record and the naked fact, they stand four-square. So must we strip the courts; so must we test them. The stripping is a tribute. An institution we could not honor naked we should not dare to strip. . . .

Yet the effect of our teaching cannot but be to make the courts, for a while, seem vaporers, uttering falsehood as to what they do, ignorant, misguided, blind. This will not last—but while it lasts it devastates the little there is left in you undevastated. . . .

Yet I say again, I see no help. I see no way to train you but to give you the light your teachers think they have, whatever it may cost in shattering. I see no way but to risk all upon it. I see no way but to pass you through this further fire.

Comment

The first months of law school, for both student and teacher, are exhilarating. Students almost joyfully take risks. They yearn to know about the people in the cases and how the "rules of law" relate to the problems these people have. However, after this initial period of wonderment students become dulled to the richness of human potential in the cases. Instead of yearning for more information about the people they yearn for the "rules of law" and "the answer." It seems as if students leap from a sense of wonder to a sense of cynicism without passing through a stage of healthy skepticism. They then become desensitized to the "people issues" in the cases, blind to the human dimension in law as people are often blind to the human dimension of life.

At such times, students remind me of the characters portrayed by John Cheever: outwardly insensitive to the world of feelings around them, but inwardly full of pernicious feelings. They could cut with a glance or would steal with a smile. They cause emotional and psychological wounds. Prolonged use of these tools of emptiness is devastating, a self-reinforcing downward spiral that is deadening. Such perverse games kill the spirit and wound the body.

Another side of Cheever people is fear—a fear of involvement—a fear of risk taking, a fear of being wrong. Perhaps his characters are us at our self-centered worst. But why should we read of the exploits and struggles of these emotionally hollow shells? After reading a few of Cheever's stories I yearned for the artist to portray the positive side of these individuals or at least write of an individual with potential for positive growth and development. I feel cheated that Cheever's indirection gives us such an impressionistic view of the positive side of individuals. The point is that by dwelling on the negative we do not necessarily see other positive alternatives.

Law students move from wonder, to fear, to moral myopia almost imperceptibly. Is there a positive side to law school? Or, more appropriately, how does one tap into it? The deeper question here is what is my role or to what degree am I responsible, as a teacher, for this state of affairs. I notice the cynicism in the classroom, then I notice myself making snide comments about an appellate opinion and the values inherent in an opinion. This then produces a sense of guilt in that I am contributing to the cynicism. Far too often we, as teachers, justify the cynicism by proclaiming that a sharp critical retort is merely the honing of a lawyer's analytic skills. In reality, cynical comments are often intended as a negative judgment rather than designed to elucidate a point. I feel that I am only beginning to lose the cynicism I find in myself about the law and legal education. Recognizing that cynicism is an important part of helping students develop a healthy attitude toward the study of law.

J.T.

Comment

Joe Tomain is stirring some very fundamental questions here. I brought to my work as a law teacher—as I believe many of my colleagues do—two qualities that I value, and do not want to lose: a critical faculty for exposing sloppy reasoning, and a capacity for recognizing and responding to injustice. Consciously and unconsciously, I want to transmit these to my students. Indeed, one of the most frustrating things about teaching is to see students so anxious to learn the way things really are "out there" that they hear nothing else, and I have often reacted to my fear that students' critical abilities were not being engaged by escalating the acidic quality of my classroom style. For many who teach—and of course for many others too—this is a sensible road. Our moral sensibilities and intellectual acuity can be enhanced by confrontation with miserable examples of their absence. There is often nothing so ennobling as even a pathetic portrayal of human tragedy in fiction or drama; and for many of us, there was nothing so helpful to our emergence as legal scholars as the decimation of judicial work product, which we observed in our student days. When students characterize my views as "cynical" (as they often do), I typically respond that it seems more pertinent to inquire whether they are right.

Karl Llewellyn wrote eloquently of the utility and the dangers of that technique. Tomain crystallizes my awareness of the dangers, and of the difficulties I face in abandoning it. He is right to be saying, as I think he is, that I am reluctant to disclose my values, my concerns and my own sense of justice to the class, reluctant to disclose my caring feelings and the more hopeful, softer, less defended side of myself. It is difficult to appear more vulnerable in class than as a "cynical idealist." Yet I am repelled by a similar cynical stance in students; I want my toughness to soften them, my cynicism to give them hope that things can be better and a will to work to make them so. Conscious of the limits of my power, I seek refuge in irony and indirection, but I expect my students to ride headlong into the windmill and up-end it. I react to the evident feeling of powerlessness that many students have with disapproval and disappointment, impatiently sloughing off any suggestion that I am far stronger and more secure than they.

Tomain is right in saying that the willingness to risk greater self-disclosure is an essential question: I do not read him to urge that he, and I, and all of us in teaching, simply pull ourselves together and start taking risks. We can only begin to move beyond the safety of a critical pose if we at the same time begin to acknowledge to ourselves, share with each other, and share with our students, what the risks are, and what the difficulties are of our taking them and of our asking others to do the same—and share with ourselves and them too the bases for our judgment and our feeling that it is critical to the work of being a lawyer, a law teacher, or a law student that we be willing to disclose a fuller picture of what is important to us than we usually do.

H.L.

John Ayer, *The Make Believe World of the Lawyer*
Learning and the Law, Vol. 4 No. 1 pp.43-44, 47 (1977).

Another false premise is the notion that law school, since it need not create destructive human beings, need not itself be a destructive place. But this is no more than half true. For almost every law student, to become a lawyer means to change, and to change is to destroy. I do not mean to let this fact stand unqualified. Stating that some destructiveness is inevitable does not justify all destructiveness. An atmosphere that does no more than destroy probably is worse than an atmosphere that provokes no change at all.

An improved legal education would not exist in an atmosphere of beatitude, but it would get rid of the needless destructiveness. It would channel the rest—and perhaps provoke more—so the student could use his education as an engine for growth.

What should be the goal of this process. . . ? Put shortly, the answer is this: we should seek to create a person who . . . is capable not merely of answering questions, but of asking them; someone who has an accurate sense of himself, his environment and of the "relatedness" between the two; who can use his experience and his peculiar resources with virtuosity; who is, in the last analysis, autonomous. . . .

[T]he kind of "true" Socratic question that seems to be at the heart of genuine dialogue [is] one which genuinely confronts the student as a person and honestly seeks to know what he thinks. . . . It should be obvious that an honest, searching question can be just as anxiety-producing as any . . . because it speaks to the student himself, with all his vagaries and contradictions, rather than addressing merely what he has learned.

This "true" Socratic question . . . is the type that legal education can and ought to depend upon. It yields a classroom situation in which students talk much more than is ordinarily the custom and teachers, much less. It requires that students spend more time talking to each other, and less to the professor, but most importantly, it entails a shift in the strategy of the discussion—it must be more collaborative, less evaluative and less calculated to induce a preordained result.

I do not for a moment suppose that this revised model is likely to be attractive to students or professors. Quite the contrary . . . [it] is bound to raise anxieties on both sides of the question.

For the professor, it means having to deal with his students as persons—one by one and day by day—rather than cutting them adrift. For the student, it means having to participate in his education, rather than being a mere receptor.

And this may be the most difficult part of all, for up to now, however frustrating the law or legal education might be, it was always somebody else's problem. Once a student conceives of himself as a participant, he must recognize his own responsibility. . . .

Scott Turow, *One L*
pp.258-259 (Putnam 1977).

Early in the second term, Perini announced that, as he did annually, he would be hiring a few members of the section as summer research assistants. Several people were hopeful of getting one of the jobs. Most 1Ls have a hard time finding legal work over the summer, and being students, many people needed the money. After grades came out, Perini announced he would be receiving résumés.

"They should include," he said, "all relevant information." In case anybody doubted that that meant the two fall-term grades, Perini went on. "I'm very proud," he said, "that so many of my summer people make the Law Review. I have a very high batting average."

Perini's announcement concerning the jobs were always made during class, and the race to work for Perini became another of the dramas and competitions within the section. One time I overheard two men commiserating because, with two Bs each, both knew they'd be wasting their time applying. Eventually, Perini narrowed his choice to eight candidates. He wrote their names on a piece of paper which he affixed prominently to the seating chart. When people saw that Cauley, who'd so long pleased Perini in class, had been excluded, the criterion of selection became clear: These were the eight applicants with the highest grades. In the last two weeks before spring vacation, Perini gave each of the eight a workout in class, interrogating them on cases while the rest of us looked on. And in the end, the jobs were awarded anyway to the three men with the best marks.

It had been a vulgar episode in all respects. Once more he'd used the classroom for his own purposes, turning a private matter into a public spectacle. He'd glorified himself and the job of working for him. He'd rubbed our noses in the crucial effects of grades. And once again, he'd played on our worst vulnerabilities, everything from status fears to the need for money. It was a thoroughly contemptible performance and it doused whatever weak light of regard I'd maintained for Perini. I hated him now, and I thought less of Harvard Law School because he was there.

Comment

For me as a teacher, the most powerful aspect of this account is its reflection of Perini's inability or unwillingness to acknowledge and take responsibility for his own standard of selection. Accepting for the moment the appropriateness of choosing a research assistant by the standard of academic excellence in its most traditional sense, I am struck at how a teacher so committed to that standard, and so confident of his ability to judge people by it, nonetheless surrenders his judgment to his colleagues. Cauley, "who'd so long pleased Perini in class," is not even admitted as a finalist because his grades were not in the highest eight. And the "finals" themselves, conducted with vigor and rigor, are not sufficient to give Perini a basis for judgment that is as reliable as the recorded judgment of his fellow faculty members.

When I hire a student whose grades are not outstanding, or I recommend that student to a colleague or employer, I take a risk that reliance on grade averages does not entail. If the person with mediocre grades does not work out, it reflects badly on *my* judgment; but if I hire or recommend the "number one" student in the class, who proves to be a mediocre research assistant, law clerk or attorney, it is not nearly so much my fault. I believe that this factor is as strong as any in wedding many of us—teachers, judges, attorneys, students, alike—to the tyranny of grades. Even for me to speak well to my colleagues of a student who is not excelling at school requires a certain willingness to stick my neck out. Turow's account is, again, powerful for me because it shows that even one who is presumably most robustly self-confident about his standards and judgment proves unwilling to stick his neck out.

Perini's more serious failing to me is not, however, that he lacks the strength to make and rely on his own judgments. It is that he is unwilling to admit that lack to himself and others. The charade of putting the finalists through a series of tests—which he would doubtless assert are far more searching and valid than the examinations—serves not merely to glorify himself and demonstrate his power, as Turow bitterly notes. It serves also to permit Perini to maintain, to himself and the law school community, the fiction that he is a person of searching and confident judgment. "I have a very high batting average": The true charade is his claim that the batting average is *his,* rather than the first semester teachers'.

The pressure not to stick my neck out against opinions bearing historic credentials of weight and legitimacy is not, of course, limited to the area of grades. If I teach a traditional course using traditional methods, I feel safe from reproach if something does not go right. But if I try something new in class, and it does not work, it is much harder to lay the blame on the students or the materials. Using the style of writing that I do in this comment, and writing about these issues, entails a risk that I do not run when writing on a more traditional topic in law review style. I am often unwilling to run the risks involved in any particular context. When I decide to take the safer route, I try at least to acknowledge what I am doing to myself. That is the essential first step in assuming responsibility. Often, the next step suddenly seems easier to take—and, sometimes at least, the dangers most feared never come to pass, or prove not all that difficult to live with.

H.L.

Robert Pirsig, *Zen and the Art of Motorcycle Maintenance*
pp.194-196 (Bantam 1975).

A bad instructor can go through an entire quarter leaving absolutely nothing memorable in the minds of his class, curve out the scores on an irrelevant test, and leave the impression that some have learned and some have not. But if the grades are removed the class is forced to wonder each day what it's *really* learning. The questions, What's being taught? What's the goal? How do the lectures and assignments accomplish the goal? become ominous. The removal of grades exposes a huge and frightening vacuum.

What was Phaedrus trying to do, anyway? This question became more and more imperative as he went on. The answer that had seemed right when he started now made less and less sense. He had wanted his students to become creative by deciding for themselves what was good writing instead of asking him all the time. The real purpose of withholding the grades was to force them to look within themselves, the only place they would ever get a really right answer. . . .

For many of the students, this withholding created a Kafkaesque situation in which they saw they were to be punished for failure to do something but no one would tell them what they were supposed to do. They looked within themselves and saw nothing and looked at Phaedrus and saw nothing and just sat there helpless, not knowing what to do. . . .

He could think of no possible way he could tell them what they should work toward without falling back into the trap of authoritarian, didactic teaching. But how can you put on the blackboard the mysterious internal goal of each creative person?

The next quarter he dropped the whole idea and went back to regular grading, discouraged, confused, feeling he was right but somehow it had come out all wrong. When spontaneity and individuality and really good original stuff occurred in a classroom it was in spite of the instruction, not because of it. This seemed to make sense. He was ready to resign. Teaching dull conformity to hateful students wasn't what he wanted to do.

Comment

As a teacher, I have had moments, sometimes strung into a semester, when the issue Pirsig is here grappling with seemed paramount, and my feelings reflected the confusion and despair that Pirsig seemed to feel. The issue for me is broader than that of grades. Indeed, I think grading can often become a red herring, taking us away from the underlying concern with the proper role of authority, which is present whether or not a course is graded.

I, too, have looked for ways of creating a learning environment where students actively pursue the connection between their own sense of meaning and what they are learning about. Sometimes that attempt falls far from the mark, with a hovering feeling of cynicism and despair because of the promise I, or we, have held out for ourselves. I have come to believe that to the extent I am missing the connection between my sense of meaning and what I am teaching, or lose the belief that such a connection exists or my willingness to search actively for it, I help to create a learning environment that leaves the inquiry tinged by a mocking dis-ease.

I know that there have been times when I have used authority— assignments, requirements, enforcement—to cover up my own failure to be in touch with my goals in the learning environment. In fact, as I experience it now, some of my exertions of authority had only that purpose. The more I felt unsure about what I was about as a teacher, the more rigid I might become (I don't think the two *necessarily* have this reciprocal relationship) in requiring products of the students that were often unrelated to the goals, although one could (and I did) argue for their relevance. That way I could be "sure" the students would be doing something of importance for their learning.

I certainly do not know "the answer" to the tension between teacher authority on the one hand and student responsibility and self-motivation on the other. What seems to me true now is that we hamper the search for individual meaning (carried on alone or collectively) if we hold too tightly to authority in ways that do not allow the quieter voice of meaning to be acknowledged within and between us. That is true within me and, I imagine, within others. It also appears to be the case within the learning environment. I believe the issue here is elusive, subtle, escaping our grasp or sending up many incomplete, misleading or false takes on what appear to be answers, only to find the underlying issue still facing us. This issue seems vitally and particularly important in legal education because the tension between authority and meaning underlies as well much of the struggle in law. And whether it is in us, in the classroom, or in law, when authority conflicts with the pursuit of value and meaning we have lost our way.

J.H.

Comment

A facility for independent thinking is said to be one of the major benefits of a legal education. Yet it is a very hard thing to learn. For me, the problem rarely comes from following orders blindly. It is more a matter of assuming that things have to be done a certain way, or thought about along familiar lines, and never exercising the freedom to break free from these routines.

From the start of my first year, and especially around exam time, I was warned repeatedly not to assume anything. I was told it was dangerous for a lawyer to make assumptions, whether it is about what clients meant when they said something, what the statute of limitations is, or what an appellate judge will want to hear at an oral argument. I found that lesson easy enough to absorb in the context of exam writing but very hard to apply generally. My teachers continued to repeat their warning but it didn't seem to have any broader meaning than maintaining a skeptical attitude toward any statement of fact.

Perhaps one reason why I found this lesson so hard to absorb in any full way is that many of my teachers conducted their classes based on unexamined assumptions of what they were compelled to do as teachers. I watched a first-year teacher tell his class at the end of the spring semester that he regretted the pressure of first year, hoped the students would relax over the summer, and hoped the year had not been too hard on the students, ending his speech by saying that he was sorry there was nothing he could do to change this state of affairs. He was saying, in effect, that no one is responsible for the harsh effects of the first year.

In her book about humanistic elementary schooling, *Left Handed Teaching,* Gloria Castillo explains how she began to change her teaching style. She felt that the traditional curriculum inhibited the changes she wanted to make yet it existed and was supposed to be used. Caught in this bind, she realized there was a way out. In order to cope effectively with the materials she disliked teaching from, she had to stop assuming that she was required to use them.

To make such a switch, teachers might begin by looking at what they are doing in the classroom from a different perspective: one that postulates complete freedom. From that perspective, they could choose methods and techniques that further the goals of the class. Then they could match the class plans they have created against the reality of what is explicitly and implicitly forbidden by outside forces and their own values. It is possible that teachers would find out they have a lot more freedom to act than they had previously realized.

If law teachers provide the example of people who, in professional life, follow only the rules that truly have to be followed and those that they choose to follow, it might be easier for law students to be open to the possibility that many of their "shoulds" and "have to's" are self-imposed.

E.D.

John Enright, *One Step Forward: Situational Techniques For Altering Motivation for Therapy,* 12 Psychotherapy: Theory Research & Practice, No. 4 (Winter 1975).

Motivation is a complex variable. However one facet of it, the *expressed willingness to be there* . . . can be isolated and studied quite easily. Expressed willingness to be there can vary from almost total unwillingness—for instance a patient brought in restraints by the police to the therapist's office—to the opposite extreme of desperate eagerness to be there. . . . There are many, many people who get to the therapist's office under their own steam without physical external restraints who nonetheless say, "I have to be here." In a sense it is a lie to say, "I have to be here." All this phrase means is that the person chooses to be there rather than pay the price of refusal—whatever that might be: nagging parents, spouse, being fired, etc. *and prefers not to acknowledge* his choice. This refusal to acknowledge that he chooses to be there can become the focus or nodal point of resistance and holding back. . . .

Setting: State Mental Hospital

About 20 patients drawn from several wards had been brought to a room for a demonstration therapy session for the purpose of training about 15 staff members of the hospital. The training therapist was a visiting consultant, not a staff member at the hospital. The patients were sitting around the room looking rather lackadaisical, some of them leaning against the wall looking half asleep. The first few minutes of the meeting were desultory one sentence exchanges between therapist and patient, usually initiated by the therapist and leading nowhere. (Sample exchange: Therapist: "What brings you to this group?" Patient: "The nurse brought me here.") After a few minutes the therapist stopped the proceedings to give a brief, enthusiastic description of the possible benefits of group therapy, including several instances of positive gain from his own experience as a patient in group therapy. At the end of this brief discussion he invited any of the patients in the room who were interested to move their chair a foot or so closer in the center of the circle and participate in some of the ways he had outlined and suggested. Six patients rather hesitantly pulled their chairs forward and the sub-group began to interact at a noticeably higher level of involvement and action than the whole group had shown. After a few minutes a patient still leaning against the wall threw in a comment. He was immediately interrupted by the therapist and told he was welcome to participate *if* he moved his chair in and he was welcome to remain out if he preferred not to participate, but he could not participate from outside the inner circle. He slowly moved his chair in, apparently wishing to make his comment more than he wished to lean against the wall. A few minutes later 2 more patients moved their chairs in, followed by several others. By the end of the hour and a half, every one of the 20 patients had pulled his chair in and was participating.

Setting: The Psychiatric Ward of a General Hospital

A therapy group meeting twice a week for an hour had been going very badly for the past few weeks with very little involvement and participation. Boring, tense and unproductive meetings had been the rule. . . .

At one meeting . . . the therapist began by acknowledging that the group had been going rather badly and sharing responsibility for this. He then announced that the group would only have to meet for half an hour. However, at the end of that time, since he had nothing else scheduled, he would be willing to remain and chat with anybody who wished to on a purely voluntary basis. At the end of the usual desultory half hour the therapist got up and stretched and announced that the group was over, and repeated his offer to remain if anybody wished. All but one patient remained and by the end of that second half hour a quite involving, interested discussion between the therapist and several patients was underway. This pattern was repeated on several occasions; desultory, almost total non-communication for the first half hour, followed by rather relatively lively exchanges in the second, completely voluntary, half hour. On some other occasions one or two patients would leave at the official break; at times not a single patient did. . . .

Setting: A Counseling Center Associated with a County Probation Department

The Juvenile Court in this county had a program whereby adolescents involved in minor misdemeanors or minor parole violations were allowed to choose 6 hours of counseling at the counseling center instead of going back to juvenile hall or going on probation, depending on the situation that brought them in. Not surprisingly, as soon as the word was out, most individuals given this choice chose 6 hours of counseling on the grounds that it was obviously easier and less interruptive of their life to do that than go to juvenile hall or be on probation for a number of months. However, they did not actually use the counseling situation for counseling, and the counselors became thoroughly frustrated and discouraged. The adolescents in general refused to talk about anything serious and just sat around "doing time." A careful look at the Juvenile Court ruling showed that it did not specify that 6 hours had to be in the form of 6 actual hours and the actual spacing of time was up to the Counseling Center. The consulting psychologist therefore proposed that the length of the session be determined by whether or not the adolescent was interesting the counselor as he talked. After the session had gone for 10 minutes, if the counselor was not interested and involved, he was free to end the session, giving the counselee only as much time credit as he had actually spent there, be it 10, 15, 20 minutes or whatever. Thus an adolescent who was systematically frustrating the intent of the counseling program by refusing to get involved might have to come for 36 10-minute sessions in order to fulfill his court requirement. We expected this condition to be met with howls of protest. Many of them checked out the counselors for one or two sessions to see if they really meant business, and when they found that the counselor would indeed end the session if he was not interested, they managed to become interesting for an hour at a time and fulfill their contract in the usual 6 hours. A third of a fairly large number who entered this program voluntarily continued counseling at the end of their 6 hours, which had been unheard of before this innovation was instituted, and there were several other indications of rather satisfactory counseling occurring during this time under the terms of this contract.

An underlying theme in all of these vignettes is that the element of choice or free self determinism was introduced into the situation. This was perhaps clearest in the first vignette. Society had dragged the patient to the mental hospital, locked the doors and kept him there. The nurse had gently but firmly brought him to the group therapy room. But he and only he had moved his chair one foot forward. With that act he announced that he was present; a willing individual, open to the risks and pleasures of participation. As small as it may seem, this act was a *commitment*.

All of us, it seems, lead lives between risk and holding back; between reaching out into the world and expressing what is in us, and cautiously holding back and staying safe. Many, perhaps most of us, generally lean toward caution in holding back and this is the choice it seems that most patients have made or make quite routinely. In the long run it is probably a destructive one. But from moment to moment it seems safer. Psychotherapy at its best is, as Jourard has so beautifully put it, an *invitation* to openness and letting go of some of the caution in life. . . . If the patient can find or construe the slightest hint of coercion in the situation, it then becomes much easier to reinterpret the situation as one in which caution and holding back is necessary, and he can feel justified and all right about refusing the invitation. I think this is why the expressed willingness to be here is important in making therapy go well. A patient who has just said out loud, "I want to be here" is going to find it very hard to construe the situation as coercive and justify his holding back. The balance of power for a moment at least is shifted on the side of risk. . . .

In my early days of experimenting with these techniques I had the idea that these steps were opening the way to therapy, as though getting the person to acknowledge his willingness to be there would make therapy possible. More and more I have seen the procedures that get a person to acknowledge his willingness to be there *are* therapy, and in some cases the most effective and important phases of a person's therapy. What he does, after he acknowledges his willingness to be there, is almost less important than getting to the position of that conscious responsible choice. . . .

Comment

Most teachers see students as attending law school voluntarily: They have chosen to become lawyers, they have chosen to attend a particular law school, they have chosen (usually) to take any particular course. To many students, I imagine, such perceptions are oblivious to much relevant reality. There is, first of all, pressure to work, and to choose a line of work that brings social approval and reward; admission to practice as a lawyer is today impossible without attendance at law school; the differences among law schools are minor and, in any event, there is much pressure to attend the most selective law school to which one can be admitted; there is much pressure to take many courses nominally deemed electives and, in any event, one must take the requisite number of courses and the differences among courses are often not great. In all, a student might well respond in bitter irony: I am in no real sense in your course voluntarily.

The web of unacknowledged coercive pressures entraps and attracts both students and faculty. The passivity of students in embracing the victim role finds its mirror in the passivity of faculty in refusing to take into account the force of critical strands in that web. Since I am a teacher and not a student, I do not want to speak further to the students' responsibility. As teachers, I believe that we need to be very clear—far clearer than I ordinarily am, with myself or my students—about what we decide to require of students, and what is left to their free choice.

Within any requirement, there are levels of freedom. If I want my students to choose actively their level of involvement, I must be clear about the choices to be made. In deciding, for example, whether to require attendance at a particular seminar or course as a condition of enrollment, I need to be careful not to turn the question of justification for the requirement aside on the ground that, after all, students are free not to take the seminar. If I decide not to require attendance, I believe that I have a responsibility to make that decision clear and not passively take advantage of the congeries of unexamined pressures on many students to enhance attendance. I need, in particular, to avoid indirect or unspoken messages, for which I would disclaim responsibility, about the correlation between attendance and final grade, for such messages, to a student, contradict the statement that attendance is not required.

This is not to say that full and unrestrained student freedom of election is my hidden goal. I do have requirements, and at the same time I want to present a learning context in which the students make decisions for themselves about some important aspects of their involvement in their learning. All of this is very difficult. It necessitates a willingness to accept a student's decision not to participate, if I prefer that all students participate but my decision is that the choice should be left with them. It necessitates a willingness to acknowledge that I am imposing a requirement, if my decision is to the contrary. The Enright examples, drawn from a mental hospital, make me realize that one result of my making clear to students that they are free to attend or not (if that is my decision) is that those then choosing to attend may well find themselves free of the deadening passivity that the victim psychology engenders in the classroom. If my decision is to withdraw the issue of attendance from student choice, I will nonetheless be led to consider at what degree of involvement I wish to let student choice prevail. At that point, the same process, whereby awareness of choice fosters active learning, can work.

H.L.

John Holt, *Freedom and Beyond*
pp.108-113 (Dutton 1972).

A few years ago, when I was only teaching part time, I worked very hard on the cello for two years or so, practicing or playing as much as six hours a day. I could not practice at home, so I worked out a deal with the Commonwealth School—I would coach their soccer team, and they would let me practice in the building, in the morning before classes and in the evening after the end of school. So, during those two years, it was my regular custom to get up at about four or four-thirty in the morning, get dressed, pack up cello, music, and music stand, walk to the school, open the building, find an empty room, set up stand and music, and start to practice. When the building began to fill up, around eight o'clock, I would pack up, returning again in the evening, if I was not playing with a group. My friends were baffled by this regime. They didn't know whether to call it work or play. It didn't seem to be work, because nobody was making me do it or paying me for it, and there was no other kind of reward or benefit I would get from it. At the same time, they couldn't think of it as play—how can anyone call "play" getting up at four and walking through dark winter streets just to practice for three hours. They explained everything with awed remarks about my will power. This missed the point. I suppose one might give the name "will power" to whatever it was that got me up at that hour on those winter mornings to do what nobody was compelling me to do. But this suggests that inside of me somewhere there were two people, one of them a lazy, good-for-nothing lying in the bed, enjoying the warmth and wanting to stay there, and the other a stern taskmaster saying, "Get up, you no-good bum, get out of bed and go practice that cello," and finally winning the argument because he was stronger. But there are not two people inside me, only one. The fact was that I loved to play the cello. I don't just mean that I wanted very much someday to play it well, though I wanted that too. I mean I loved playing it as I played it, a struggling beginner. I loved the scales, the exercises, the feeling of strength, skill, accuracy, quickness gradually coming into my hands and fingers, the sounds I could get from the instrument. Many other things in my life have given great pleasure, but nothing more than those hours of early morning practice. I wanted to play the cello and since the only time I could play it was early in the morning, that was when I had to get up in order to play it.

On some pitch black mornings, hearing what I knew was a cold wind howling outside, I might think, "Well, it is certainly comfortable in this bed, and maybe it wouldn't hurt if I just skipped practicing today." But my response to this was not to draw on something called will power, to insult or threaten myself, but to take a longer look at my life, to extend my vision, to think about the whole of my experience, to reconnect present and future, and quite specifically, to ask myself, "Do you like playing the cello or not? Would you like to play it better or not?" When I put the matter this way I could see that I enjoyed playing the cello more than I enjoyed staying in bed. So I got up. If, as sometimes happened or happens, I do stay in bed, not sleeping, not really thinking, but just not getting up, it is not because will power is weak but because I have temporarily become disconnected, so to speak, from the wholeness of my life. . . .

On those winter mornings I did not feel so much that I was getting out of bed and getting dressed and walking to school *so that* I could play the cello, as that they were all *part of* playing the cello. When I start to play, I take the cello out of its case and tune it—always a slow job for me. When the cello is tuned, I very often do what are called percussive exercises with the left hand, banging my fingers down on the fingerboard as hard as I can. And so from there into various other warm-ups, scales, position exercises, left-hand stretching exercises, bowing exercises, trills, and some of the music I may be working on, with a good deal of improvising thrown in. But all this *is* playing the cello. I don't divide my practice into pleasant and unpleasant parts, and then use "will power" to make myself do the unpleasant ones so that I may later have the fun of doing the pleasant. It is all one. . . .

Perhaps an exaggerated and ridiculous example will show what's wrong with always dividing experience into Cause and Effect, Ends and Means, Skills and Acts, Getting Ready and Doing It. Suppose I am thirsty. Do I tell myself that I must take the trouble, use will power to force myself to go to the cupboard, then open the door, then take out a glass, then go to the sink, then turn on the faucet, then fill the glass, then raise the glass to my lips—go through all this Disagreeable Hard Work so that I may *then* have the pleasure of feeling the cool water in my mouth and going down my throat? It's ridiculous. If I am thirsty, and if there is anything to drink, I take a drink, which means *I do all the things I need to do to get the drink.* I don't have to use will power to do them; they are part of the act of getting the drink. Does it take will power to get in bed when we're sleepy? Babies have more sense than we do about this. No one could explain to a baby, even if he had the words, what we mean by will power. Babies live their lives all of a piece. Imagine a baby on the floor, playing or exploring. He sees a toy or ball or bear on the floor at the other side of the room, and the feeling or thought comes to him that he wants to play with it. Does there then arise a little conflict inside the baby over whether it is worth the trouble to crawl all the way across the room just so he may then seize the toy? No. To want the toy is to want to do whatever must be done to get it. Instantly the baby sets out across the floor, probably already feeling some of the excitement and pleasure of playing with the toy. In his mind, he is playing with it. His play with it *begins* when he thinks of playing with it and begins to move toward it. . . .

Comment

This makes no sense to me—I mean that it doesn't work for me. I have many times wanted a drink of something, but found it more trouble than it was worth to go and get it. I am an impatient person, crotchety and irritable about a lot of the little (and not-so-little) tasks of life. I see the desired end, I often even see that the means can be viewed as desired as easily as disagreeable: Yet the means are too burdensome, and I stay in bed (figuratively *and* literally).

I have come to think of it as a mistake to think of this as a failure of will or of willpower, or as a defect of character or personality. To do that is an exercise of self-flagellation, and is not the beginning of a movement towards change; it is therefore itself an evasion of responsibility. I also think that it is a mistake to say that the answer is simply to exercise will and get the drink, practice the cello, or whatever. Rather it now seems clear to me that my decision not to "work at" something which in one sense I want to do, but which I am finding disagreeable, is itself an act of will. I choose to stay in bed, or to stop practicing, because I value more being in bed, or remaining indolent (though thirsty), or avoiding repetitive irritating work. I judge this preference of mine harshly because it seems clear that I do not "really" prefer my slothfulness, crotchetiness, or insistence on refusing to take a longer view. The fact, however, is that I do: I prefer my "laziness" to being able to play the cello. In an important sense, I exercise my will when I act on this preference, no less than I would if I acted differently.

It is true that I am not acting out of a connection between my actions and the goal or activity that I value. But using the concept of "will" in this latter sense does not help me, as the former sense does, to realize that I must look at the choice among values as consciously as possible, and take responsibility for the choice I make. If I am unhappy with my preferences and choices, I can change them—and my will and action—only by genuinely coming to care less about the comfort of the moment and to discover a meaningful connection between the present task and the end I desire. And I cannot find the connection if it is not there, simply because it seems more appealing to be a person who sees it than one who denies it. It is uncomfortable to admit, to Holt and the world, that I truly am lazy or irritable in some important respects. But I will never make an aware and honest choice of values, and never validly engage my will, if I simply succumb to the compelling rhetoric of the case for Holt's view of the competing values.

This is not said to excuse my present choices. In many ways, I want to make Holt's views mine. To do that, I must look at what I value in crotchetiness and laziness with a fuller sympathy and understanding than those epithets permit. If I stop insulting those aspects of myself, they can safely loosen their grip on me. I will still give them weight in making choices, but I will be able to give them no more weight than I want to.

H.L.

Comment

I am intrigued by what Holt writes, and particularly by my and others' reactions to what he states so very simply. While at one moment the concept seems to embody a familiar experience, at another I feel as if he is describing something quite beyond me. At such all too frequent moments, ends and means seem worlds apart, and the idea that they can fuse, or indeed that they are one, a distant illusion.

Yet I believe we are all aware of what Holt describes. We all have had the feeling of being totally involved in an activity, so much so that notions of overcoming resistance seem completely out of place. We have had it, and we have struggled to find it, having become "temporarily disconnected."

What is it then that Holt is talking about? It is not simply succeeding in getting something done. As law teachers or law students we all have succeeded in getting things done. Somehow we did everything we had to do to get where we are. And it is not only doing something without having to force ourselves to do it. There are lots of times when we have done just that—taking an exam or getting a motion in by a deadline. I believe what Holt is talking about is loving, deeply loving, what we are doing and being connected to that love in the doing. That happens less frequently, and the infrequency intrigues me in general and frustrates me in myself.

I have had moments in teaching a class or in writing a brief or an essay when I felt deeply and fundamentally connected with what I was doing. What characterizes those moments is that I am responding to what feels like a deep inner urging. It is not what someone is telling me to do; it is not what I think I "should" do; it is not what I think I might like to do. It is what I believe in and who I am.

On other occasions my action is often in response to some external requirement (or internalized "should"). I never played the cello, but I did play the clarinet, and I practiced. I was told to and I thought I should (and later at least thought I should think so) but I didn't love it. My half hours of practice were longer than Holt's stolen mornings and evenings. The clarinet was for me then, and remains, a statement of who I am not.

The classes and writing that I love to do, these have been for me my cello. There were deadlines but at a core level I was responding to my own inner urgings. That hasn't always been so, but it has been frequent enough to recognize the voice.

The distinction between having to do something and loving to do something is a simple and fundamental one. The notion that we can love our work, that there is work that we do love (and that we may even have the responsibility to ourselves and others to find that work we love), does not always have much support in our culture. What I find particularly alarming is that our educational system seems to reinforce this lack. I have frequently talked to students who are in the process of becoming lawyers and increasingly unhappy with the direction their careers are taking. On one occasion I remember talking to a particular student who felt he had lost all his joy for life as he plunged into the job interview process. Lawyering had become, ever so subtly, a new requirement. He had almost forgotten, and was certainly disregarding, *why* he decided to become a lawyer. I suggested he try an experiment—to take three months and act as if he had decided not to go the usual job route—including telling his peers he had abandoned the chase. After a short chorus of "but I can't"; "what would . . . ," he agreed to try and immediately felt a huge burden lifted from his shoulders. He continued the "experiment" past the three months and his job interests returned to those that had brought him to law school. Others have not taken me up on the offer.

What disturbs me is how hard I and, I know, others find it to keep hold of that experience of loving what we are doing. One day's love feels like another day's labor. I *feel* disconnected. And, I believe, my work *is* different. If it were simply a question of making myself feel better, the concern would be of somewhat limited scope. But the disconnection is not only from me. When my work is connected and I am loving what I am do-ing, I feel connected with a process or movement in the world that transcends me. I am connected with others. Teaching and writing become dynamic and creative. I experience my work and myself as part of a larger context.

I do believe Holt is right—what I need at such times of disconnection is "to extend my vision, to think about the whole of my experience, to reconnect present and future." But I can realize that as an idea only, one that I don't know how to accomplish. And I often find I have strayed far even from remembering the idea.

Here the concept of will does become important. Holt appears to have discipline, and in that he is fortunate. I believe discipline is a trait that our culture simply does not do all that well in engendering. So while we may find what we love to do, we do not necessarily pursue it with that love. We easily become disconnected. And when that happens, the issue of will looms large. In fact, it is sometimes in just those areas where our work is most important to us that we can procrastinate endlessly. I know for myself I can willingly and obsessively accomplish immeasurable things in the process of avoiding what is most fundamentally important to me.

When that happens, and I feel "disconnected," it is as if there were a bridge to cross. Once across, I am reconnected. Before crossing I am faced with an immense chasm. And I get little relief from badgering myself with the awareness that it is largely of my own making.

Like Holt, I do try at those moments to allow in a broader perspec-tive. Sometimes I need to discover what is in the way of the broader perspective. Sometimes I simply need to will myself to take the steps across the bridge, until I suddenly find I am well on my way.

What thinking and writing about Holt has made me do is ask myself and others whether we have learned from school (and are teaching in school) to do things because we have to rather than because we love to. And is there a way we can help undo that for ourselves and for each other?

J.H.

4. EXPLORING PATTERNS OF THINKING

A. REASON AND EXPERIENCE

Oliver Wendell Holmes, Jr. "The Profession of the Law," in
Collected Legal Papers pp.29-32 (Harcourt Brace 1920).

And now, perhaps, I ought to have done. But I know that
some spirit of fire will feel that his main question has not been
answered. He will ask, What is all this to my soul? You do not bid
me sell my birthright for a mess of pottage; what have you said
to show that I can reach my own spiritual possibilities through
such a door as this? How can the laborious study of a dry and
technical system, the greedy watch for clients and practice of
shopkeepers' arts, the mannerless conflicts over often sordid interests, make out a life? Gentlemen, I admit at once that these
questions are not futile, that they may prove unanswerable, that
they have often seemed to me unanswerable. And yet I believe
there is an answer. They are the same questions that meet you in
any form of practical life. If a man has the soul of Sancho Panza,
the world to him will be Sancho Panza's world; but if he has the
soul of an idealist, he will make—I do not say find—his world
ideal. Of course, the law is not the place for the artist or the poet.
The law is the calling of thinkers. But to those who believe with
me that not the least godlike of man's activities is the large survey
of causes, that to know is not less than to feel, I say—and I say
no longer with any doubt—that a man may live greatly in the law
as well as elsewhere; that there as well as elsewhere his thought
may find its unity in an infinite perspective; that there as well as
elsewhere he may wreak himself upon life, may drink the bitter
cup of heroism, may wear his heart out after the unattainable.
All that life offers any man from which to start his thinking or
his striving is a fact. And if this universe is one universe, if it is
so far thinkable that you can pass in reason from one part [of] it
to another, it does not matter very much what that fact is. For
every fact leads to every other by the path of the air. Only men do
not yet see how, always. And your business as thinkers is to
make plainer the way from some thing to the whole of things; to
show the rational connection between your fact and the frame of
the universe. If your subject is law, the roads are plain to anthro-
pology, the science of man, to political economy, the theory of
legislation, ethics, and thus by several paths to your final view of
life. It would be equally true of any subject. The only difference

146

is in the ease of seeing the way. To be master of any branch of knowledge, you must master those which lie next to it. . . .

But do not think I am pointing you to flowery paths and beds of roses—to a place where brilliant results attend your work, which shall be at once easy and new. No result is easy which is worth having. Your education begins when what is called your education is over—when you no longer are stringing together the pregnant thoughts, the "jewels five-words-long," which great men have given their lives to cut from the raw material, but have begun yourselves to work upon the raw material for results which you do not see, cannot predict, and which may be long in coming—when you take the fact which life offers you for your appointed task. No man has earned the right to intellectual ambition until he has learned to lay his course by a star which he has never seen—to dig by the divining rod for springs which he may never reach. In saying this, I point to that which will make your study heroic. For I say to you in all sadness of conviction, that to think great thoughts you must be heroes as well as idealists. Only when you have worked alone—when you have felt around you a black gulf of solitude more isolating than that which surrounds the dying man, and in hope and in despair have trusted to your own unshaken will—then only will you have achieved. Thus only can you gain the secret isolated joy of the thinker, who knows that, a hundred years after he is dead and forgotten, men who never heard of him will be moving to the measure of his thought—the subtile rapture of a postponed power, which the world knows not because it has no external trappings, but which to his prophetic vision is more real than that which commands an army. And if this joy should not be yours, still it is only thus that you can know that you have done what it lay in you to do—can say that you have lived, and be ready for the end.

Comment

Like his colleague Cardozo, Mr. Justice Holmes often wrote with such eloquence and grandeur that it is easy not to pay close attention to the meaning of his words. He has often been thought to stand for the glorification of intellect and rationality, disembodied from a connection with (merely) human activities. There is much in this passage that could be read this way. Yet what strikes me so vividly is how his words explicitly deny that the "spiritual possibilities" of a life in law are to be found in the heroic pursuit of reason and knowledge for their own sake. The "joy" of the thinker comes from the knowledge—unprovable at the time it is felt; proven true or false long after death; but nonetheless something which the thinker is willing to say he "knows"—that "a hundred years after he is dead and forgotten, men who never heard of him will be moving to the measure of his thought."

Here we have no Olympian detachment, no apotheosis of pure reason, but a deeply felt emotion, a deeply committed faith. More, it is a faith that finds sufficient justification for a life in striving to do work which will have meaning to a person yet unborn, identified only by a common humanity and dedication to a similar striving. This, the Justice says, is what in the end makes the life of the mind worth living. I do not know a finer statement which combines a tribute to a life committed to the mind, to rationality and thought, with a recognition that the value of those aspects of life rests in their connection with something more, in their connection with other humans.

H.L.

Karl Llewellyn, *The Bramble Bush*
pp.127-128 (Oceana 1960).

I have hinted before at what can be gotten even from the cases. I know no more fascinating record of the human tribe if you have the wit to read it. The wit to read it! Within a hair we have lost the art of reading. There was a time when men read by putting all of themselves and their experience into what they read. Reading was active, reading was creation. There is one book on which that has been proved. See what the Bible meant to Puritan culture. Read over Pilgrim's Progress once again, and see what John Bunyan put into his Bible. Each terse, sharp story, each pregnant word, became a focus for experience, as the theme of the Annunciation became to a medieval artist the vehicle to work out all the message and miracle of impending motherhood.

Now, reading is different. . . . The author does your thinking for you—as your instructors, you sometimes hope, will do your thinking for you. A pleasant evening with the Satevepost, each thought sprawled out at length and twice repeated.—And what you read there as much as three months ago, is washed away. Why, indeed, should it stick? You cannot read the Bible so. Either it bores you, and you drop it; or it stays with you. Either you get nothing, or you do the bulk of the work yourself.

So of the cases. Put yourself into them; dig beneath the surface, make your experience count, bring out the story, and you have here dramatic tales that stir, that make the cases stick, that weld your law into the whole of culture. There are the parties. There are, as well, the judges: working at shaping the law to human needs. In every case the drama of society unrolls before you—in all its grandeur, in all its humor, in all its futility, in the eternal wonder of the coral-reef. The clash of ideals, the courage of high hope—and man's purblind inadequacy with man's problems. This, for the seeing. Humanity and law—not two, but one.

Comment

I read these words as a plea for experiential learning. By experiential learning in law I do not mean clinical courses, although clinics have grown in part because of, and respond in part to, that need. By experiential learning, I mean, as I read Llewellyn to mean, the integration of idea and human experience.

In writing on this subject, I face an obvious difficulty: How, if at all, can I communicate with ideas about the limitation of ideas? To put the same question more broadly, how can we as students of law make an immediate and vital connection between learning and experience? How can we as legal practitioners connect the words of law with the fullness of human reality?

This problem is also hard to write about because it is so central and potentially so vast. From different sources in the profession we are beginning to grasp how much the problems in law and legal education have to do with how we think about and how we deal with law and legal institutions. It can become almost overwhelming to take the next step and glimpse how deeply rooted these problems are in the ways we see the world—particularly in our tendency to give ideas a priority over experience rather than recognizing them as *part* of experience.*

And the problem is personal—certainly for me, perhaps for many of us connected to law. It is not just a tendency that exists out there. It is a struggle inside the individual. The one trap I consistently fall into, least know how to deal with, and find most troubling is this one. Recognizing that ideas are only a part of experience is a *continual* personal process encompassing fear, release, retrenchment, surrender. In the law school setting particularly, I find it easy to hold fast to ideas in an increasingly limiting way. I know, or think, that with an idea I have my bearings. I can look it up. I've written many good ones down and can return to them. If I rely on experience, I feel I am on my own. Launched. I must use the winds and sail to get back to shore and may then discover that shore is itself an illusion.

But I am gradually learning to recognize how limiting it is to use ideas in ways that exclude much of human experience. The reliance on ideas alone can deaden a classroom, stifle an institution, rigidify a system, and restrict a life. Here again I fear the limits of communicating in ideas. I'll try to clarify.

I am not suggesting that we need abandon ideas, although anything that questions our exclusive reliance on them (particularly in legal education) will surely be interpreted that way. I am saying that ideas are, and need to be recognized as, only a part of human experience. And I am say-

---

*   Jack Ayer's essay, Isn't There Enough Reality to Go Around? An Essay on the Unspoken Promises of Our Law, 53 N.Y.U.L. Rev. 475 (1978), was an enormous aid to my understanding of these problems. The quotations in this Comment are from that article, pp.477, 501-503.

ing that we have a tendency to use ideas to replace or guard against the rest of human experience. This happens easily, without our even understanding that that is what we are doing. After all, an idea, a word or phrase can summarize so much. The temptation to replace an experience with an idea is unavoidable and often irresistible.

In law, it is more than a temptation. It is a way of organizing our experience. Law imposes theory on facts, ideas on experience, words on reality. This is as it should be. This is as it must be. Law *does* deal with concepts and principles. Law *is* a system that we as human beings have and continue to develop to protect ourselves from our baser drives and to strive to make life richer in some way. To that end, we draw from human experience certain principles and concepts. The difficulty is that the words in the concept or principle can come to replace human experience or, in time, even become unyieldingly at war with the underlying human experience. As Jack Ayer has said: "It is the tragedy of thought that yesterday's insights become tomorrow's dogmas." Concepts become masters, rather than a tool, of mankind.

Perhaps the most destructive potential of legal education is its ability *implicitly* to elicit, reinforce and define this way of viewing reality. Legal education can be a process of learning to separate ourselves from human reality. To put it simply, we have made a little too much of a good thing. Ideas are important and powerful. We seem to have gone too far in giving them power, often over us. As Ayer puts it:

> [S]uccess [in these respects] can be its own undoing. Charmed as we are by the insight of our analysis, we run the risk of remaining perpetually mesmerized by the words themselves, and, as a result, of reifying them. We may make events conform to language, rather than language to events. . . .

> What we confront in reification is the persistent unwillingness of individual people to recall the roots of their knowledge and remain aware of its uncertainty. To reify, or hypostatize, is to endeavor to minimize this uncertainty and make the world a familiar place by creating the illusion that some of our concepts and our forms of thought are facts about the world. The less we examine ourselves, the more we are likely to find our image mirrored in our perception of the world, without being able to recognize it as our image. Merely to state the issue is not to resolve it, of course. But we ought to have at least some sense of the obstacles in our way.

To engage in this critique does not, as Ayer points out, solve the problem. I frankly do not think it is a simple matter to have a legal education and legal system that are inclusive of experience, in the way I describe here, although I do think that refusing to see the problem is the surest way to perpetuate it. What we can do is do what we can do. And we can work towards connecting legal education (and ourselves as educators) more directly and immediately to the depth of human experience. There is much out there and inside us that stands in the way of such a change; that fact is not so much for me a reason not to act, but an accenting of my realization that I have no other real alternative.

I am hopeful because in placing ideas over human experience, I believe we inflict a deep pain and loss on ourselves. This is because the supremacy of ideas not only causes upsetting consequences but it lessens our own immediate experience and our lives. I am hopeful because ultimately we may find the cost too great, for ourselves as well as the world. And as we do, an idea will be seen more as an idea, with all the power and limitations of that element of our experience. And then perhaps we will become more secure, as we recognize that we are adrift, together.

J.H.

Comment

For me, the initial burst of energy on a writing project flames brightly in ways closely paralleling religious revelation or artistic inspiration, which are essentially irrational processes. That flame is never constant; it snuffs out as quickly and mysteriously as it comes, and is often followed by a feeling of emptiness.

It remains for the muscles of the mind to construct a means of carrying the messages to the reader. It is inevitable that this translation process will convert the often formless, irrational spirit of the theme to something that can be spoken about. And if it can be spoken about, it can be discussed, even argued over. Further reductions of the initial vision take place. My mind knows that it is much easier to grasp means rather than ends and, as with the topics of religion, politics, and sex, it may be more practical to engage readers at the level of conduct—what they will agree to do rather than what their grounds of belief are. To be accepted by my audience, I am inclined to formulate a rule instead of describing a quality of being, outline a technique rather than elaborate a personal point of view. So if inspirational sources, the irrational, feelings and intuitions are related to "softness," my writing inevitably displays some "hardness" as a result of rendering the soft on paper.

But even more so, by dint of my training and experience as a lawyer. Here the "hard" is not only practical and discussable, it is proof-oriented, precise and logical. Having experienced the adversarial confrontation in the courtroom, I anticipate a confrontation with my reading audiences. It is often a defensive posture. For example, if I believe a certain "soft" humanistic approach is the better one in matters of ethical conflict arising in law practice, I will avoid saying I think it should be adopted because it is morally and humanly right. Rather, I will try to prove it is better because it "works" better, or because supposedly neutral cost-benefit analysis shows it reaps advantageous benefits, or because significant authority figures have recognized its worth.

I depersonalize the point of view to the extent that, like Franken-stein's monster, I have lost connection with the source of my being: My habitual disassociation takes me out of touch with the very feelings that are my inspiration and my guide. This transformation parallels the com-parable loss of ideals that commonly occurs in law students in response to experiences of law school education, and in lawyers in response to ex-periences of law practice.

These acts of writing pose a paradox for me. Writing demands hard-ness. Yet for the writing truly to reflect what seems most important about my subject, I must be in touch with its mysterious source: I must also be receptive to softness.

M.S.E.

Richard Wasserstrom, *Postscript, Lawyers and Revolution*
30 U. Pitt. L. Rev. 125, 129 (1968).

> [T]he law is conservative in the same way in which language is conservative. It seeks to assimilate everything that happens to that which has happened. It seeks to relate any new phenome-non to what has already been categorized and dealt with. Thus, the lawyer's virtually instinctive intellectual response when he is confronted with a situation is to look for the respects in which that situation is like something that is familiar and that has a place within the realm of understood legal doctrine. In the early development of the Anglo-American legal system this fun-damental tendency manifested itself most obviously in the operation of the writ system. Rather than enlarge substantially the number of causes of action, the law found it more congenial to [adapt]—to some degree—to a changing world through the use of elaborate, complicated, fictions. But it also rejected—because unfamiliar—much that was important and that should have been cognizable by the legal order.

> We still, I am convinced, have our own analogues of the writ system with us today. And this fundamental tendency of mind still manifests itself whenever we as lawyers boggle at a claim, an interest, or a case because it is unlike what has gone before; or whenever we attempt to force the unfamiliar (no matter how much we distort it in the process) into a category that fits into our world of legal concepts. I think that persons who are genu-inely concerned with far-reaching and radical—in the generic sense of the term—solutions to social ills ought to be on guard against and ought to mistrust this powerful tendency on the part of the lawyer to transmogrify what is new into what has gone before or to reject as unworkable or unintelligible what cannot be so modified. . . .

Comment

In reading this passage by Wasserstrom, I am reminded how any human or institutional attribute can be an asset or a liability, and how easy it is for us to turn the one into another. I believe I have often used with advantage the capacity of my mind to analogize to and draw upon past experience to interpret, assimilate and communicate about present reality. I have found myself doing that as a lawyer writing briefs or arguing a case. I have done it with my students, as I help them move from one experience and perception to a new and expanded one. I do it as well with friends, as we might seek to explore together where we have come or help each other in a period of readjustment or reassessment. And I do it with myself, as I seek to draw on some past experience to face some new situation.

That approach has also been vastly limiting. In my attempt to draw upon the past to help me through the present, I have found myself hanging tenaciously to a perceptual framework that simply will not yield to my present reality. I convince myself that this situation is just like a past one I have been in with my students. I search in vain in my notes and thoughts for the analogue, knowing somewhere within that the attempt is simply a refusal to give in to the newness of the moment and what I am about to, and need to, learn. When that feeling occurs frequently enough, I realize (sometimes) that I am holding too firmly to precedent, but my legal thinking sure doesn't make it easy.

J.H.

Robert Pirsig, *Zen and the Art of Motorcycle Maintenance* pp.272-279 (Bantam 1975).

Stuckness. That's what I want to talk about today. . . .

A screw sticks, for example, on a side cover assembly. You check the manual to see if there might be any special cause for this screw to come off so hard, but all it says is "Remove side cover plate" in that wonderful terse technical style that never tells you what you want to know. There's no earlier procedure left undone that might cause the cover screws to stick.

If you're experienced you'd probably apply a penetrating liquid and an impact driver at this point. But suppose you're inexperienced and you attach a self-locking plier wrench to the shank of your screwdriver and really twist it hard, a procedure you've had success with in the past, but which this time succeeds only in tearing the slot of the screw.

Your mind was already thinking ahead to what you would do when the cover plate was off, and so it takes a little time to realize that this irritating minor annoyance of a torn screw slot isn't just irritating and minor. You're stuck. Stopped. Terminated. It's absolutely stopped you from fixing the motorcycle.

This isn't a rare scene in science or technology. This is the commonest scene of all. Just plain *stuck*. In traditional maintenance this is the worst of all moments, so bad that you have avoided even thinking about it before you come to it.

The book's no good to you now. Neither is scientific reason. You don't need any scientific experiments to find out what's wrong. It's obvious what's wrong. What you need is an hypothesis for how you're going to get that slotless screw out of there and scientific method doesn't provide any of these hypotheses. It operates only after they're around.

This is the zero moment of consciousness. Stuck. No answer. Honked. Kaput. It's a miserable experience emotionally. You're losing time. You're incompetent. You don't know what you're doing. You should be ashamed of yourself. You should take the machine to a *real* mechanic who knows how to figure these things out.

It's normal at this point for the fear-anger syndrome to take over and make you want to hammer on that side plate with a chisel, to pound it off with a sledge if necessary. You think about it, and the more you think about it the more you're inclined to take the whole machine to a high bridge and drop if off. It's just outrageous that a tiny little slot of a screw can defeat you so totally. . . .

I think the basic fault that underlies the problem of stuckness is traditional rationality's insistence upon "objectivity," a doctrine that there is a divided reality of subject and object. For true science to take place these must be rigidly separate from each other. "You are the mechanic. There is the motorcycle. You are forever apart from one another. You do this to it. You do that to it. These will be the results."

This eternally dualistic subject-object way of approaching the motorcycle sounds right to us because we're used to it. But it's not right. It's always been an artificial interpretation *superimposed* on reality. It's never been reality itself. When this duality is completely accepted a certain nondivided relationship between the mechanic and motorcycle, a craftsmanlike feeling for the work, is destroyed. When traditional rationality divides the world into subjects and objects it shuts out Quality, and when you're really stuck it's Quality, not any subjects or objects, that tells you where you ought to go. . . .

To put it in more concrete terms: If you want to build a factory, or fix a motorcycle, or set a nation right without getting stuck, then classical, structured, dualistic subject-object knowledge, although necessary, isn't enough. You have to have some feeling for the quality of the work. You have to have a sense of what's good. *That* is what carries you forward. This sense isn't just something you're born with, although you *are* born with it. It's also something you can develop. It's not just "intuition," not just unexplainable "skill" or "talent." It's the direct result of contact with basic *reality,* Quality, which dualistic reason has in the past tended to conceal. . . .

Let's consider a reevaluation of the situation in which we assume that the stuckness now occurring, the zero of consciousness, isn't the worst of all possible situations, but the best possible situation you could be in. After all, it's exactly this stuckness that Zen Buddhists go to so much trouble to induce; through koans, deep breathing, sitting still and the like. Your mind is empty, you have a "hollow-flexible" attitude of "beginner's mind." You're right at the front end of the train of knowledge, at the track of reality itself. Consider, for a change, that this is a moment to be not feared but cultivated. If your mind is truly, profoundly stuck, then you may be much better off than when it was loaded with ideas.

The solution to the problem often at first seems unimportant or undesirable, but the state of stuckness allows it, in time, to assume its true importance. It seemed small because your previous rigid evaluation which led to the stuckness made it small.

But now consider the fact that no matter how hard you try to hang on to it, this stuckness is bound to disappear. Your mind will naturally and freely move toward a solution. Unless you are a real master at staying stuck you can't prevent this. The fear of stuckness is needless because the longer you stay stuck the more you see the Quality-reality that gets you unstuck every time. What's *really* been getting you stuck is the running from the stuckness through the cars of your train of knowledge looking for a solution that is out in front of the train.

Stuckness shouldn't be avoided. It's the . . . predecessor of all real understanding. An egoless acceptance of stuckness is a key to an understanding of all Quality, in mechanical work as in other endeavors. It's this understanding of Quality as revealed by stuckness which so often makes self-taught mechanics so superior to institute-trained men who have learned how to handle everything except a new situation.

Comment

Stuckness may have something to do with the poor quality of some examination answers, those in which only a small percentage of the issues appear. While considering the examination question, it may be that some students, to avoid the feeling of being stuck, leap for an easy answer in the form of a readily-known rule. Perhaps the fear of being stuck prevents them from noticing the many issues that should arise in considering whether the rule applies or the possibility that some other rules apply. This same phenomenon must also occur in the practice of law—the fear of stuckness squelching creativity and even competence.

Some problems (on an examination or in practice) *can* be handled by "running from the stuckness through the cars of the train of knowledge." But the students I have described so fear stuckness that they sit down, with a sigh of relief, in the first or second boxcar. They're comfortable, and maybe even pass the examination, but they have not done quality work. And their fear of stuckness may prevent them from recognizing this.

There are other problems that *cannot* be handled by simply searching through one's files of objective information. For these the problem-solver must operate "at the front end of the train of knowledge, at the track of reality itself." This, of course, requires more courage than running through the boxcars.

I have seen the problem in my own teaching—I was "stuck" for my first two years as a law professor. I imitated several teachers whose styles I admired, even when it became clear that my teaching was less effective than I had hoped it would be. I continued in this mode because of my own insecurity. I was not confident enough to try other ways. I wanted to get through the hour. It took me a few years to feel confident enough to experiment with forms of teaching, to reach beyond the first "answer" I came to when I asked myself how I wanted to be as a teacher.

I now want to help students develop their confidence to tolerate ambiguities, to be imaginative and creative. I know they need to feel relatively secure in order to take the risks necessary for true competence. My feeling is that I can ease students' insecurity with being stuck by making it clear that all normal persons (including lawyers, law teachers, and judges) are befuddled at times and that befuddlement can be consistent with competence. My expectation is that students with a realistic sense of self-confidence can and will care about the quality of their work, and that this caring will impel them to overcome the seductive appeal of a static and harmfully narrow view of law.

L.R.

Comment

Pirsig, in his metaphorical description of being stuck, really hits home. How I hate to feel stuck, to be without an answer, *the* answer. My character, my training lead me to run from the situation. "I'm going to know the answer," I vowed, like so many others, during my first days in those large classes.

In this work in humanistic education, I think I'm learning, slowly and grudgingly, to allow the moment of stuckness to last a bit longer—not to reach immediately for the first answer, but to allow an answer or answers to emerge. And each time the situation is upon me anew, there is that split second when I need to decide to allow the moment of stuckness, defying the cries of the voices, inside and out, "What, you don't know the answer?" "What kind of work is this if the answers aren't at hand?" "I knew this couldn't work." "Where's the practical value?"

Nowhere has this been truer than when I try to work with these ideas and approaches with law students and law teachers. Whether they learned it from the law schools or the culture, whether they are responding to their own inner voices or to their anxiety over what it will be like "out there," law students demand practical answers. And that search or, better, demand for the practical can lock them into the moment so that they lose the larger perspective of meaning and the involvement of their own lives. And I, in not allowing that split second where I can accept stuckness, have often responded with an answer that bought off their frustration. I could cite the rule of the statute and put aside the human quandary that was questioning the rule. I could tell a student the explanation that would appear to satisfy a client (or at least keep him or her quiet) while hiding the fear, pain or sense of struggle in the client's urgings. I could, oh so subtly, use my authority to give students a direction while shielding myself and them from the underlying questions about learning and *our* relationship in the study of law that their frustration embodied. Together, in such instances, we have colluded in a little denial of reality and made our world a bit smaller.

Pirsig uses the metaphor of the motorcycle to say something about the subject-object duality. What he says applies to law and learning about law. We learn, and teach, it seems to me, to see the law as outside and cut off from us. In fact, we put tremendous energy into making that seem the case. We are comforted by that way of seeing law, for it masks our questions about the sense of it all and our responsibility in it. When I stand back from that dualistic view, I see it as continually undermining much of what it purports to be constructing. Reality is not so dualistic, and we, individually and as a society, cannot afford to try to hold it so.

Pirsig expands on the duality:

Zen Buddhists talk about "just sitting," a meditative practice in which the idea of a duality of self and object does not dominate one's consciousness. What I'm talking about here in motorcycle maintenance is "just fixing," in which the idea of a duality of self and object doesn't dominate one's consciousness. When one isn't dominated by feelings of separateness from what he's working on, then one can be said to "care" about what he's doing. That is what caring really is, a feeling of identification with what one's doing. When one has this feeling then he also sees the inverse side of caring, Quality itself.

So the thing to do when working on a motorcycle, as in any other task, is to cultivate the peace of mind which does not separate one's self from one's surroundings. When that is done successfully then everything else follows naturally. Peace of mind produces right values, right values produce right thoughts. Right thoughts produce right actions and right actions produce work which will be a material reflection for others to see of the serenity at the center of it all. . . .

I think that if we are going to reform the world, and make it a better place to live in, the way to do it is not with talk about relationships of a political nature, which are inevitably dualistic, full of subjects and objects and their relationship to one another; or with programs full of things for other people to do. I think that kind of approach starts it at the end and presumes the end is the beginning. Programs of a political nature are important *end products* of social quality that can be effective only if the underlying structure of social values is right. The social values are right only if the individual values are right. The place to improve the world is first in one's own heart and head and hands, and then work outward from there. Other people can talk about how to expand the destiny of mankind. I just want to talk about how to fix a motorcycle. I think that what I have to say has more lasting value.   (pp.290-91)

Nothing is plainer in law and legal education than the importance of objectivity, and yet here too there *is* the evil that can cloud any good. For me the danger is that in learning to be objective, what we learn, practice and teach is to objectify. People, human concerns, my own deepest beliefs become problems, issues, points of contention. What started out as an attempt to be clear and true has resulted in a situation where words and ideas dominate to such an extent that the self, which is doing all the objectifying, is lost. What has happened in the attempt not to be overly subjective is that we have lost ourselves as subject; in our attempt to approach law in a way that we thought would bring us closer to the world around us we have adopted ways that cut us off from ourselves and the world.

Pirsig is surely not against all objectivity, but only that which "objectifies." For him to do what he seeks, cultivating right values, right thoughts and right actions requires clarity, self-honesty, and holding firmly and caringly to oneself in all that one does. That is hard for me to do, and I believe it's vital.

If I am to try to bring about social change while at the same time ignoring or defiling the values that I seek in my own actions, then somehow, however subtly, I am destroying what I am seeking to create. That subtle *un*doing is what I have felt myself and others so often doing, despite ourselves, in lawyering and teaching. To speak and learn about justice, equality and fairness in an atmosphere marked by contention, hostility and arrogance is to be guilty of the dualism and objectification of which Pirsig writes. For me this realization does not mean that we must abandon all efforts towards social and political action. It does mean that it is of the essence of such efforts that our individual values and actions be true to what we espouse. When I realize the extent of the duality in me, I believe I have a glimpse of the immensity of the problem *and* the possibilities for change.

J.H.

B. POLARITIES AND PARADOX

Without contraries there is no progression.

—William Blake, *The Marriage of Heaven and Hell*

The reconciliation of the irreconcilable, the merger of antithesis, the synthesis of opposites, these are the great problems of the law. "Nomos," one might fairly say, is the child of antinomies, and is born of them in travail. We fancy ourselves to be dealing with some ultramodern controversy, the product of the clash of interests in an industrial society. The problem is laid bare, and at its core are the ancient mysteries crying out for understanding—rest and motion, the one and the many, the self and the not-self, freedom and necessity, reality and appearance, the absolute and the relative. . . . Is this dreamland or reality? The ground seems to slip beneath our feet, yet a foothold must be found. "Fundamental opposites," I quote from a different context the words of Lytton Strachey in his essay on Pope, "fundamental opposites clash and are reconciled."

—Benjamin N. Cardozo, *The Paradoxes of Legal Science*

Charles Hampden-Turner, Essay (Unpublished, 1978).

When Oedipus first came to Thebes he found it besieged by an anomalous monster, the Sphinx, meaning "she who binds." She had the face and breasts of a woman, the haunches and claws of a lion, and wings. She barred the mountain pass to Thebes and asked all travelers a riddle as monstrous and contradictory as she was. "What creature is it that walks on four legs in the morn-

159

ing, two legs at noonday, and three legs in the evening?'' When Oedipus answered "Man" she sprang from the precipice.

Now the traditional rationale for "value free" social science is precisely that values are so double-binding and Sphynx-like that rational persons should keep away. Consider just four familiar value judgments, the virtues of courage and caution, and the vices of recklessness and cowardice. Each pair includes opposite injunctions, while the virtue of the first two reproaches the vice of the second two. Logical positivism and language analysts have persuasively objected to the non-sense of such judgments.

Suppose we told a man like Oedipus, "Show courage, not cowardice!" Or again, "Show caution, not recklessness." Is anything at all being said? Can this emotionally colored language lead to anything but blows? Positivists have analyzed such language into descriptive and prescriptive parts. Statement one advocates risk-taking, "since in my opinion this is a good thing." Statement two opposes risk-taking, "since in my opinion this is a bad thing." These prescriptive addenda about opinions and good/bad things are said to be subjective, superfluous, unverifiable, mutually contradictory, and hence meaningless. Science can attempt to describe such things as risk-taking, but should leave to the humanities vague exclamations of preference and prescriptive utterances. . . .

No wonder there are few thinkers who even try to lift the siege of crime and decay on our modern cities. The thought processes by which Oedipus solved his riddle are clues to a more general solution to the value perplexity of our times. Consider the following arrangement of the riddle over and under a line.

	creature		four legs		morning
What		is it that walks on		in the	
	noonday	three legs		evening?	
two legs in the		and		in the	

The words above the line are metaphors, while those below are more literal descriptions of man. Hence "morning," "noon," and "evening" are metaphors for stages of man's life, "four legs" are hands and knees, while "three legs" includes a stick. The "monstrous" appearance of the riddle comes from mixing language levels. . . . Genuine contradiction is avoided provided opposite values are laminated together at different levels of logical typing. Let us see how this illumines the nature of value judgments.

Suppose I fell into a dangerous river while walking with a friend. At once he faces dilemma and seeming paradox. "Be courageous, not cowardly! Be altruistic, not selfish!" cries one inner voice. "Be cautious, not reckless! Protect your self-interest from self-destruction!" cries another voice. Is all this meaningless? Not if we organize these values sequentially in time, and by different levels of language. If my friend leaps in to rescue me, courage and altruism are *initially manifested* in his behavior, while caution and egoism are the *latent context* of his motives to be realized later. We may say of him that his present courage is for later caution, and present altruism for later self-interest. Indeed, no sooner has he swum through the waves and secured me, than he should logically let his caution and self-interest start coming to the fore, thus motivating him to get us both out of the river in the shortest order possible! Once on the bank, caution is restored and his self-interest can enjoy being congratulated. This process can be modeled by a feedback loop, thus:

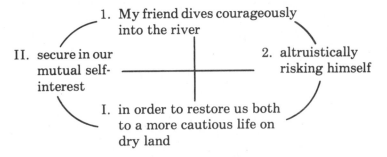

The process moves cyclically clockwise from 1 to II, and dialectically crosswise to and fro between 1 and I and 2 and II. In order to avoid a logical contradiction at any one point of time, the two lines which cross in the center divide object levels from meta-levels of language. Where courage figures, caution is the ground, and vice versa. Wherever altruism figures, self-interest is the ground, and vice versa. Whichever is manifest at one moment is constrained and contained by its latent opposite, which in turn becomes manifest and is contained by *its* opposite. The result is a cybernetic, ecological, open system of values in transaction with its environment. . . . A large variety of bi-modal values can, of course, be substituted for the four illustrated here.

The model also helps us to distinguish courage from recklessness and caution from cowardice, altruism from self-destruction and self-interest from selfishness. There is nothing inherently good or bad in the fact of risk-taking alone. Vice or virtue lies in the manner in which different degrees of risk-taking have been sequentially organized and optimally related. In cases where terms implying virtue are justified, there is between courage and caution and between altruism and self-interest a synergistic relationship (from the Greek syn-ergo "to work with"). My friend develops all four values in an optimal synthesis as a consequence of his rescue. In contrast, where "courage" is cut off from "caution" and the impulses to risk and not to risk are mutually impeding one another, then each split half deteriorates into recklessness and cowardice. Were my friend to leap into the river only to drown while I drowned, then his "altruism" would never reach his "self-interest," even as he failed to reach me, and we might better call him self-destructive. If he sat on the bank crying while I drowned, then his "caution," by failing to reach even the courage of another rescuer, is better called cowardice.

As in *The Fall* by Camus, the personality of a man who fails to rescue a drowning person may literally disintegrate into broken pieces of disvalue, selfishness vs. self-destruction, cowardice vs. recklessness. . . . The failure of human relations and the failure of value-relations are one. No wonder that traditional personifications of evil all possess anomalous aspects. The Sphynx binds us between motherly face and savage claws, as do Jekyll and Hyde, Frankenstein and monster, and the sociopath. Every ghost symbolizes living death, the ultimate contradiction. It attacks our rational ways of processing information and threatens us with madness.

To summarize: Good is an optimal sequential synthesis of binary values integrally "laminated" at different levels of language. Evil is the mutually conflicting juxtaposition of value contradictions at the same level of language. But what passes for good in our culture? My answer is one-dimensional values. Courage with a capital C, Toughness, Loyalty, Individualism, Tenacity. In the words of John Mitchell, "When the going gets tough, the tough get going." Each one-dimensional value represses its opposite virtue, e.g., caution, tenderness, rebellion, cooperation, etc. and regards these as vices, thus dooming our culture to a virulent ecological lop-sidedness, and turning moral arguments into shouting matches. When we do find moral leaders, Socrates, Christ, More, Gandhi, King, we kill them because the dual nature of their moralities is mistaken by one-dimensional people for embodiments of evil. We cannot stand the "crucifix" at the center of the model, the tension between the poles. We reject the essential ambiguity of good for the "pure" banality of evil. We escalate Toughness, Loyalty, Individuality to extremes, and get murderous with those who reproach our brutality, conformity and alienation, since we have no way to reason with them, and the sheer dissonance between the different evaluations enrages us.

Comment

The approach set out by Charles Hampden-Turner seems to me an enormously useful and productive way of looking at a wide range of human problems. We are, all of us, thoroughly indoctrinated in a linear way of thinking about "competing" values. Whether considering such far-ranging questions as the choice between liberty and equality or capitalism and communism, or (in the narrower world of legal education) debating between academic and clinical instruction, or the demands of analytic rigor and those of emotion and value, we are strongly predisposed to see the question as a tug-of-war, in which one pole can "prevail" only at the expense of another. Forced, as we are led to believe, to choose one pole, each of us will do so, and the more we are answered by the arguments of the opposite pole, the more "pure" our insistence on the centrality of that which we are defending will become. The only alternative to the victory of one side in an all-out war is a more or less grudging compromise.

It is often true that the underlying concerns of each pole are not contradictory. Hampden-Turner's metaphor of fidelity to each pole in the context of fidelity to its opposite has for me truly profound wisdom. I will not multiply examples: Justice Holmes long ago spoke of "the equality of position between the parties in which liberty of contract begins" (Coppage v. Kansas, 236 U.S. 1, 27), and one can articulate the same insight for other polarities. It is significant that the method of thinking that Hampden-Turner describes is quite similar to that espoused by authors working in several different disciplines, as the two succeeding excerpts—from writings of Fritjof Capra and E.F. Schumacher—demonstrate.

What these writers are telling us, viewed as philosophy, is that we need to try to develop a way of thinking about human problems that will guide us to a synthesis of important polarities, rather than to battle or compromise. I believe that, viewed psychologically, what is involved is the realization that, if a person is defending one pole by attacking the other, one I hold dear, I can more readily expect to be able to induce him or her to desist from that attack by supporting the first pole than by attacking it. For example, teachers who reject clinical education as insufficiently academic or intellectual often provoke me into expressing vigorously skeptical views about the real value of much academic or intellectual work. Such a response only proves that we are in a zero-sum game. The problem can be transformed through honest assurance (which I believe can be given) that clinical education can provide a context of practice that enhances the academic value of theory, just as theory is a necessary context—too often insufficiently recognized by clinicians committed to the practical—for realizing the meaningfulness of practice.

I do not think that it minimizes human controversy, even in such "narrow" contexts as legal education, let alone in the broader world, to realize that defensiveness is often the result of our being conditioned to think in linear ways, which impair our ability to see in a demand for a more inclusive perspective something other than a demand to surrender the portion of it we most value.

H.L.

Fritjof Capra, *The Tao of Physics*
pp.114-117 (Shambhala 1975).

The Taoists saw all changes in nature as manifestations of
the dynamic interplay between the polar opposites *yin* and *yang*,
and thus they came to believe that any pair of opposites constitutes a polar relationship where each of the two poles is dynami-
cally linked to the other. For the Western mind, this idea of the
implicit unity of all opposites is extremely difficult to accept. It
seems most paradoxical to us that experiences and values which
we had always believed to be contrary should be, after all,
aspects of the same thing. In the East, however, it has always
been considered as essential for attaining enlightenment to go
"beyond earthly opposites," and in China the polar relationship
of all opposites lies at the very basis of Taoist thought. . . .

From the notion that the movements of the *Tao* are a continuous interplay between opposites, the Taoists deduced two
basic rules for human conduct. Whenever you want to achieve
anything, they said, you should start with its opposite. Thus Lao
Tzu:

> In order to contract a thing, one should surely expand it
>   first.
> In order to weaken, one will surely strengthen first.
> In order to overthrow, one will surely exalt first.
> In order to take, one will surely give first.
> This is called subtle wisdom.

On the other hand, whenever you want to retain anything, you
should admit in it something of its opposite:

> Be bent, and you will remain straight.
> Be vacant, and you will remain full.
> Be worn, and you will remain new.

This is the way of life of the sage who has reached a higher
point of view, a perspective from which the relativity and polar
relationship of all opposites are clearly perceived. These opposites include, first and foremost, the concepts of good and bad
which are interrelated in the same way as *yin* and *yang*.
Recognizing the relativity of good and bad, and thus of all moral
standards, the Taoist sage does not strive for the good but rather
tries to maintain a dynamic balance between good and bad.
Chuang Tzu is very clear on this point:

> The sayings, "Shall we not follow and honour the right and
> have nothing to do with the wrong?" and "Shall we not
> follow and honour those who secure good government and
> have nothing to do with those who produce disorder?" show
> a want of acquaintance with the principles of Heaven and
> Earth and with the different qualities of things. It is like

following and honouring Heaven and taking no account of Earth; it is like following and honouring the *yin* and taking no account of the *yang*. It is clear that such a course cannot be pursued.

It is amazing that, at the same time when Lao Tzu and his followers developed their world view, the essential features of this Taoist view were taught also in Greece, by a man whose teachings are known to us only in fragments and who was, and still is, very often misunderstood. This Greek "Taoist" was Heraclitus of Ephesus. He shared with Lao Tzu not only the emphasis on continuous change, which he expressed in his famous saying "Everything flows," but also the notion that all changes are cyclic. He compared the world order to "an everliving fire, kindling in measures and going out in measures," an image which is indeed very similar to the Chinese idea of the *Tao* manifesting itself in the cyclic interplay of *yin* and *yang*.

It is easy to see how the concept of change as a dynamic interplay of opposites led Heraclitus, like Lao Tzu, to the discovery that all opposites are polar and thus united. "The way up and down is one and the same," said the Greek, and "God is day night, winter summer, war peace, satiety hunger." Like the Taoists, he saw any pair of opposites as a unity and was well aware of the relativity of all such concepts. Again the words of Heraclitus—"Cold things warm themselves, warm cools, moist dries, parched is made wet"—remind us strongly of those of Lao Tzu, "Easy gives rise to difficult . . . resonance harmonizes sound, after follows before."

It is surprising that the great similarity between the world views of those two sages of the sixth century B.C. is not generally known. Heraclitus is often mentioned in connection with modern physics, but hardly ever in connection with Taoism. And yet it is this connection which shows best that his world view was that of a mystic and thus, in my opinion, puts the parallels between his ideas and those of modern physics in the right perspective.

Comment

My normal practice is to swing from one end of a contradiction to another—from "I have to be a sister to this client, her life is such a mess, she needs my help so badly," to "I can't get involved at all. I'll be overwhelmed." To save myself from the hazards of this way of thinking, I will grab onto one side tenaciously, never letting go for fear that the only other choice open to me is a leap to the opposite side. In a law school course on collective bargaining, involving a series of negotiation exercises, my style tended to be obstinate, taking a hard line on everything because I assumed there were no alternatives but total collapse.

I understand that it is possible to proceed in other ways—to lay out both sides of the polarity I am struggling with and see what other courses of action appear, or see what I value in each side and figure out whether there is a way of satisfying both sides. For example, how can I both help the client and protect myself from being overwhelmed? Both are worthy ends; why should I have to sacrifice one to the other? In the collective bargaining session we were bogged down in conflict over a minor issue, until one of the negotiators questioned both sides closely to clarify what was really important to each. She then proposed a resolution—very different in form from what each side had been demanding—that met all the concerns. She embraced the contradictions and left them behind.

So, although I see how it can be different, this is a tricky pattern of mine. It is hard to catch myself in the act. I don't feel stuck in one way of looking at a problem—at each moment, I tend to feel that I am looking at it in the only possible way of seeing it.

E.D.

E.F. Schumacher, *A Guide for the Perplexed*
pp.120-128 (Harper & Row 1977).

Unsolved problems tend to cause a kind of existential anguish. . . . [O]ne of the weapons in the modern battle against anguish is the Cartesian approach: "Deal only with ideas that are distinct, precise, and certain beyond any reasonable doubt; therefore, rely on geometry, mathematics, quantification, measurement, and exact observation." This is the way, the only way (we are told) to solve problems; this is the road, the only road, of progress; if only we abandon all sentiment and other irrationalities, all problems can and will be solved. We live in the age of the Reign of Quantity. Quantification and cost/benefit analysis are said to be the answer to most, if not all, of our problems, although where we are dealing with somewhat complex beings, like humans, or complex systems, like societies, it may still take a bit of time until sufficient data have been assembled and analyzed. Our civilization is uniquely expert in problem-solving. There are more scientists and people applying the "scientific" method at work in the world today than there have been in all previous generations added together, and they are not wasting their time contemplating the marvels of the Universe or trying to acquire self-knowledge: they are solving problems. . . .

This extraordinary situation might lead us to inquire into the nature of "problems." We know there are solved problems and unsolved problems. The former, we may feel, present no issue; but as regards the latter: Are there not problems that are not merely unsolved but insoluble?

First, let us look at solved problems. Take a design problem—say, how to make a two-wheeled, man-powered means of transportation. Various solutions are offered which gradually and increasingly converge until, finally, a design emerges which is "the answer"—a bicycle—an answer that turns out to be amazingly stable over time. Why is this answer so stable? Simply because it complies with the laws of the Universe—laws at the level of inanimate nature.

I propose to call problems of this nature *convergent* problems. The more intelligently you (whoever you are) study them, the more the answers *converge*. They may be divided into "convergent problem *solved*" and "convergent problem *as yet unsolved*." The words "as yet" are important, for there is no reason *in principle* why they should not be solved some day. Everything takes time, and there simply has not yet been time enough to get around to solving them. What is needed is more time, more money for research and development . . . and, maybe, more talent.

It also happens, however, that a number of highly able people may set out to study a problem and come up with answers which contradict one another. They do not converge. On the contrary, the more they are clarified and logically developed, the more they *diverge*, until some of them appear to be the exact opposites of the others. For example, life presents us with a very big problem—how to educate our children. We cannot escape it; we have to face it, and we ask a number of equally intelligent people to advise us. Some of them, on the basis of a clear intuition, tell us: "Education is the process by which existing culture is passed on from one generation to the next. Those who have (or are presumed to have) knowledge and experience teach, and those who as yet lack knowledge and experience learn. For this process to be effective, authority and discipline must be set up." Nothing could be simpler, truer, more logical and straightforward. Education calls for the establishment of authority for the teachers and discipline and obedience on the part of the pupils.

Now, another group of our advisors, having gone into the problem with the utmost care, says this: "Education is nothing more nor less than the provision of a facility. The educator is like a good gardener, whose function is to make available healthy, fertile soil in which a young plant can grow strong roots; through these it will extract the nutrients it requires. The young plant will develop in accordance with its own laws of being, which are far more subtle than any human can fathom, and will develop best when it has the greatest possible freedom to choose exactly the nutrients it needs." In other words, education as seen by this second group calls for the establishment, not of discipline and obedience, but of freedom—the greatest possible freedom.

If our first group of advisors is right, discipline and obedience are "a good thing," and it can be argued with perfect logic that if something is "a good thing," more of it would be a better thing, and perfect discipline and obedience would be a perfect thing . . . and the school would become a prison house.

Our second group of advisors, on the other hand, argues that in education freedom is "a good thing." If so, more freedom would be an even better thing, and perfect freedom would produce perfect education. The school would become a jungle, even a kind of lunatic asylum.

Freedom and discipline (obedience) here is a pair of perfect opposites. No compromise is possible. It is either the one or the other. It is either "Do as you like" or "Do as I tell you."

Logic does not help us because it insists that if a thing is true its opposite cannot be true at the same time. It also insists that if a thing is good, more of it will be better. Here we have a very typical and very basic problem, which I call a *divergent problem,* and it does not yield to ordinary, "straight-line" logic; it demonstrates that life is bigger than logic.

"What is the best method of education?" presents, in short, a divergent problem par excellence. The answers tend to diverge, and the more logical and consistent they are, the greater is the divergence. There is "freedom" versus "discipline and obedience." There is no solution. And yet some educators are better than others. . . . If we explained to them our philosophical difficulties, they might show signs of irritation with this intellectual approach. "Look here," they might say, "all this is far too clever for me. The point is: You must *love* the little horrors." Love, empathy, participation mystique, understanding, compassion—these are faculties of a *higher order* than those required for the implementation of any policy of discipline or of freedom. To mobilize these higher faculties or forces, to have them available not simply as occasional impulses but permanently, requires a high level of self-awareness, and that is what makes a great educator.

Education presents the classical example of a divergent problem, and so of course does politics, where the most frequently encountered pair of opposites is "freedom" and "equality," which in fact means freedom versus equality. For if natural forces are left free, i.e., left to themselves, the strong will prosper and the weak will suffer, and there will be no trace of equality. The enforcement of equality, on the other hand, requires the curtailment of freedom—unless something intervenes from a higher level.

I do not know who coined the slogan of the French Revolution*; he must have been a person of rare insight. To the pair of opposites, Liberté and Egalite, irreconcilable in ordinary logic, he added a third factor or force—Fraternite, brotherliness— which comes from a higher level. How do we recognize this fact? Liberty or equality can be instituted by legislative action backed by force, but brotherliness is a human quality beyond the reach of institutions, beyond the level of manipulation. It can be achieved only by individual persons mobilizing their own higher forces and faculties, in short, becoming better people. . . .

Divergent problems . . . cannot be solved in the sense of establishing a "correct formula"; they can, however, be transcended. A pair of opposites—like freedom and order—are opposites at the level of ordinary life, but they cease to be opposites at the higher level, the really *human* level, where self-awareness plays its proper role. It is then that such higher forces as love and compassion, understanding and empathy, become available, not simply as occasional impulses (which they are at the lower level) but as a regular and reliable resource. Opposites cease to be opposites; they lie down together peacefully like the lion and the lamb in Dürer's famous picture of Saint Hieronymus (who himself represents "the higher level"). . . .

It is important for us to become fully aware of these pairs of opposites. Our logical mind does not like them: it generally operates on the either/or or yes/no principle, like a computer. So, at any time it wishes to give its exclusive allegiance to either one or the other of the pair, and since this exclusiveness inevitably leads to an ever more obvious loss of realism and truth, the mind may suddenly change sides, often without even noticing it. It swings like a pendulum from one opposite to the other, and each time there is a feeling of "making up one's mind afresh"; or the mind may become rigid and lifeless, fixing itself on one side of the pair of opposites and feeling that now "the problem has been solved." . . .

In the life of societies there is the need for both justice and mercy. "Justice without mercy," said Thomas Aquinas, "is cruelty; mercy without justice is the mother of dissolution"—a very clear identification of a divergent problem. Justice is a denial of mercy, and mercy is a denial of justice. Only a higher force can reconcile these opposites. . . . Similarly, societies need stability and change, tradition and innovation, public interest and private interest, planning and laissez-faire, order and

---

* Some people say it was Louis-Claude de Saint-Martin (1743-1803) who signed his works Le Philosophe inconnu, the Unknown Philosopher.

freedom, growth and decay. Everywhere society's health depends on the simultaneous pursuit of mutually opposed activities or aims. The adoption of a final solution means a kind of death sentence for man's humanity and spells either cruelty or dissolution, generally both.

Divergent problems offend the logical mind, which wishes to remove tension by coming down on one side or the other, but they provoke, stimulate, and sharpen the higher human faculties, without which man is nothing but a clever animal. A refusal to accept the divergency of divergent problems causes these higher faculties to remain dormant and to wither away, and when this happens, the "clever animal" is more likely than not to destroy itself.

Comment

Before going to law school, I perceived law as a means of solving human, societal and economic problems. I was very excited at the prospect of gaining skills that would enable me to help others and myself out of difficult problems instead of using my analytical skills to study bacteria, as I had originally intended. I thought what I would learn would give me a perspective for understanding many aspects of American life and government that I found confusing and distressing.

I did find problem-solving skills being taught in the law school, but somewhere along the way I became dissatisfied with the means of solving the problems and the solutions. I felt constrained; everything seemed to have been simplified, streamlined and made unreal. The world as presented in law school felt two-dimensional to me: yes/no, win/lose, action/reaction, question/answer, guilty/not. Everything is set up in dichotomies and many times that feels very wrong. I feel I am being taught to solve problems by dissecting away the messy, less concrete parts of the problems and then devising stop-gap half measures that do not begin to deal with the original, or basic, problem. I am being trained to create practical solutions that may be fine for some things, but I find the techniques incapacitating for approaching other areas of law and life—especially the broader societal problems. The two dimensional win/lose syndrome gets in my way when I look for common themes and higher principles. It also makes it very hard for me to recognize the social consequences of the simple "answers" and even to recognize the narrow perspective I am using to "solve" the problem. I also wonder how many problems we actually solve. I find an overwhelming desire for control, order and certainty manifested in our method of solving problems. We lawyers and students help create so much particularistic garbage we can't see the forest anymore.

I was feeling pretty smug about this perception I had about the lawyers' approach to problem solving until I realized how nervous I get in areas of the law that are fuzzy, undecided and broad. I also want badly to have order in my world so I can deal with situations and problems and not be overwhelmed. I know I find it more comfortable to deal with finite objects—amounts of money, contracts and closed systems of black-letter law—than with social questions. The answers to the type of questions and problems I am comfortable with are in books and the courts. For counseling, litigation and planning all I have to do is gather the facts; play with the facts until they fit within a statute or an exception and the "problem" is solved; the course can be plotted. I don't think about the implications of the answers and have no strong feelings about the answers. I've got the only answer that matters—what needs to be done. The judge, jury or client decides. I do not have to search my soul, which makes it emotionally easier for me to handle the situation. The fact that the answers and solutions are found elsewhere (in other people, books and courts) means that I need feel no connection with the problem, as a lawyer or as a person. It is easier to shrug off disappointment when the answers are outside of me, with cynical remarks like "this is the law, not justice."

What is missing for me is a larger perspective that includes myself. I am frustrated because the way I have learned to analyze has never been connected with the world I inhabit. It is very hard for me to maintain a focused awareness of my own thoughts and feelings about a problem, and it is, many times, very uncomfortable. I'd rather not do it. And doing it seems like the best way to make the connection between the legal problem and the problem as it exists in the world.

M.E.

Comment

The polarity between my need for control and my wish to have students take responsibility for their own learning has been a source of considerable tension for me, and I have sought various ways to deal with it. During my first two years of teaching I tried to achieve both objectives by being "Socratic." I refused to answer most questions, and I laid out very little information. I *knew* that students were not learning much in class, and I hoped to force them to learn outside of class. By my third year, I realized that I had to lay out sufficient information to provide a structure secure enough to harbor a creative discussion.

It was at this point that I was struck with the conflict. The more I laid out, the more reinforcement I got from students. It was easy (though not fulfilling) for me, and they seemed happy; clearly they were "learning law." Yet I was markedly uncomfortable. There was a conflict of goals, a discrepancy in levels. My principal goal was to get them to take responsibility for their own learning. They often wanted me to take that same responsibility (or a similar one—for teaching them). We both wanted them to learn the rules of law, but I viewed that as just one operation in a much larger process of learning and development. A good lawyer—which is what I wanted each of them to be—must take responsibility for his or her own learning.

I have come to realize lately that I need some higher principle to resolve this polarity about what to do in the classroom. The resolution derives from the primary feeling that motivates me in teaching: a kind of love or caring for others, a wish to help and to make contact. That makes me see the students' justifiable need for security, and I try to attend to it by giving them some answers that can be easily grasped—teaching "the law," convergent, solved problems. Having done that, I can draw attention to the more open-ended divergent type of problems, which require active student learning. The recourse I have made to my primary motivation in teaching has made my classes more of a collaboration and has largely eliminated the separation I felt from both students and the law during my first five years of teaching.

L.R.

Robert Bolt, *A Man For All Seasons*
pp.37-38 (Vintage 1962).

> (RICH exits. All watch him; the others turn
> to MORE, their faces alert.)

ROPER   Arrest him.

ALICE   Yes!

MORE   For what?

ALICE   He's dangerous!

ROPER   For libel; he's a spy.

ALICE   He is! Arrest him!

MARGARET   Father, that man's bad.

MORE   There is no law against that.

ROPER   There is! God's law!

MORE   Then God can arrest him.

ROPER   Sophistication upon sophistication!

MORE   No, sheer simplicity. The law, Roper, the law. I know what's legal not what's right. And I'll stick to what's legal.

ROPER   Then you set man's law above God's!

MORE   No, far below; but let *me* draw your attention to a fact—I'm *not* God. The currents and eddies of right and wrong, which you find such plain sailing, I can't navigate. I'm no voyager. But in the thickets of the law, oh, there I'm a forester. I doubt if there's a man alive who could follow me there, thank God . . . (He says this last to himself)

ALICE   (Exasperated, pointing after RICH) While you talk, he's gone!

MORE   And go he should, if he was the Devil himself, until he broke the law!

ROPER   So now you'd give the Devil benefit of law!

MORE   Yes. What would you do? Cut a great road through the law to get after the Devil?

ROPER   I'd cut down every law in England to do that!

MORE   (Roused and excited) Oh? (Advances on ROPER) And when the last law was down, and the Devil turned round on you—where would you hide, Roper, the laws all being flat? (He leaves him) This country's planted thick with laws from coast to coast—man's laws, not God's—and if you cut them down—and you're just the man to do it—d'you really think you could stand upright in the winds that would blow then? (Quietly) Yes, I'd give the Devil benefit of law, for my own safety's sake.

ROPER   I have long suspected this; this is the golden calf; the law's your god.

MORE   (Wearily) Oh, Roper, you're a fool, God's my god. . . . (Rather bitterly) But I find him rather too (Very bitterly) subtle . . . I don't know where he is nor what he wants.

ROPER   My god wants service, to the end and unremitting; nothing else!

MORE   (Dryly) Are you sure that's God? He sounds like Moloch. But indeed it may be God—and whoever hunts for me, Roper, God or Devil, will find me hiding in the thickets of the law!

Comment

At his trial, More asserts: "The law is a causeway upon which, so long as he keeps to it, a citizen may walk safely." The values he is expressing so eloquently here are, I think, a powerful aspect of the attraction of the law for many who become lawyers: Law—including its technicality, its separation from morality—serves as an important protection against arbitrary action, and from this perspective, extends that protection to all, whether the Lord Chancellor or a mere citizen.

I have often experienced Roper's eagerness to get after the Devil, and exasperation to realize that the law is so often available for *his* use. Yet I remain committed to the idea that More is, after all, right. Sometimes that commitment seems based on a utilitarian belief that we have a more just society to the extent that it observes a division between what is right and what is lawful than if it did not. That belief often appears to lack firm empirical support. The Devil seems more able to make use of his benefit of law than others whom I regard as more deserving. Robert Bolt refers, in his Preface—p. 17, above—to "Cromwell's contemptuous shattering of the forms of law by an unconcealed act of perjury, [showing] how fragile for any individual is [the] shelter" of the law.

Soundly based or not, I continue to share More's belief. The more pertinent point seems to me that, recognizing and accepting the enormous attraction that law has in its expression of the value More articulates, we need nonetheless to remain concerned about the actual results that the legal system produces. Too often, the sentiments More expresses are voiced in a way that is smug about their rightness and indifferent to their failures to express reality. They need not lead that way.

H.L.

Comment

More is no sophist. His beauty is in his insistence on a subtle but simple path that allows seeming opposites to be one. He will not accept the way of either-or, for neither alternative alone encompasses for him the fullness and reality of the human condition.

The opposites he is dealing with here are familiar ones to those of us who live with law as a study or profession. On the one hand, law is a set of conventions or conveniences easily adaptable for those with the power or wit to move it their way. Truth, justice, goodness exist outside the law. On the other, law defines the boundaries of our ability to pursue the right. We must act, and can only achieve justice, by following the laws that we have created or the procedures for changing those laws. Within this dilemma, individuals and societies have struggled, more perhaps than we can comprehend.

More's words and life suggest a logic of self in the world that transcends that polarity. When he recognizes a right that goes beyond law, he does so with a full, deep and abiding respect for the laws of man. When he argues for the need for fealty to law, he does it in a way that robs no one of duties that can exist beyond law. And in both, he is speaking with the same voice, acting with the same truth.

For me, More speaks and acts with humility. He experiences himself as inextricably bound to a social network. He believes it his duty to work with others within the structures, the laws, that mankind has evolved for mutual protection and well-being. He knows that within that structure he and others can best gain the freedom to live and to live with each other. *And* he knows that he cannot subordinate himself to the social structure in a way that denies the very experience of self that gives meaning to his life, and makes possible his fidelity to law. He is *an individual* in society and must honor his own truth in so far as he knows it.

What is so often for us an elusive way between two irreconcilable positions, or the narrowest of paths seemingly impossible to apprehend or follow, More walks simply, confidently and, what I think enables him to walk it, humbly.

J.H.

5. THE EXPRESSION OF THE SELF

No man is an island, entire of itself;
every man is a piece of the continent,
  a part of the main;
if a clod be washed away by the sea,
  Europe is the less,
    as well as if a promontory were,
    as well as if a manor of thy friends
    or of thine own were;
any man's death diminishes me,
    because I am involved in mankind;
and therefore never send to know
    for whom the bell tolls;
it tolls for thee.

—John Donne, *Devotions*

Carl Rogers, *On Becoming a Person*
pp.26-27 (Houghton Mifflin 1961).

There is one deep learning which is perhaps basic to all of the things I have said thus far. . . . It is simply this. *It has been my experience that persons have a basically positive direction.* In my deepest contacts with individuals in therapy, even those whose troubles are most disturbing, whose behavior has been most anti-social, whose feelings seem most abnormal, I find this to be true. When I can sensitively understand the feelings which they are expressing, when I am able to accept them as separate persons in their own right, then I find that they tend to move in certain directions. And what are these directions in which they tend to move? The words which I believe are most truly descriptive are words such as positive, constructive, moving toward self-actualization, growing toward maturity, growing toward socialization. I have come to feel that the more fully the individual is understood and accepted, the more he tends to drop the false fronts with which he has been meeting life, and the more he tends to move in a direction which is forward.

I would not want to be misunderstood on this. I do not have a Pollyanna view of human nature. I am quite aware that out of defensiveness and inner fear individuals can and do behave in ways which are incredibly cruel, horribly destructive, immature, regressive, anti-social, hurtful. Yet one of the most refreshing and invigorating parts of my experience is to work with such in-

175

dividuals and to discover the strongly positive directional tendencies which exist in them, as in all of us, at the deepest levels.

Comment

Carl Rogers here develops what he means by his daring to believe that human beings have a "deep and underlying thread of commonality" (p. 113, above), which would make full development of human potential a constructive and not a harmful force in the world. Roberto Unger has described the belief "in a correspondence between being and goodness" as one "neither arbitrary nor capable of conclusive proof. To accept it and to act upon it is to run a serious risk. Yet it is a risk a wise man might have reason to assume." *Knowledge and Politics,* p. 248 (Free Press 1975).

I believe that one's espousal or rejection of the faith that Rogers expresses is the single most fundamental choice to be made. To one who is committed to a Hobbesian view of the world, much of what this book is about must seem wrong. One struck by the rightness of much that is here will find, I think, in himself or herself a positive response to Rogers' statement.

I have had many moments when I have felt that the beliefs he expresses are simply pious dreams. I have had a number of moments when they seemed deeply right. When I reflect on the occasions when I have believed one version or the other, I come away convinced to share his faith. The specific occasions in my own life that I am referring to seem more personal right now than what I would want to share with all who might read this. And, here more than in any other area, each of us can be persuaded one way or the other only by the life we are ourselves living.*

H.L.

Peter Marin, *The New Narcissism*
Harper's, Oct. 1975, pp.47-56.

Most of us realize at one level of consciousness or another that we inhabit an age of catastrophe—if not for ourselves then

---

* Nevertheless, Unger's expressed basis for his choice bears recalling here:

> Even when it portrays evil as an independent force at work in the cosmos, religion starts with the notion that the realm of values is somehow grounded in the reality of things; that truth and goodness are partners. This frequent religious perception has a counterpart in the primitive sense that it is better to exist than not to exist. Thus, when philosophy chooses the tie between being and goodness as a first principle, it does no more than embrace an intimation that runs through much of human experience.

> This intimation could, however, be disappointed. Short of relying on revelation, speculative thought cannot deny that there may be some ultimate antagonism between the ideal and actuality, or between the inclinations of consciousness and the objective reality of the world. Nevertheless, to the extent we recognize hope as a virtue inseparable from love and love as something we cannot do without, we may still be willing to risk a commitment to the idea that being and good are joined.

Ibid.

for countless others. Try as we do, we cannot ignore the routine inequities of consumption and distribution which benefit us and condemn others to misery. Each of us must feel a kind of generalized shame, an unanswerable sense of guilt. So we struggle mightily to convince ourselves that our privilege is earned or deserved, rather than (as we must often feel unconsciously) a form of murder or theft. Our therapies become a way of hiding from the world, a way of easing our troubled conscience. What lies behind the form they now take is neither simple greed nor moral blindness; it is, instead, the unrealized shame of having failed the world and not knowing what to do about it. Like humiliated lovers who have betrayed what they love, we turn our faces from the world, if only (in Paul Goodman's phrase) "just to live on a while."

That is what makes our new therapies so distressing. They provide their adherents with a way to avoid the demands of the world, to smother the tug of conscience. They allow them to remain who and what they are, to accept the structured world as it is—but with a new sense of justice and justification, with the assurance that it all accords with cosmic law. We are in our proper place; the others are in theirs; we may indeed bemoan their fate or even, if we are so moved, do something to change it, but in essence it has nothing to do with us.

What disappears in this view of things is the ground of community, the felt sense of collective responsibility for the fate of each separate other. What takes its place is a moral vacuum in which others are trapped forever in a "private" destiny, doomed to whatever befalls them. In that void the traditional measures of justice or good vanish completely. The self replaces community, relation, neighbor, chance, or God. Looming larger every moment, it obliterates everything around it that might have offered it a way out of its pain.

The end result of this retreat from the complexities of the world is a kind of soft fascism: the denial, in the name of higher truth, of the claims of others upon the self. Our deification of the self becomes equal in effect and human cost to what Nietzsche long ago called the "idolatry of the state." Just as persons once set aside the possibilities of their own humanity and turned instead to the state for a sense of power and identity no longer theirs, so we now turn to the self, giving to it the power and importance of a god. In the worship of the state, life gives way to an abstraction, to the total submission of individual will. In the worship of the self, life also gives way to an abstraction, in this case to an exaggeration of the will. The result in both cases is the same. What is lost is the immense middle ground of human community. The web of reciprocity and relation is broken. The world diminishes. The felt presence of the other disappears, and with it a part of our own existence.

The real horror of our present condition is not merely the absence of community or the isolation of the self—those, after all, have been part of the American condition for a long time. It is the loss of the ability to remember what is missing, the diminishment of our vision of what is humanly possible or desirable. In our new myths we begin to deny once and for all the existence of what we once believed both possible and good. We proclaim our grief-stricken narcissism to be a form of liberation; we define as enlightenment our broken faith with the world. Already forgetful of what it means to be fully human, we sip still again from Lethe, the river of forgetfulness, hoping to erase even the memory of pain. Lethe, lethal, lethargy—all of those words suggest a kind of death, one that in religious usage is sometimes called accidie. It is a condition one can find in many places and in many ages, but only in America, and only recently, have we begun to confuse it with a state of grace. . . .

The natural direction of human ripening is from the smaller to the larger world, is toward the realization and habitation of ever-widening realms of meaning and value. Just as the young are moved from the inside out through increasingly complex stages of perception and thought demanding corresponding changes in their environment, so, too, adults are moved from inside themselves through increasingly complex stages of relation: past the limits of ego and into a human community in which the self becomes other than it was. Seen in this way, human fulfillment hinges on much more than our usual notions of private pleasure or self-actualization, for both of those in their richest forms are impossible without communion and community, an acknowledgement of liability, and a significant role in both the polis and the moral world. To be deprived of those is to be deprived of a part of the self, and to turn away from them is to betray not only the world but also the self, for it is only in the realms in which others exist that one can come to understand the ways in which the nature of each individual existence is in many ways a collective act, the result of countless other lives.

The traditional image for what I am talking about has always been the harvest: the cooperative act in which comrades in a common field gather from it what they need. One finds the image repeated in the work of Camus, Giono, Kropotkin, Lawrence, Silone, and many others, but the most vivid example I know is the scene in *Anna Karenina* in which Levin labors in a field with the peasants, losing all sense of himself in the shared rhythms of the work, the deep blowing grain, and the heat of the sun on his body. It is an image of ecstatic relation which is as much an expression of Eros as is the emblem of two lovers tangled in embrace, and it can stand for almost every aspect of our lives. Every privilege, every object, every "good" comes to us as the result of a human harvest, the shared labor of others: the language we use and the beliefs we hold and the ways we experience ourselves. Each of these involves a world of others into which we are entered every moment of our lives. . . .

That, I believe, is what each of us already knows—no matter how much we pretend we do not. Our lives are crowded with the presence of unacknowledged others upon whom our well-being and privilege depend. The shadows of those neglected others— dying in Asia, hungry in Africa, impoverished in our own country—fall upon every one of our private acts, darken the household and marriage bed for each of us. We try to turn away, but even the desperate nature of our turning is a function of their unacknowledged presence, and they are with us even in the vehemence with which we pretend they are not. Something in each of us . . . aches with their presence, aches for the world, for why else would we be in so much pain?

The question of the age, we like to think, is one of survival, and that is true, but not in the way we ordinarily mean it. The survival we ordinarily mean is a narrow and nervous one: simply the continuation, in their present forms, of the isolated lives we lead. But there is little doubt that most of us *will* survive as we are, for we are clearly prepared to accept whatever is necessary to do so: the deaths of millions of others, wars waged in our name, a police state at home. Like the Germans who accepted the Fascists, or the French citizens who collaborated with the Germans, we, too, will be able to carry on "business as usual," just as we do now. Our actual crisis of survival lies elsewhere, in the moral realm we so carefully ignore, for it is there that our lives are at stake. . . .

Physicists sometimes use a lovely word, *elsewhere*, to describe the realms of being which we can postulate in thought but can never enter or demonstrate to exist. It is as if they existed side by side with the known world but were beyond all human habitation or touch. In a sense, *elsewhere* also exists in the moral realm, for whatever we fail to love or inhabit fully fades into it, is like a ghostly presence around us, a reality we vaguely remember or intuit, but which is no longer ours. Thus, in a very real way the nature of the shared human world does depend on our actions and words, and we can destroy it not only with bombs, but through our failure to inhabit it as fully and as humanly as we should.

Comment

What Marin writes raises the fundamental question of the relation between self and others: whether responsibility to one's self means or precludes one's responsibility to humankind. For me the saving promise of the humanistic approach as we have been trying to understand and develop it, what makes it ultimately meaningful, rests in the commitment (not always honored) to self-truth. The commitment to self-truth that I understand, feel and believe includes the commitment to my fellow humans, not so much because that is a moral edict but because it *is* the essential truth of the human condition.

The danger of narcissism in the humanistic approaches to growth, therapy and education is real, and if we do not see the dangers in what we believe, no matter how good and noble our beliefs, then we will surely lose our way. Like Marin, I have seen the notion of self-responsibility used and abused as a way of avoiding responsibility to and with others. I have experienced using it that way myself, but never without a deep feeling of there being something wrong and untrue in doing that.

Where I have difficulty with Marin, as I read this passage, is in the implication that looking within ourselves is necessarily narcissistic while looking to the outside is necessarily inclusive of humanity. My experience has been that looking outward is no sure proof that I will see the other. Indeed, it seems to me that there are ways of looking outward—social, political, and philosophical—that can run from the essence of the human condition. In the law school, as elsewhere, I have seen us abuse each other vociferously in the name of truth and social justice. We can limit our vision and become misguided, whether in looking within or looking outward. It is the truth in the vision, not the direction, that is telling. When it is true, I see both within and without. We can discover the truth within others as we look within ourselves. We can see the truth within ourselves as we look to others.

The danger of narcissism is real. My belief is that it is real precisely because when we look within, and here I believe I am in agreement with what Marin has written, we inevitably come upon how deep our responsibility to others truly is. We can become confused, defensive, and want to hide from this realization in some other reality. In accepting that responsibility we see how deep our grief is for the plight of the human condition, how important the contribution we can make, how little we can do, and how much we need others to do it.

J.H.

Comment

I don't see my commitment to the concept of responsibility for oneself as in any way implying lack of responsibility for anyone else or for the world. And so, when I read this article, I was horrified by Marin's examples; but I did not read them as a warning to *me*. Yet I know that in law school when we discuss a legal topic, I enjoy its complexity and have fun arguing. I get absorbed in the intellectual challenge—and often don't consider its effect on real people. This is a form of retreat to personal pleasure, a way I detach myself from the world.

This problem is particularly real when we're dealing with a complex statutory scheme. When the class is studying the Internal Revenue Code or the UCC I can have a lot of fun. It's exciting to follow the drafters' ingenuity (or lack thereof). I get a kick out of seeing the different meanings and varied purposes a simple word can serve. The feeling is comparable to doing a crossword puzzle or reading a murder mystery. I can have a lot of fun because my active participation (through understanding, remembering, and developing the ability to manipulate the sections) is so necessary to complete the work of the drafters. Their work will fail if it can't be grasped. And each time a new person understands and makes use of their scheme, it is given new life and added validity. When I am studying at home or taking notes in class, that sort of admiration for the drafters is the closest I get to relating the statutes and concepts to real people writing checks, going bankrupt, or being brought down by someone else's bankruptcy.

But the point of Article 4 of the UCC isn't only how slick the banking lawyers were in controlling its content. The intricacy of any such statutory scheme is not an end in itself, created for pleasure or frustration in working with it. While I know that these two statements are true, at the same time I often don't understand and fully absorb their truth. I don't bother to: It's enough to know that I understand the statute.

I am capable of learning law as a closed system, a series of interrelated concepts, free of morality, without any impact on anyone's life. I sometimes prefer to approach law as an abstraction. If it is absorbing enough, that's what I do. When I do that, although I am holding myself responsible for learning and understanding the legal concepts, I am absolving myself from responsibility for the effect of the concepts.

This sort of separation is harmful. It hurts me because it puts me in a fantasy world. It hurts the law because I (and, I imagine, other law students) don't develop the habit of demanding that the law be responsive to the people whose lives it regulates. Most painful of all, I lose any sense of community (beyond the community of legal minds) and responsibility to the community of people I will join as a person who is a lawyer.

E.D.

Robert N. Bellah, *The New Religious Consciousness and the Secular University*
Daedalus, pp.110-115 (Fall 1974).

One way of getting at the ethos of the secular university today is to characterize its central value as "cognitive rationality." ... [Talcott] Parsons is probably right in saying that this is the central value around which the university is organized. But I am not quite so happy about that fact as Parsons tends to be. It is not ... that I don't respect cognitive rationality, but that I think there are other things in the world with which the university might be concerned as well. At its best, "cognitive rationality" means "disciplined knowing," not simply the acquisition of knowledge . . . but learning to learn, the process of inquiry itself. This statement of the normative commitment, the basic value system of the secular university, obviously has a link to traditional, philosophical, and religious commitments and to traditions of education that stretch back far before the emergence of the secular university. The pursuit of truth for its own sake can become, and has become, a kind of supreme rationality, like that which Spinoza expresses in the notion of the intellectual love of God. . . . [T]here is a point at which rationality transcends itself, merges with nonrational ways of knowing, and becomes one way of attaining the vision of divine truth, of ultimate reality. Even when that particular chain of connections is not made in traditional ways of thinking about the pursuit of knowledge, the quest of reason has been seen as involved in a complex of human activities that includes feeling, moral evaluation and action in the world.

For most of what the secular university does, however, cognitive rationality or disciplined knowing does not go beyond a simple desire to understand things—how they operate, why they came to be, and what they may do next. But even in that relatively mundane form, cognitive rationality exists precariously in the university. It exists on sufferance, so to speak, in relation to a pervasive notion in our culture that, after all, knowing is not an end in itself. It is simply a means. Knowledge is a tool for the manipulation of the world. The pervasive emphasis on the manipulative instrumental use of knowledge has tended to make of the university a kind of universal filling station where students tank up on knowledge they will "need" later. . . . The ethos behind this conception of education is very general in the culture. It is rooted in the deep American value of pragmatism. . . .

The Old Right and the New Left agree that education is useless unless it is related to rather immediate ends in "the real world." The implication is that the university is *not* the "real world," that the "real world" is somehow outside the university, and that work within the university can be justified only insofar as it is a means to an end in the "real world." According to this conception, the university is composed of atomized, individualistic students with certain fixed impermeable goals. The university's only purpose is to help students attain their goals by communicating to them certain discrete skills and certain discrete bodies of fact about the external world which they can then "use."

Education in the great traditional societies as well as in primitive and archaic societies is by and large as different from this picture as one could imagine. . . . Education traditionally is initiation in the sense of initiation into reality with a capital "R."

It involves heart, and soul, and body. Initiation is . . . a radical process involving the whole person in relation to his whole environment; it differs sharply from the idea of a closed, atomized individual manipulating an equally closed, objective world. Traditionally, education was involved in the formation of a new person ideally more perceptive than when he began, one more aware of the whole of existence, including its tragic dimension, and more responsive as a human being. Such education involved not only cognitive skills but a discipline of body, of feelings, of imagination, as well as of mind.

Traditionally education was not a relationship between a closed subject and an alien object, but the development of a transformed person in relation to the organic whole which included his society, the natural world, the whole cosmos. If that description has any validity, it will be apparent how sharp the contrast is with the kind of education typical of the contemporary, secular university. Even though there is perhaps no word used more often today than "experience," the experiential dimension is extraordinarily weak in the kind of education that we purvey. . . .

The victory of cognitive rationality as the central value in higher education had its roots in the rise of the graduate school in the late nineteenth century, was advanced by the emergence of mass-educational institutions in the twentieth century and was not complete until after World War II. Only recently have the remnants of a fuller conception of education been finally washed out of the American university. . . .

Thus far, I have painted the traditional form of consciousness in its brightest hue. The other side is a narrow dogmatism, a repressive authoritarianism, and an absolute lack of openness. During the seventeenth century the growing empirical consciousness challenged all established powers. In the name of rationality, it undermined every status quo, every doctrinaire assertion of social and religious institutions. It helped in the immense release of . . . human energies. . . . The secular consciousness had a genuine transcendent element especially where it challenged established tyrannies. In the religious field, it led to the undermining of established authorities, both clerical and textual, and the rise of higher criticism. It unmasked all assertions about religious man, ending in the late nineteenth and early twentieth centuries with Marx and Nietzsche, and Freud, the three great unmaskers of the pretensions of *Homo religiosus*. And that, too, was a liberation. . . .

Modern secularism, while releasing human beings from one kind of tyranny, often imposed a new, more terrible tyranny, however—the tyranny of the pragmatic world of every day, of the givenness of immediate reality with all its constraints. It has resulted in the rise of the bureaucratic, technological, and manipulative man, who rejects all transcendence, who has what Blake called "single vision." There is something deeply demonic in the single vision of modern secular consciousness with the vast range of human experience that it tends to shut out.

From its beginning, the modern secular culture has faced critical opposition and, eventually, movements from inside that cautioned: "Beware! What kind of human being will this liberating revolution finally produce?". . .

These possibilities are at the moment only incipient. We have a long way to go before their full implications will be clear. But here at least is one small point where the profound schism in our culture, the schism between the disembodied intellect and our whole humanity, might possibly begin to be overcome, where the initiatory element of education might begin to be regained.

Roger Cramton, *The Ordinary Religion of the Classroom*
29 J. Leg. Educ. 247, 262-263 (1978).

Modern dogmas entangle legal education—a moral relativism tending toward nihilism, a pragmatism tending toward an amoral instrumentalism, a realism tending toward cynicism, an individualism tending toward atomism, and a faith in reason and democratic processes tending toward mere credulity and idolatry. We will neither understand nor transform these modern dogmas unless we abandon our unconcern for value premises. The beliefs and attitudes that anchor our lives must be examined and revealed.

Our indifference to values confines legal education to the *"what is"* and neglects the promise of *"what might be."* It confirms a bias deeply engrained in many law students—that law school is a training ground for technicians who want to function efficiently within the status quo.

The aim of all education, even in a law school, is to encourage a process of continuous self-learning that involves the mind, spirit and body of the whole person. This cannot be done unless larger questions of truth and meaning are directly faced.

If all law and truth are relative, pressing one's own views on others would be arrogant and mischievous. But if there is really something that can be called truth, beauty or justice—even if in our finiteness we cannot always agree on what it is—then law school can be a place of searching and creativity that aspires to identify and accomplish justice. If ethical relativism reigns supreme, law will become ever more complex and detailed, and finally boring, and law school will merely be a dull and unpleasant place on the gateway to a supposedly learned profession. At least the scientist, even if he is an ethical relativist, has something new to discover about the world of nature. If truth and justice have no reality or coherence, what does the lawyer have to do? And why should a trade school—for that is what it would be—occupy space on the university campus?

Law schools and legal educators are inevitably involved in the service of values. For the most part they serve as priests of the established order and its modern dogmas. The educator has an obligation to address the values that he is serving; and there is room for at least a few prophets to call the legal profession and the larger society back to a covenant faith and moral commitment that it has forsaken. The New Testament, Paul Tillich reminds us, speaks of "doing the truth." "Truth," he says, "is hidden and must be discovered. . . . Truth is something new, something which is *done* by God in history, and, because of this, something which is *done* in the individual life. . . . [T]ruth is *found* if it is done, and *done* if it is found. . . . Saving truth is in him that does the truth."

Paul Nash, *Theory & Practice of Humanistic Education* (unpublished, 1979).

Dialogue

An essential requirement of interpersonal competence is the ability to engage in dialogue. By this I do not mean merely being able to talk. I am using the word "dialogue" in a strict sense, with certain quite specific characteristics. . . .

Listening. . . . Why is good listening so rare? Because it is difficult and because its difficulties are commonly underestimated. We often think we are listening when in fact we are engaged in a conventional, social, academic, or commercial game in which a period of "listening" is called for by the rules. It is not considered polite or acceptable for one person to talk all the time (except in carefully structured situations of audience control such as lectures), so we must give the other person his share of air time even though we know his views are of trifling importance compared with our own nuggets of golden wisdom. We politely await our turn to speak, adopting the well-learned manners and body language of a person "listening." During the waiting period, the customary way to pass the time is to prepare our next remark, perhaps picking up a slip of weakness in the other's argument, which we can in our turn correct or refute, using our correction as a launching pad for our next demonstration of forensic brilliance.

Openness—Dialogue requires a particular kind of openness from the participants. Basically, this means my respecting and being open to the other person and his persuasion. Respect includes the belief that he has a right to participate and express his views, that he is worth listening to, and that he may be in touch with insights that are not apparent to me. Consequently, I must be open to being changed or persuaded by him. This is not possible if I enter into the interacting in the spirit of the traditional missionary, seeking the conversion of the other from a base of absolute certainty about the rightness of my own position. Since this latter attitude is taken by a large proportion of the teachers in schools and colleges, dialogue in the typical classroom is rare. This need for openness applies also to recognizing the other as a unique person rather than as a member of a category. A major hazard to dialogue is the temptation we have to put the other person into a "box" or classification.... If I do this, the danger is that I will then see and hear only the box, not the person.... Or we put this suggested idea into a box. "I've tried it before, it doesn't work." Thus, we save ourselves the trouble of really listening to the person or idea....

Building—Dialogue must be built by the participants. This may sound trite, but it is worth saying because so much human interaction appears to ignore it. Building is the opposite of what we are trained to do in academic seminars, that is, to point out the flaws and weaknesses in others' facts and arguments, to destroy others' hypotheses and suggestions, to put down others and elevate oneself by showing one's intellectual superiority. To build means to see the potentially creative part in the other's contribution, to relate one's own contributions to it and to add to it in such a way that something new emerges that neither person could have created alone....

Equality—All partners in the dialogue are equals. Superordination and subordination of status are harmful to dialogue. It is hard for most of us to avoid trying to please our superiors or to resist the temptation to control, browbeat, or patronize our inferiors. And all such activities are enemies of the search for truth, which is the object of dialogue. It is more difficult to save ourselves and others from illusion and delusion if we operate in hierarchical situations. It is possible to pursue dialogue in such situations if the participants are able to discipline themselves so that, in the exchange of views, distinctions of status and power disappear and each statement is assessed only on its own merit. But this is enormously difficult to achieve in practice, as anyone can attest who has watched a teacher steer, control, and manipulate a classroom discussion so that the conclusion she had previously reached is eventually arrived at by "democratic" process. One rough test of the quality of the dialogue is to assess how much change occurs in the views of the members. If people, especially those of higher status or power, habitually leave the situation by the same door that they entered, we can have justifiable doubts as to whether dialogue is occurring.

Comment

I want to relate a situation that occurred toward the end of the year in my freshman criminal procedure class. To describe it I must first elaborate on my primary teaching methodology. After reassuring myself, via a gentle Socratic dialogue with much positive reinforcement, of the class' basic understanding of a principal case's rationale and conclusion, I then try to encourage a more thorough appreciation of the issue by leading them through the development of the arguments on both sides of some related but unresolved point.

In the particular class in question we had just finished our initial consideration of the case in which the Supreme Court concluded that for fourth amendment purposes, the risk one assumes in talking to another that the other will betray his confidence is not appreciably heightened by the fact that the other is at that time surreptitiously recording or electronically transmitting the conversation: that regardless of whether the listener is wired for sound, the speaker must assume the risk that the statement will be turned over to the police or that the listener will in fact already be a police officer, and that neither eventuality is an unreasonable search and seizure in violation of the fourth amendment. I then asked the class how the issue might be presented to a state supreme court when litigated under the terms of a state constitutional provision that basically tracks the fourth amendment but with additional explicit guarantees against unreasonable invasions of privacy.

After we developed the arguments that would be presented by both counsel for the defendant and for the state, I startled myself by observing to the class that I could not present the state's side of that particular issue. I was not at all startled that I should have such a position. Indeed, during my pre-teaching criminal practice, half of which was as prosecutor and half as defense counsel, in both roles I not infrequently declined to pursue a particular possibility because of ethical considerations. While one might argue that those ethical constraints that delimit acceptable trial strategy are somehow qualitatively different from philosophical concerns about the proper relationship between the individual and the state in a free society, I would strongly disagree. Both concerns are grounded in values that should guide one's decisions if those decisions are to be principled. *What* one argues is, to me, every bit as important as *how* one argues. This is not to suggest, of course, that all need reach the same conclusion on any given issue.

No, I was hardly surprised that I should take such a position. What was genuinely startling was that I should have announced it to the class. During my entire teaching career I have meticulously attempted to avoid abusing the power inherent in that position by imposing, even unintentionally, my views on my students.

To the extent that students do mimic their perception of a professor's positions, I think that it is largely a function of the students' demeaning (to the professor) idea that the professor will somehow think better of them. Such repetition probably has no long-term ill effect other than possible reinforcement of the misguided notion that such a hypocritical stance is appropriate behavior. However, there may be a few, who, in the process of parroting a position, subconsciously internalize it; and there may be a few, who, for whatever reason, are simply too readily swayed by what they think an authority figure believes.

With the foregoing in mind I have, with very rare exception, deliberately avoided revealing my personal views on issues that would arise in the classroom. I realize that one in the role of teacher cannot be completely effective at masking his positions, but I tried to do the best I could. Outside of the classroom, after attempting to lay a groundwork of mutuality, I would be happy to share my views on almost any subject.

My revealing to the class my personal position on the criminal procedure issue (no doubt a common practice for many professors) may have been a major breakthrough for me. This abrupt about-face of such a long standing rule of classroom behavior must have been the spontaneous manifestation of two interrelated ideas that seem basic to humanistic education. One *shares* values rather than imposing them, and one relates to others as whole persons. I had always been sensitive to the former but rarely to the latter. By trying to establish a groundwork of mutuality in extra-classroom exchanges, I had been paying heed to both. But my fastidious concern with avoiding the imposition of values in the classroom had been at the expense of any regard for the students as whole persons. Indeed, my use of control and responsibility in class, which allowed me to deal with students in a highly compartmentalized manner, made sharing of values impossible. I had not regarded them with that respect that would have facilitated, and been characterized by, the *exchange* of ideas. I was caught in the dilemma of either risking imposing my values or withholding an important aspect of myself. My unexpected willingness to avoid that dilemma was related, I think, to my having begun to share responsibility and control with my students.

Clearly there are important differences in the roles of student and teacher, and clearly there must be differences in the allocation of control and responsibility between the two. Yet I realize that the balance I had traditionally struck undermined our mutual opportunity for learning and growth.

W.M.

William Simon, *The Ideology of Advocacy: Procedural Justice and Professional Ethics,* 1978 Wis.L. Rev. 30, 130-143.

The choice between the Ideology of Advocacy* and nonprofessional advocacy rests on one's view of the relative priorities of individuality and stability, and of the prospects of

* [For Simon's conception of the Ideology of Advocacy, see pp.26-27, above.]

reconciling the tension between them.[236] Non-professional advocacy is difficult to describe with precision, but it is not at all mysterious. On the contrary, it relies on a style of thought and conduct with which everyone has at least some familiarity. The foundation principle of non-professional advocacy is that the problems of advocacy be treated as a matter of *personal* ethics. As the notion is generally understood, personal ethics presupposes two ideas diametrically opposed to the foundation principles of the Ideology of Advocacy. First, personal ethics apply to people merely by virtue of the fact that they are human individuals. The obligations involved may depend on particular circumstances or personalities, but they do not follow from social role or station. Personal ethics are at once more particular and more general than professional ethics. On the one hand, they require that every moral decision be made by the individual himself; no institution can define his obligations in advance. On the other hand, the individual may be called upon to answer for his decisions by any other individual who is affected by them. No specialized group has a monopoly which disqualifies outsiders from criticizing the behavior of its members. Second, personal ethics require that individuals take responsibility for the consequences of their decisions. They cannot defer to institutions with autonomous ethical momentum.

Personal ethics involve both a concern for one's own integrity and respect for the concrete individuality of others.[237] The

236. The principle thrust of the present argument is that adversary advocacy is incompatible with the norms of individuality to which it appeals. . . .

Individuality and community are best viewed, not as opposing norms, but rather as interdependent aspects of what Unger calls the Paradox of Sociability. Unger, [Knowledge and Politics] 215-17. The notion of individuality depends on the norms of community because individuality is a social phenomenon. Because an individual's sense of self depends on recognition by others, individuality can flourish only in a community committed to the autonomy, responsibility, and dignity of each of its members. At the same time, the notion of community depends on the norms of individuality because it implies voluntary commitment to the values which are the basis of the community, and voluntary acceptance of membership in the community. For the members to exercise the voluntary choice necessary to form a genuine community, their capacities as individuals must be developed.

Thus, the notion of individuality discussed here implies a complementary rather than an antagonistic notion of community. For instance . . . a style of advocacy which seriously respected individuality would be more likely to promote mutuality and altruism in the judicial process than partisan advocacy. This is because people actually do hold communitarian values which partisan advocacy represses. . . .

237. The concern for both one's own integrity and the integrity of others makes personal ethics somewhat problematical. It raises difficult questions in situations where one's own ends and the ends of others conflict. . . . [O]ne of the ways in which personal ethics deal with such situations is by referring to social norms and institutions such as those associated with law. Conceived in this way, personal ethics differ from two other alternatives to professional ethics: radical individualist ethics and radical politicization.

Radical individualist ethics hold that moral decisions should be a matter of entirely autonomous, independent, non-professional advocate presents himself to a prospective client as someone with special talents and knowledge, but also with personal ends to which he is strongly committed. The client should expect someone generally disposed to help him advance his ends, but also prepared to oppose him when the ends of advocate and client conflict. . . .

Non-professional advocacy does not preclude conflict. Conflict is possible both inside and outside of the relationship. Where their ends are opposed, the advocate may engage in conflict with the client (although obviously any large measure of conflict will end the relationship). Where their ends are shared, advocate and client may join together to engage outsiders in conflict. On the other hand, non-professional advocacy does not presuppose conflict. . . . The advocate may lead the client to modify or abandon a collision course so as to make voluntary, informal resolution possible. Indeed, one of the most important effects of non-professional advocacy should be to increase the client's concern for the impact of his conduct on others, and to enlarge the minimal role which norms such as reciprocity and community now play in attorney-client decisions.

If the major foundation principle of non-professional advocacy is that advocacy be deemed a matter of personal ethics, the major principle of conduct is this: advocate and client must each justify himself to the other. This justification need not embrace the person's entire life, but merely those aspects of it which bear on the dispute. Each must justify the goals he would

and self-conscious choice by the individual decision-maker. . . . From this point of view, social norms and institutions, and even the concrete ends of other people, are at best irrelevant and at worst oppressive constraints on the moral freedom of the individual. The radical individualist approach is unsatisfactory because it fails to take adequate account of the social dimension of individuality. Because the individual's sense of self depends on recognition by others, individuality depends on social relations. To a significant extent, individuality can only be expressed in terms which are meaningful to others. A person whose ethical choices were entirely independent of social norms and the ends of others could not have a coherent moral personality. . . .

The approach of radical politicization holds that moral decisions should be entirely instrumental to the establishment of a new social order. . . . From this point of view, existing social norms and institutions and the concrete ends of individuals are merely reflections of the in-

justice and repressiveness of the existing order. Moral decision on the basis of personal ethics must await the establishment of the new order. This view suffers from the defects of moralities of the long run. . . . It treats existing norms, institutions, and personal ends as means to future ones, and hence collapses process into result. The problems of justice and freedom must be confronted in the course of social change; they cannot be deferred to an idealized future order. Moreover, the radical politicization approach ignores the extent to which the ideals for which it strives are themselves rooted in existing social norms and institutions and the concrete present concerns of individuals. To a significant extent, the realization of these ideals may require the resolution of problems and contradictions within the existing order. In relying solely on a vague idealized negation of the existing order, radical politicization begs the questions presented by these problems and contradictions. . . .

pursue and the way he would pursue them. In this manner, the advocate-client relation is reconstructed in each instance by the participants themselves. It is not set in advance by formal roles. Such relationships will sometimes arise spontaneously, but they will often arise only after patient, step-by-step efforts. Advocate and client may become friends . . . in the . . . familiar sense of an intimacy made possible by shared ends and experience. Yet, friendship is not necessary to the relationship. The basic requirement is that each have respect for the other as a concrete individual. In addition, some sharing of ends will be necessary, but this sharing need not approach a complete coincidence of ends.

Trust is an important value in non-professional advocacy. But it is not a formal, definitional property of the advocate-client relation. It is a quality which the parties must create or fail to create in each instance. When confidentiality may be important to the client, advocate and client should arrive at some understanding at the outset concerning this issue. The scope of confidentiality need not be defined for the entire relation at the outset. It can be defined in stages as lawyer and client gain greater understanding of each other. The client's claim to assurances of confidentiality is a strong one, and once assurances have been made, his claim that they be honored is much stronger still. Yet, these claims must be viewed in the context of other, potentially conflicting values. They must be considered in the context of the specific ends which the client seeks to further. The claim of a client who seeks legal services to exploit or oppress another cannot have the same priority as the claim of one who seeks to escape exploitation and oppression. This approach to the problem of confidentiality means that the client must take a risk in seeking an advocate, and that the advocate-client relation will sometimes end in betrayal. This element of risk is inherent in any effort by lawyer and client to come to terms with each other as concrete individuals. It is in part because of this risk that trust, when it is created, can be a vital and concrete psychological reality rather than an empty, formal claim.

The non-professional relation is quite different from the "helping" or "accepting" lawyer-client relation described by recent writing which draws on the concepts and jargon of existentialist psychotherapy. This writing is valuable because it recognizes that the task of understanding the client's ends is a difficult one, and that the client's consciousness of his own ends is shaped in the lawyer-client relation. It also acknowledges, at least partially, that the lawyer's posture of detachment can threaten, rather than safeguard, the client's autonomy. Yet, the relation of relatively intimate, sympathetic, and personal involvement prescribed by the psychotherapists is unsatisfactory. Although these writers purport to be concerned with respecting the client's concrete individuality, the style of practice they propose will often be more of a threat to it than traditional advocacy. As they describe him, the lawyer claims to be dedicated to his client's concrete individuality, but he does not present *himself* to the client as a concrete individual. Individuals have ends about which they care deeply. Even the most tolerant individual cannot view everyone's ends with the same undifferentiated sympathy. Yet, the psychotherapists seem to contemplate that the same homogeneous acceptance be dispensed indiscriminately to the exploiters and the exploited, the creative and the destructive, the smug and the despairing. No individuality of any depth could be expressed through such an attitude.

A relation defined in advance in terms of acceptance is more likely to be a relation of bureaucratic impersonality than one of respect and understanding. . . . The fact that the lawyer withholds or denies his private ends, while he seeks to ascertain his client's, undermines the credibility of his claim of loyalty to the client. The lawyer's posture of selflessness often will seem either false and hypocritical, or a defensive retreat to the refuge of role. In either event, the client will be led . . . to retreat himself rather than . . . to open himself to understanding by the lawyer. Moreover, . . . tension and even conflict is often essential to the growth of both self-consciousness and mutual understanding. The flaccid, undifferentiated sympathy so extravagantly dispensed by the psychotherapists may discourage precisely the kind of doubt, questioning, and reflection which would best enhance the client's understanding of his own ends. Non-professional advocacy must recognize that a relation of respect and understanding between autonomous individuals can rarely be an entirely accepting relation. Respect and understanding will often depend more on resistance than on acceptance.

One of the most important questions raised by non-professional advocacy concerns the bases for the establishment of a relationship in the absence of a coincidence of ends. The question is not as difficult as it initially appears. In the first place, in many situations in which ends are not shared, there will not be opposition, but merely indifference. In these situations, there will be a large range of courses of action on which the parties will be able to agree. In the second place, even in those situations in which ends are actually opposed, there are a variety of quite familiar bases for compromise. These are the formal values of liberal theory, such as reciprocity, promise keeping, the ideal of law, and the ideal of representative government. These values do not provide a precise, objective, neutral mechanism for the resolution of differing ends. Moreover, they can never be dispositive by themselves. However, as values, they will often provide a substantial basis for an alliance between people with

differing concrete ends. Consider, for instance, the ideal of law.
. . . We do not always know what the law says, and we sometimes
feel that what it says is unjust. But there are many situations in
which we do know what the law says and have no reason to think
it unjust. At least in these situations, many people still feel that
the ideal of law does have independent moral authority, that it
can still provide a reason for doing something even when it conflicts with many more concrete ends. Thus, where the lawyer is
convinced that the claim against his client is unsupported by
law, or that his client's claim against another is supported by
law, the ideal of law will often provide a basis for association
even in the absence of a sharing of more specific, concrete ends.

[N]on-professional advocacy . . . does not ignore procedural
values entirely. The non-professional advocate recognizes that
the *way* in which a dispute is settled or a decision made can be a
matter of importance. In particular, he recognizes the strong
value of assuring the client an opportunity to attempt to explain
or justify himself publicly. Moreover, the non-professional advocate may encounter situations in which he feels that he cannot
effectively assess his client's position, and thinks that a judge or
jury would be in a much better position to do so after an adversary hearing.

Such procedural considerations provide a further basis for
accommodation between parties with opposing ends. The non-
professional advocate should take them very seriously. He does
not, however, regard them in the same manner as the Ideology of
Advocacy does. First, he will never consider them independently
of the substantive legal and moral values involved. [T]he non-
professional advocate cannot answer any [question] without
knowing the nature of the result to which his decision is likely to
lead. Second, the non-professional advocate . . . refuses to
assume that [procedural values] are necessarily present in every
case, or that when present they will invariably be advanced by
any particular mode of conducting the case. The value of enabling the client to explain and justify himself in public is im-
plicated only when the client sincerely wants to explain or justify
himself and proposes to do so. The utility of adversary advocacy
in facilitating informed decisionmaking is relevant only when
there is some reason to believe that the truth is not clear, and
that the judge will be in a better position to decide after a trial
than the advocate is now. Neither of these procedural considerations can ever justify attempts to exclude probative evidence, to
discredit testimony which is not misleading, or to engage in any
of the routine procedural tactics designed to obfuscate rather
than clarify the issues. There may be other considerations which
would justify such actions, but they must be identified and considered in each case along with the competing considerations
which favor the exposure of truth.

So far in this essay, the terms procedural justice and procedural values have been used to refer to norms associated specifically with the judicial process. The terms can also be used to refer to a more general notion which is also relevant to non-professional advocacy. This is the notion of a legitimacy or fairness arising from equality of access and participation in the society as a whole. Where there is substantial inequality and the lawyer can assist the relatively powerless to a greater measure of access and participation, this general notion of procedural justice will often provide a basis for advocate-client relationships in the absence of shared substantive values. The general notion of procedural justice will have a particularly strong claim on the advocate where his prospective client has little or no prospect of finding another advocate. In such situations, given the drastic inequality of power between lawyer and client, it will be unusually difficult to work out a genuinely voluntary relationship, and there is a great danger that the lawyer's insistence on his substantive ends may force the client to compromise his own in order to secure some measure of access and participation. For this reason, many who reject the determinative role of the specific notion of procedural justice contend that the general notion should be the exclusive basis of the advocate-client relationship, at least where the client is among the relatively powerless. From this line of thought, a modified version of the Ideology of Advocacy has emerged in the field of public interest law.

Yet, non-professional advocacy cannot regard general procedural considerations as exclusively determinative of the advocate's ethical obligations even within the area of representation of the powerless. The importance of substantive considerations is most apparent in situations where the oppressed client proposes a course of action which will injure others who are equally powerless. In such situations, the public interest lawyer . . . first commits himself to his client on the basis of his belief that institutional processes do not operate fairly, and then rationalizes the harm he does to others by asserting that institutional processes should be relied upon to protect their interests. Moreover, even where the client's course of action does not implicate the interests of other oppressed people, the interests of the client's own autonomy, responsibility, and dignity will sometimes require that the advocate insist on his own substantive ends.

Thus, non-professional advocacy . . . rejects the notion that the advocate-client relation must invariably be characterized by both partisanship and neutrality, but it does not rule out the possibility that either principle might sometimes be relevant. There may be situations in which the non-professional advocate will find it appropriate to present to a tribunal a claim to which he is not willing to commit himself personally. And there may be situations in which he will find it appropriate to present a claim aggressively even to the point of engaging in obfuscation or deception. Yet, from the point of view of non-professional advocacy the two principles appear, not complementary, but antagonistic. . . .

Ideally, everyone should be his own advocate, but this ideal does not seem capable of realization. The very existence of the occupation of the advocate pre-supposes some measure of alienation from law. Unlike the professional, the non-professional advocate can reduce, rather than aggravate, this alienation. Yet, except where advocate and client can develop a relation of genuine understanding and fraternity, he will not eliminate it. Except where the relation is based on shared substantive ends and experience, the client's dependence on the advocate will compromise his autonomy. It is important to recognize that, like the soldier's, the advocate's occupation arises from social imperfection. This imperfection may be inevitable, but it is important that the advocate not feel that he has a vested interest in it. If the non-professional advocate is to perform his job, he must be willing and even anxious to work to diminish the power and importance of his own role in order to enhance the client's autonomy. . . .

[I]t will be objected that non-professional advocacy puts an unrealistically large moral and psychological burden on the lawyer. . . . The often voiced premise of this criticism—that the lawyer's conditions of work involve greater responsibility or ethical pressure than others—seems wrong. Most occupations involve, directly or indirectly, constant, and often intimate and confidential, dealings with strangers which implicate moral responsibilities. The real difference between the position of the lawyer and that of, for instance, the corporate bureaucrat lies not in the greater pressure on the lawyer, but in his greater freedom. The autonomy of the lawyer should not be exaggerated. Most lawyers work under conditions of bureaucratic routine. Nevertheless, compared with most other occupations, lawyers have achieved a remarkable measure of autonomy in their conditions of work. Not every lawyer has the opportunity to act like Brandeis, but some do, and many have more latitude in defining the nature of their work than the most powerful corporate executives. The strain which the lawyer feels results less from the weight of his responsibilities than from the weight of his freedom. The corporate executive sacrifices his personal values more easily because he perceives his choices as more limited. The lawyer must undertake more strenuous efforts to rationalize his compromises because the pressures on him to compromise are weaker. Non-professional advocacy merely asks the lawyer to make the most of the freedom he has. . . .

Comment

Students beginning their work in the clinical seminar I teach generally tend to control the relationship with their clients without realizing that they are doing so; they tend to assume that they understand the client's goals without explicitly formulating them; they tend to be businesslike and to limit conversation to what is necessary to processing the task at hand. Their major concern is to appear competent, and this desire seems to control their decisions about how to behave with clients.

To open for examination these preconceived, although unarticulated, rules for attorney-client interaction, we attempt to make the students conscious of the rules and concerns that are guiding their behavior and draw out the possibility of alternative approaches. To demonstrate that choices are being made, we point out the ways that students may be asserting more control than necessary and may be imposing their values and priorities on the clients.

For example, our examination of the interviewing process begins with an exercise in which each student is asked to interview another and then to introduce him or her to the rest of the class. The students almost always find that in adopting the roles of interviewer and interviewee they place strict limits on what they can do and, worse, what they can think of doing. The interviewers do not consider asking: "What do you think is important for me to say about you to the class?" And the interviewees become passive and do not realize they can say: "This is what I'd like you to emphasize in introducing me." The limitations, on both sides, are a product of the belief that power and control lie solely in the hands of the interviewers. It is accepted that it is they who will structure the interview and the resulting presentation to the class. While that notion has a rational basis, rigid adherence to role leads it to be carried to an absurd extreme. What is most remarkable here is that the participants, both law students, would experience themselves as equal outside of the context of the exercise. None of the usual aspects of the lawyer-client relationship (the lawyer having an expertise, the client coming for help) are present.

Opening up these restricting attitudes for discussion and evaluation raises a danger that the students will swing to a polar opposite way of working with clients. Perhaps because it is easier to learn rules than to adapt to each new situation, students often hear our message as "it's wrong to be controlling." They then see their job as one of listening passively to clients and doing whatever a client asks them to do.

This pattern was vividly illustrated for me last year, when two students told me that they were prepared to help forge documents for a client to explain away a source of income that might reduce a claim she had made. When asked why they had decided to do this, they explained that although they thought it was wrong to take this action (apart from any issue under the Code of Professional Responsibility), their understanding was that they were not supposed to impose their will on a client, but were only to help the client get what she wanted. Wasn't this what we had been teaching them?

The issue is obviously complex. The lawyer who determines the client's goals and the lawyer who automatically accedes to the client's goals trouble me equally. I am trying to encourage students to see that there are alternatives to flipping back and forth between these poles. One alternative I believe in is to emphasize the importance of understanding the implicit value premises underlying the decisions the lawyer makes—whether to take a case, how to work with clients and the range of actions taken during the course of representation—and finding ways of expressing the values that are meaningful to them as lawyers. I encourage students to work with clients in a similar manner: continually clarifying the client's values so that the values of both affect the course of representation.

This effort to make the participants' values part of the reality that must be dealt with when acting as a lawyer cannot work if it is conceived of as a routine check—a space to be filled in on a form. It requires a continuous awareness of how these values are realized or frustrated in the course of representation. The lawyer and client need to understand each other's goals and values and their implications for decision-making, so that any actions they take are based on mutual understanding. This is not an easy process. It can be time consuming. It requires a willingness to listen to one's self and to another. It means facing up to disagreements that could easily be papered over and ignored. And it must take other people into account as well, for neither lawyer nor client exists in a vacuum and the values of a particular matter inevitably reach to the larger community.

For all that this is a difficult ideal to accomplish, it is exciting to attempt. When the students' thinking about how they want to relate to their clients is linked to such a continuous process of awareness, their decisions to exercise or abdicate control will rarely be automatic reactions to one set of rules or another. Whether the decision—in the example above or in others—is to agree or refuse to agree to any particular action desired by the client is not the only issue. The process of learning to be a lawyer, and lawyering itself, require that the students learn to acknowledge and take responsibility for their own choices and give their own answers to the questions of the values in legal representation—in the contexts of the relationship with the client, the profession, and the larger human community in which law takes place and has its effect.

E.D.

Rollo May, *Love and Will*
pp.289-292 (Norton 1969).

Care in Love and Will

Care is a state in which something does matter; care is the opposite of apathy. . . .

Care is given power by nature's sense of pain; if we do not care for ourselves, we are hurt, burned, injured. This is the source of identification: we can feel in our own bodies the pain of the child or the hurt of the adult. But our responsibility is to cease letting care be solely a matter of nerve endings. I do not deny the biological phenomena, but care must become a conscious psychological fact. Life comes from physical survival; but the good life comes from what we care about.

For Heidegger, care *(Sorge)* is the source of will. This is why he practically never speaks about will or willing, except when he is refuting other philosophers' positions. For will is not an independent "faculty," or a department of the self, and we always get into trouble when we try to make it a special faculty. It is a function of the whole person. "When fully conceived, the care-structure includes the phenomenon of Selfhood," writes Heidegger. When we do not care, we lose our being; and care is the way back to being. If I care about being, I will shepherd it with some attention paid to its welfare, whereas if I do not care, my being disintegrates. Heidegger "thinks of care as the basic constitutive phenomenon of human existence." It is thus ontological in that it constitutes man as man. Will and wish cannot be the basis for care, but rather vice versa: they are founded on care. We could not will or wish if we did not care to begin with; and if we do authentically care, we cannot help wishing or willing. Willing is caring made free, says Heidegger—and, I would add, made active. The constancy of the self is guaranteed by care.

Temporality is what makes care possible. The gods on Mount Olympus do not care—we here have our explanation for this fact which every one has patently seen and wondered about. The fact that we are finite makes care possible. Care also, in Heidegger's concept, is the source of conscience. "Conscience is the call of Care," and "manifests itself as Care."

Heidegger quotes an ancient parable of care, which Goethe also used at the end of *Faust:*

"Once when 'Care' was crossing a river, she saw some clay; she thoughtfully took up a piece and began to shape it. While she was meditating on what she had made, Jupiter came by. 'Care' asked him to give it spirit, and this he gladly granted. But when she wanted her name to be bestowed upon it, he forbade this, and demanded that it be given his name instead. While 'Care' and Jupiter were disputing, Earth arose and desired that her own name be conferred on the creature, since she had furnished it with part of her body. They asked Saturn to be their arbiter, and he made the following decision, which seemed a just one: 'Since you, Jupiter, have given its spirit, you shall receive that spirit at its death; and since you, Earth, have given its body, you shall receive its body. But since "Care" first shaped this creature, she shall possess it as long as it lives. And because there is now a dispute among you as to its name, let it be called *"homo,"* for it is made out of *humus* (earth).' "

This fascinating parable illustrates the important point brought out by the arbiter Saturn, Time, that though Man is named *Homo* after the earth, he is still constituted in his human attitudes by Care. She is given charge of him in the parable during his temporal sojourn in this world. This also shows the realization of the three aspects of time: past, future, and present. Earth gets man in the past, Zeus in the future; but since "Care first shaped this creature, she shall possess it as long as it lives," i.e., in the present. . . .

This gives us, indeed requires of us, a clear distinction between care and sentimentality. Sentimentality is thinking *about sentiment* rather than genuinely *experiencing* the object of it. Tolstoy tells of the Russian ladies who cry at the theater but are oblivious to their own coachman sitting outside in the freezing cold. Sentimentality glories in the fact that I *have* this emotion; it begins subjectively and ends there. But care is always caring *about* something. We are caught up in our experience of the objective thing or event we care about. In care one must, by involvement with the objective fact, do something about the situation; one must make some decisions. This is where care brings love and will together.

Paul Tillich's term, concern—used normally with the adjective "ultimate"—I also take to be a synonym for what we are now discussing. But I prefer for our purposes here the simpler and more direct term, care. I could also use the term compassion, which may connote to many readers a more sophisticated form of care. But compassion, a "feeling with" someone, is already an emotion, a passion which may come and go. I choose the term care because it is ontological and refers to a state of being.

Care is important because it is what is missing in our day. What [we have] is the seeping, creeping conviction that nothing matters; the prevailing feeling that one can't do anything. The threat is apathy, uninvolvement, the grasping for external stimulants. Care is a necessary antidote for this. . . .

The struggle is for the existence of the human being in a world in which everything seems increasingly mechanical, computerized, and ends in Vietnam. . . . It is the refusal to accept emptiness though it face one on every side; the dogged insistence on human dignity, though it be violated on every side; and the stubborn assertion of the self to give content to our activities, routine as these activities may be.

Love and will, in the old romantic and ethical sense, are dubious concepts and, indeed, may be both unavailable and unusable in that framework. We cannot support them by the appeal to romance in this day when romance is on the way out, or by the appeal to "ought." Neither of these carry cogency any longer. But there remains the old, bed-rock question, Does something, or some person, *matter* to me? And if not, can I find something or someone that *does* matter?

Comment

It seems bizarre on its face to assert that *caring* is the key to a question of substantive law, even one involving decisional authority as between attorney and client. Yet exactly that conclusion suddenly became clear to me during a seminar discussion.* The question we were considering was whether an attorney had any legitimate independent interests in the way a case was to be handled on behalf of a client, that is, accepting that the client should in most cases have the ultimate authority, whether there were grounds that could properly be advanced on the attorney's own behalf to limit client decision-making authority. We were discussing a case in which the lawyer proposes to call a child as a witness on behalf of the client; the client believes that the experience will be seriously harmful to the child and is unwilling to be the cause of that harm; the lawyer honestly believes that the child would not be seriously or unnecessarily harmed, and that without the child's testimony the case stands a substantially enhanced likelihood of being lost; the client, told that, nonetheless insists: Has the lawyer a sufficient independent interest to justify refusing to agree not to call the child?

In arguing "yes" here, some students asserted that the lawyer will indeed be harmed if the client loses the case. The attorney's interest in his or her reputation may be at risk and is a legitimate concern. Moreover, if the loss entails real pain to the client—loss of custody, conviction of a crime, even substantial financial burden—there will be genuine pain to the attorney as well, which he or she may legitimately want to avoid. Finally, the attorney may reasonably predict that, however the client judges the matter now, once the moment of choice has passed and the client must en-

---

* I am indebted to my colleague, Mark Spiegel, for presenting this problem to the seminar, and for sharing with me and the class a draft of his article, Lawyering and Client Decisionmaking: Informed Consent and the Legal Profession, 128 U.Pa.L. Rev. 41 (1979), which illuminated the issues for us and stirred our thought processes.

dure the cost, he or she will come to blame the attorney for "permitting" the client to make a mistake. Thus, it is said to be permissible for an attorney to refuse to proceed with the case unless the client agrees to call the witness, and to do that even if the lawyer's purpose is to use the client's dependence to force the latter to surrender the point.

To others, this course of action is offensively coercive, and involves the assertion of interests that are either minimally at risk or marginally legitimate, or both. On this view, the costs are the client's to bear, and it is paternalistic to seek to protect the client from subsequently coming to count them greater. It is offensive for the attorney to intrude his or her own interests, pale as they are in comparison to the client's, into the lexicon of risks.

What struck me so vividly as I listened to an excellent discussion of these pros and cons is that both sides were right, or wrong, depending on an aspect that I see as the presence or absence of a caring relationship with the client. Would the adherents of the second position be satisfied with an attorney who said to an objecting client, "Alright, it's your funeral. I think you're making a big mistake, but if that's the way you want to play, go ahead"? The client, left abruptly with this "concession," *will* feel badly represented if he or she later comes to believe that the attorney failed to provide sufficient guidance. Much of the notion of informed consent is a response to the client's need for something more than simply a hurried "have it your own way." By the same token, I doubt whether those who support the first view, giving the attorney a legitimate right of veto, would feel very comfortable with a scenario which consisted of the attorney simply blurting out: "Look, you can do it any way you like, but if I'm going to be your lawyer the kid testifies. Otherwise, you can get yourself somebody else."

What is wrong here is not that the attorney is not being "nice." I can come at my point by asking you to consider, by way of contrast, either solution with the element of caring present. First, an attorney who says: "I appreciate your reluctance to harm this witness, and I respect you for it. It's a shame that our legal system doesn't have methods for bringing information out in a less harmful way. For these reasons . . . , I don't see any way to make the point we need to make without calling the child. We can do a couple of things that I'll discuss with you to make it less of a problem for everybody. If you decide to let the case go to decision without the witness, you will have to live with the loss for a long time, and my experience is that you may feel that you took on a lot more pain than you spared the child. I'll support your decision, whatever it is, but I honestly think you'd be doing the right thing to let me call the witness, and I want you to think about it and let me know what you want to do."

In a sense that now seems most relevant to me, that response is more similar to than different from an "opposite" attorney response, which began like the preceding version, but ended in this vein: "I want to go along with your wishes wherever I can, and if I simply thought you were making a mistake, I would of course let you make it. But I see more to it than that. I have told myself that it's your business and not mine whether you walk out of court guilty or innocent [or, having custody of your child or not], and I can't let it go at that. Even if you can run that risk, I don't feel able to, where there's something we can do to stop it from happening and it involves an area like planning a trial that's so much the heart of my work, and when I honestly don't feel that it would be the wrong thing to do to the child, given what's at stake and things we can do to minimize the harm. I thought too whether I'm simply trying to protect my won-and-lost record, and I want to tell you that I'm confident that any knowledgeable lawyer or judge will realize that the reason I didn't call the child was that you told me not to, not that I didn't have the sense to do it. A lot of them will still think that I sold you out because I should have recognized that my judgment was sounder than yours, and it's hard for me to disregard that concern, partly because, as I'm saying to you, I agree with them. I don't want to make you do what you don't want to do, and if you decide that you're dead set against calling the child, I think the best thing for you would be to get another lawyer. I can suggest a couple of things to do about the case to make it less disruptive to you to do that. So think it over; I would like to stay on the case, but I can't if you decide not to let me call the child.''

I've come to a curious conclusion: I honestly do not think it matters which position the attorney takes—to leave the final decision with the client or insist on keeping it—so much as I think it matters whether the attorney makes either decision in a way that respects the concerns of both attorney and client, and treats the client as an understanding independent person, with interests and sensibilities separate from the attorney, and the ability and obligation to assume responsibility for his or her decisions. I do not advance this notion as a proposed rule of law—in part because I despair of expecting it to be applied, or even be capable of application, in post-hoc adversary litigation. I do believe that it is a valid insight in the context of thinking about the question of choice facing a lawyer with the situation at hand.

H.L.

Mark Twain, ''The War Prayer'' in *The Complete Short Stories and Famous Essays of Mark Twain*, pp.861-863 (Collier 1928).

It was a time of great and exalting excitement. The country was up in arms, the war was on, in every breast burned the holy fire of patriotism; the drums were beating, the bands playing, the toy pistols popping, the bunched firecrackers hissing and spluttering; on every hand and far down the receding and fading spread of roofs and balconies a fluttering wilderness of flags flashed in the sun; daily the young volunteers marched down the wide avenue gay and fine in their new uniforms, the proud fathers and mothers and sisters and sweethearts cheering them with voices choked with happy emotion as they swung by; nightly the packed mass meetings listened, panting, to patriot oratory which stirred the deepest deeps of their hearts, and which they interrupted at briefest intervals with cyclones of applause, the tears running down their cheeks the while; in the churches the pastors preached devotion to flag and country, and invoked the God of Battles, beseeching His aid in our good cause in outpouring of fervid eloquence which moved every listener. It was indeed a glad and gracious time, and the half dozen rash spirits that ventured to disapprove of the war and cast a doubt upon its righteousness straightway got such a stern and angry warning that for their personal safety's sake they quickly shrank out of sight and offended no more in that way.

Sunday morning came—next day the battalions would leave for the front; the church was filled; the volunteers were there, their young faces alight with martial dreams—visions of the stern advance, the gathering momentum, the rushing charge, the flashing sabers, the flight of the foe, the tumult, the enveloping smoke, the fierce pursuit, the surrender!—then home from the war, bronzed heroes, welcomed, adored, submerged in golden seas of glory! With the volunteers sat their dear ones, proud, happy, and envied by the neighbors and friends who had no sons and brothers to send forth to the field of honor, there to win for the flag, or, failing, die the noblest of noble deaths. The service proceeded; a war chapter from the Old Testament was read; the first prayer was said; it was followed by an organ burst that shook the building, and with one impulse the house rose, with glowing eyes and beating hearts, and poured out that tremendous invocation—

"God the all-terrible! Thou who ordainest,
Thunder thy clarion and lightning thy sword!"

Then came the "long" prayer. None could remember the like of it for passionate pleading and moving and beautiful language. The burden of its supplication was, that an ever-merciful and benignant Father of us all would watch over our noble young soldiers, and aid, comfort, and encourage them in their patriotic work; bless them, shield them in the day of battle and the hour of peril, bear them in His mighty hand, make them strong and confident, invincible in the bloody onset; help them to crush the foe, grant to them and to their flag and country imperishable honor and glory—

An aged stranger entered and moved with slow and noiseless step up the main aisle, his eyes fixed upon the minister, his long body clothed in a robe that reached to his feet, his head bare, his white hair descending in a frothy cataract to his shoulders, his seamy face unnaturally pale, pale even to ghastliness. With all eyes following him and wondering, he made his silent way; without pausing, he ascended to the preacher's side and stood there, waiting. With shut lids the preacher, unconscious of his presence, continued his moving prayer, and at last finished it with the words, uttered in fervent appeal, "Bless our arms, grant us the victory, O Lord our God, Father and Protector of our land and flag!"

The stranger touched his arm, motioned him to step aside—which the startled minister did—and took his place. During some moments he surveyed the spellbound audience with solemn eyes, in which burned on uncanny light; then in a deep voice he said:

"I come from the Throne—bearing a message from Almighty God!" The words smote the house with a shock; if the stranger perceived it he gave no attention. "He has heard the prayer of His servant your shepherd, and will grant it if such shall be your desire after I, His messenger, shall have explained to you its import—that is to say, its full import. For it is like unto many of the prayers of men, in that it asks for more than he who utters it is aware of—except he pause and think.

"God's servant and yours has prayed his prayer. Has he paused and taken thought? Is it one prayer? No, it is two—one uttered, the other not. Both have reached the ear of Him Who heareth all supplications, the spoken and the unspoken. Ponder this—keep it in mind. If you would beseech a blessing upon yourself, beware! lest without intent you invoke a curse upon a neighbor at the same time. If you pray for the blessing of rain upon your crop which needs it, by that act you are possibly praying for a curse upon some neighbor's crop which may not need rain and can be injured by it.

"You have heard your servant's prayer—the uttered part of it. I am commissioned of God to put into words the other part of it—that part which the pastor—and also you in your hearts—fervently prayed silently. And ignorantly and unthinkingly? God grant that it was so! You heard these words: 'Grant us the victory, O Lord our God!' That is sufficient. The *whole* of the uttered prayer is compact into those pregnant words. Elaborations were not necessary. When you have prayed for victory you have prayed for many unmentioned results which follow victory—*must* follow it, cannot help but follow it. Upon the listening spirit of God the Father fell also the unspoken part of the prayer. He commandeth me to put it into words. Listen!

"O Lord our Father, our young patriots, idols of our hearts, go forth to battle—be Thou near them! With them—in spirit—we also go forth from the sweet peace of our beloved firesides to smite the foe. O Lord our God, help us to tear their soldiers to bloody shreds with our shells; help us to cover their smiling fields with the pale forms of their patriot dead; help us to drown the thunder of the guns with the shrieks of their wounded, writhing in pain; help us to lay waste their humble homes with a hurricane of fire; help us to wring the hearts of their unoffending widows with unavailing grief; help us to turn them out roofless with their little children to wander unfriended the wastes of their desolated land in rags and hunger and thirst, sports of the sun flames of summer and the icy winds of winter, broken in spirit, worn with travail, imploring Thee for the refuge of the grave and denied it—for our sakes who adore Thee, Lord, blast their hopes, blight their lives, protract their bitter pilgrimage, make heavy their steps, water their way with their tears, stain the white snow with the blood of their wounded feet! We ask it, in the spirit of love, of Him Who is the Source of Love, and Who is the ever-faithful refuge and friend of all that are sore beset and seek His aid with humble and contrite hearts. Amen."

(After a pause) "Ye have prayed it; if ye still desire it, speak! The messenger of the Most High waits."

. . .

Comment

I have often made a commitment to a client's cause, felt righteous and good about doing battle for my client, and then been shocked to notice that the object of my client's scorn, fear or righteousness was indeed a person. At these moments I have a slight sinking sensation, my own moral righteousness sagging ever so slightly until I am able to dismiss this perception from my mind as an unwanted distraction bent on keeping me from doing what I know should be done. There is something exhilarating about gearing up to prepare for a confrontation. The opponent is physically absent, and I am filled with empathy for my physically present client. I am like the soldier preparing his weapons for war; I pay little or no attention to the reality of the life of the person who stands in the way of our winning.

Sometimes it is possible for me to go through an entire case without having to deal with this unwelcome perception. But the need usually arises, occurring in a completely unexpected way, often at a time when my fervor for my client's cause is running particularly high. It could be a look of vulnerability, a word that betrays the sense of hurt or pain, a humorous remark, any of the thousands of things that people do that reveal themselves to be more than the masks they wear. At these times, no matter what I want to be feeling, I cannot wholly suppress a sudden surge of sympathy—or simply a recognition of that other person as more than the adversary, the enemy. I am confused and threatened by these feelings. I am afraid that they will take over and that I will be engulfed by them. So I resist, pretending that I am not feeling what I feel and trying to rouse myself to a higher pitch of war readiness.

Yet I know too that these reactions contain something important for me in my representation of my client. My responsibility as a lawyer cannot exclude my responsibility as a citizen or a person to the human dilemma that underlies not only my client's situation but the total human situation. It seems right that I be struggling with these reactions.

G.F.

Comment

The popular injunction, "Sue the bastards," captures much of what is attractive to many of us in the adversary spirit: the lawyer identifying with a client seen as weak and wronged, who turns to law (in particular to adjudication) because of its promise of affording a fair hearing before a disinterested arbiter able and willing to call the mighty to account and to judge their conduct according to law. Thomas Shaffer has described advocacy "at its best [as] a form of reconciliation":

> "It reconciles the advocate with those whose champion he proposes to be. It reconciles the advocate with his hearers. It reconciles the person whose cause is advocated with the persons who hear advocacy. It brings to community life a new sense of the interests of those the community neglects. It seeks to make things better. It is moral discourse."

Shaffer, *Advocacy as Moral Discourse*, 57 No. Car. L. Rev. 647 (1979).

Much is of course reserved by the opening qualification; advocacy is seldom encountered "at its best." For me, *The War Prayer* contains a powerful reminder of the danger in the moral fervor we incline toward as advocates, a fervor reinforced by the claims of autonomy and fairness of the adjudicatory system. All too often, that moral fervor legitimates a moral blindness toward "the bastards" on the other side, and toward the moral ambiguities and outright failures of our system of adjudicatory justice.

It would be all too easy to reserve Mark Twain's admonition for the occasions when we are representing an unworthy client; Gary Friedman brings us up short so arrestingly because he postulates a client no less appealing than his or her adversary. One of the painful difficulties of practicing law is maintaining the connection between the valid appeal of the values of adjudicatory adversariness and client-identification, and the need to remain aware and responsible about the true operation of the adversary system, the harms we do to our adversaries, and the ambivalence of the lawyer's own moral posture. Shaffer eloquently describes one way of being, and it is an attractive vision. To make it real in a lawyer's working life, it is necessary to hear as well the warning of Mark Twain's Messenger. Else a lawyer might end up fitting the description of Edgar Lee Masters' "Editor Whedon":

> To be able to see every side of every question;
> To be on every side, to be everything, to be nothing long;

To pervert truth, to ride it for a purpose,
To use great feelings and passions of the human family
For base designs, for cunning ends,
To wear a mask like the Greek actors—
Your eight-page paper—behind which you huddle,
Bawling through the megaphone of big type:
"This is I, the giant."
Thereby also living the life of a sneak-thief,
Poisoned with the anonymous words
Of your clandestine soul.
To scratch dirt over scandal for money,
And exhume it to the winds for revenge,
Or to sell papers,
Crushing reputations, or bodies, if need be,
To win at any cost, save your own life.
To glory in demoniac power, ditching civilization,
As a paranoiac boy puts a log on the track
And derails the express train.

Masters, *Spoon River Anthology,* p.131 (Macmillan 1916).

                                                            H.L.

Seattle, *Chief Seattle's Message**.

[This address was delivered on the occasion of the transfer of
ancestral lands of the Suquamish Indians in Washington Ter-
ritory to the United States.]

The Great Chief in Washington sends word that he wishes to
buy our land.

The Great Chief also sends us words of friendship and good
will. This is kind of him, since we know he has little need of our
friendship in return. But we will consider your offer. For we
know that if we do not sell, the white man may come with guns
and take our land.

How can you buy or sell the sky, the warmth of the land? The
idea is strange to us.

If we do not own the freshness of the air and the sparkle of
the water, how can you buy them?

Every part of this earth is sacred to my people. Every shining pine needle, every sandy shore, every mist in the dark woods,
every clearing and humming insect is holy in the memory and experience of my people. The sap which courses through the trees
carries the memories of the red man.

The white man's dead forget the country of their birth when

____

*   Reprinted in Cooney & Michalowski,
eds., The Power of the People, p.6 (1977).

they go to walk among the stars. Our dead never forget this beautiful earth, for it is the mother of the red man. We are part of the earth and it is part of us. The perfumed flowers are our sisters; the deer, the horse, the great eagle, these are our brothers. The rocky crests, the juices in the meadows, the body heat of the pony, and man—all belong to the same family. . . .

This shining water that moves in the streams and rivers is not just water but the blood of our ancestors. If we sell you land, you must remember that it is sacred, and you must teach your children that it is sacred, and that each ghostly reflection in the clear water of the lake tells of events and memories in the life of my people. The water's murmur is the voice of my father's father.

The rivers are our brothers, they quench our thirst. The rivers carry our canoes, and feed our children. If we sell you our land, you must remember, and teach your children, that the rivers are our brothers, and yours, and you must henceforth give the rivers the kindness you would give any brother.

The red man has always retreated before the advancing white man, as the mist of the mountains runs before the morning sun. But the ashes of our fathers are sacred. Their graves are holy ground, and so these hills, these trees, this portion of earth is consecrated to us. We know that the white man does not understand our ways. One portion of land is the same to him as the next, for he is a stranger who comes in the night and takes from the land whatever he needs. The earth is not his brother, but his enemy, and when he has conquered it, he moves on. He leaves his fathers' graves behind, and he does not care. He kidnaps the earth from his children. He does not care. His fathers' graves and his children's birthright are forgotten. He treats his mother, the earth, and his brother, the sky, as things to be bought, plundered, sold like sheep or bright beads. His appetite will devour the earth and leave behind only a desert. . . .

The air is precious to the red man, for all things share the same breath—the beast, the tree, the man, they all share the same breath. . . . The wind that gave our grandfather his first breath also receives his last sigh. And the wind must also give our children the spirit of life. . . .

What is man without the beasts? If all the beasts were gone, men would die from a great loneliness of spirit. For whatever happens to the beasts, soon happens to man. All things are connected.

You must teach your children that the ground beneath their feet is the ashes of our grandfathers. So that they will respect the land, tell your children that the earth is rich with the lives of our kin. Teach your children what we have taught our children, that the earth is our mother. Whatever befalls the earth, befalls the sons of the earth. If men spit upon the ground they spit upon themselves.

This we know. The earth does not belong to man; man belongs to the earth. This we know. All things are connected like the blood which unites one family. All things are connected.

Whatever befalls the earth befalls the sons of the earth. Man did not weave the web of life; he is merely a strand in it. Whatever he does to the web, he does to himself. . . .

Even the white man, whose God walks and talks with him as friend to friend, cannot be exempt from the common destiny. We may be brothers after all; we shall see. One thing we know, which the white man may one day discover—our God is the same God. You may think now that you own him as you wish to own our land; but you cannot. He is the God of man, and his compassion is equal for the red man and the white. This earth is precious to him, and to harm the earth is to heap contempt on its Creator. . . . So if we sell you our land, love it as we've loved it. Care for it as we've cared for it. Hold in your mind the memory of the land as it is when you take it. And with all your strength, with all your mind, with all your heart, preserve it for your children, and love it . . . as God loves us all. . . .

Comment

It is natural that Chief Seattle, speaking these words in 1854, would attribute to the very nature of the "white man" the ways of looking at his relation to the natural world, and to his fellow humans, which so dominated Western culture at that time. Roberto Unger has described this consciousness as:

> the awareness of a radical separation between the self and nature, be-tween the self and the others, between the self and its own . . . works. Nature outside man appears as a fund of means capable of satisfying his cravings. It is a brute force that opposes the will and remains alien to its moral intentions. In its relationship to others, the self [responds to] its fear of all social bonds as threats to individuality. Men [do not recognize] the common humanity they share with persons far from them. . . . [E]very work is seen as something foreign to the will that made it.

Knowledge and Politics, p.25 (Free Press 1975). Karl Polanyi has written, in *The Great Transformation* (1944), of the "commoditization" of land and labor, that is, of people and nature, as a result of the rise of a "free market" ethic during the 18th and 19th centuries.

These ideas have remained powerful in the century since Chief Seattle spoke, but not without challenge. Unger's and Polanyi's works provide important historical and philosophical aids to understanding that the world-view that Chief Seattle attributed to the white race has been a product of a specific historical period, and not a necessary or permanent condition. The alternative perception, to which Chief Seattle gives eloquent expression—that of a deep connection between humankind and nature, between one generation and those which have gone before and are to come—is no more foreign or remote than our religious tradition. The same may be said of a connection between each of us and our fellow humans. With respect to our relation to nature, and to succeeding generations, the injunction of Leviticus is starkly simple: "The land shall not be sold in perpetuity; for the land is mine." (XXV: 23). The anthropologist Barbara Myerhoff spent eighteen months observing at close hand the life of a group of very elderly, relatively poor, first-generation-American Jews living in California. Here is her account of a conversation with a retired tailor, Shmuel:

> I never knew [the source] of Shmuel's attitude toward his work. . . . Creativity and seriousness belonged to work. It was both religion and play. When he worked, his imagination was freed.
>
> "The mind must be alive when you sew, if you are in a good shop or a bad. I have been in both, and all those in between. The outside conditions do not apply. You must bring it up from the inside, looking always for a way to express yourself.
>
> ". . . . When I am in a shop, I am told to make a whole coat for a dollar. . . . [T]he other men would . . . put down the little screw on the machine to make bigger stitches. But such a coat doesn't last the winter. This coat goes to a poor woman, her only garment for warmth.
>
> "[I]t gives out in the Bible that a pawnbroker cannot keep a poor man's caftan or cloak for deposit or for pawn overnight, because a Jew can't profit from someone else's need. 'You shall not sleep in his pledge. When the sun goes down you restore to him his pledge, that he may sleep in his own cloak.' This comes from Deuteronomy. . . . No, it is not the way of a Jew to make his work like there was no human being to suffer when it's done badly. A coat is not a piece of cloth only. The tailor is connected to the one who wears it and he should not forget it."

Myerhoff, *Number Our Days,* pp.43-44 (Dutton 1979). The lines of John Donne that open this section say no more than this, and no less, in universal and eloquent terms.

There is not then a white and an Indian view of reality. Both views have been found at different times and places in Western culture and in others. The choice is rather between maintaining a consciousness that looks solely to our separateness from one another and seeking a broader integration. To take this broader view is neither to reject wholesale the accomplishments of modern society and the strengths of individualism, nor to embrace the sentimentality of a total denial of our separateness. To say that we are linked one to another is to acknowledge that we are separate, and at the same time to insist that we are more than separate. For me, a major aim of this book is to express a commitment to the legitimacy of exploring the meaning of a legal profession and a legal system that includes values based on connection, on—as Peter Gabel has put it (*Book Review, 91 Harv. L. Rev. 302, 315*)—"a living milieu . . . in which each person recognizes the other as 'one-of-us' instead of 'other-than-me'. . . . "

H.L.

†